CHARLES FAIRFAX MURRAY

CHARLES FAIRFAX MURRAY

The Unknown Pre-Raphaelite

David B Elliott

The Book Guild Ltd
Sussex, England

The Book Guild Ltd.,
25 High Street,
Lewes, Sussex

First published 2000
© David Elliott 2000

Set in Baskerville
Typesetting by
Acorn Bookwork, Salisbury, Wiltshire

Origination, printing and binding in Singapore
under the supervision of
MRM Graphics Ltd., Winslow, Bucks

A catalogue record for this book is
available from the British Library

ISBN 1 85776 510 9

Contents

Foreword

The Pre-Raphaelite revival is a hybrid. Part swing of the pendulum, part product of market forces, it is also an exercise in nostalgia and escapism that may well say something to future social historians. Over the years, moreover, its character has changed, the *enfant terrible* of the Sixties becoming positively staid and respectable as we enter the twenty-first century. Old lags may still feel twinges of defensiveness, but a generation has emerged which finds it as natural to admire Millais and Rossetti as to idolise Rembrandt or Goya. Those who continue to dislike the Pre-Raphaelites do so out of a genuine failure of empathy, not because they were brought up to believe that good taste died in 1837. These pictures, after all, were never meant to be easy viewing.

During its forty-or-so-year lifespan, the revival has spawned a formidable amount of writing – biographies, monographs, scholarly articles, exhibition catalogues, edited collections of letters. The Pre-Raphaelite literature as it existed at the outset is conveniently encapsulated in the late Professor Fredeman's 'bibliocritical study' of 1965, and it would be interesting to see to what extent this invaluable book would expand if a new edition was compiled. There have even been moments when the outpouring has seemed so copious that it might prove counterproductive, bludgeoning us into the same state of satiated exhaustion that the Bloomsbury industry, a comparable phenomenon, is sometimes said to induce. And yet, if the flow is analysed, it will be found to be curiously partial. Anyone, for instance, wishing to use the Pre-Raphaelites' portrayal of women as a springboard for musings on gender politics might find the field a little crowded, but there are important, if less emotive, areas that are genuinely under-researched.

None of these is more glaring than the life and career of Charles Fairfax Murray. It has become something of a commonplace for aficionados to lament the lack of a good book on the subject. Not that Murray is an obscure figure. On the contrary (to use one of his own favourite expressions), everyone remotely interested in Pre-Raphaelitism has heard of him. Many probably have a picture of a short, thick-set figure, with bandy legs, snub nose, and stiff, curly hair. Some may even have reached for their Michelangelo *Klassiker* to test the truth of WS Spanton's assertion that his friend bore a strong resemblance to 'the man pulling on his cloak, just over the right hand of the prophet Daniel' on the Sistine ceiling. But although we all feel we 'know' Murray, the actual amount of information about him is incredibly sparse. Spanton's account, in his chatty reminiscences of 1927, is one of only two set-piece descriptions, the other being a chapter in AC Benson's *Memories and Friends* (1924). For the rest, it is a matter of stray references in the Pre-Raphaelite literature, those, for instance in Rossetti's correspondence with Jane Morris, in which Murray appears as a chippy, bumptious youth, very different from the benign, almost sage-like figure, 'kind, generous, and eminently human', that Benson described nearly half a century later. Certainly Murray himself does nothing to enlighten us. An excessively secretive man with much to be secretive about in both his private and professional life, he deliberately courted anonymity. He left no memoir, his diaries, so far as they exist at all, are disappointingly unilluminating, and his surviving letters deal mainly with business matters, only his letters to Spanton revealing something of his opinions, achievements and reverses. On reflection, it is perhaps surprising that his 'darkest' secret, the fact that he had two families, one in London and one in Florence, seems to be common knowledge.

But why should we want to know more about Murray, who was by no means one of the Pre-Raphaelite high-flyers? The answer lies in his ubiquity, versatility, and astonishing competence, not to mention a complex and often endearing personality. 'Murray made himself happy in the background', wrote Georgiana Burne-Jones, describing an evening at The Grange in 1868 at which Rossetti was also present. During these early years, Murray was always 'in the background'. It was where he chose to be, not out of obsequiousness or any false sense of modesty, but the fierce independence, the fear of being anyone's fool or dupe, that was such a decided feature of his character. Needless to say, it was this attitude that Rossetti construed as chippiness. As for Georgie Burne-Jones's comment, it is tempting to read into it a touch of condescension on the circle's part which, to some extent at any rate, justifies Murray's anxiety.

Whatever the case, it was from 'the background' that Murray operated so effectively, making himself invaluable to his masters and hence important to us. In the history of later Pre-Raphaelitism, Murray is the great enabler, the indispensable second fiddle, someone who makes wheels go round, the mortar (to change the metaphor yet again) which holds the edifice together, leaving others to be corner-stones or bricks. Without Murray, it could be argued, the subject would still have its familiar outlines; but it would be less cohesive and greatly impoverished, shorn of some significant dimensions.

Enabling his masters meant acting as a studio assistant to Rossetti and Burne-Jones; as a trusted adjutant to Morris, whether painting stained-glass windows or adding miniatures to his illuminated manuscripts; and as Ruskin's 'heaven-born copyist', recording the Old Master pictures and murals which figured so largely in the critic's later aesthetic system cum private mythology. Murray was ideally suited to these tasks, combining great executive skill with an imagination that was, at any rate, not as vivid as Rossetti's or Burne-Jones's. Indeed, his ability to sink his artistic personality in theirs can lead to confusion. Copies after both masters by Murray have been taken for originals in recent years, and it was not so long ago that a whole cache of Murray's drawings in an American university museum was attributed to Burne-Jones. Ever since AC Sewter drew attention to the problem in the 1970s, we have looked with caution at Burne-Jones's stained-glass cartoons, wary that they might be Murray's workshop versions.

Nor, in fact, was Murray's own talent by any means negligible. He might tell Benson that he had 'no invention', and his work certainly reflects both his contact with greater living artists and his study of the Old Masters, but it is instantly recognisable. Perhaps his best known painting is *The Violin Player* at Liverpool, but there is a little gem at Dulwich; and crowds flocking to *The Sound of Music* or *Jesus Christ Superstar* used to see *The Music Party* in the foyer of the Palace Theatre at Cambridge Circus, placed there by Richard D'Oyly Carte in 1891 when he built the theatre as a home for English grand opera. Murray's drawings are even more familiar. Portraits, figure compositions or drapery studies (his figures are nearly always heavily draped), executed in pencil or gouache, they have tended to be the small change of auctions or dealers' exhibitions. But they are never incompetent and, like all his work, they have a natural distinction and elegance – qualities rare enough in an age of unparalleled pictorial vulgarity. Certain images obsessed him, particularly the Giorgionesque conventions of a group of figures making music or seated on the ground, listening to a companion playing an instrument or reading from a book. A true child of the Aesthetic movement, he was always more interested in mood than narrative; mood, moreover, set by music, for which he himself had a good ear.

Murray's commitment to the Pre-Raphaelite great and good went far beyond their workshops and studios. No-one studies the movement for long without realising how much the rich and multi-faceted picture we have of it is due to him. He left memorable portraits of Burne-Jones, Morris and Philip Webb. Having assiduously collected the circle's drawings and literary manuscripts, he made sure that they entered public collections by giving them outright or selling them at less than their market value. Hence the great treasure-houses at Birmingham and Cambridge. He was also at pains to pass on his unrivalled knowledge. Had he possessed more time and inclination for literary composition, he could have written books on the artists he had known that would carry the greatest authority to this day. As it was, he went out of his way to help those who did put pen to paper: Lady Burne-Jones, JW Mackail, HC Marillier, AC Benson, and others.

There is something touching about Murray's devotion to his heroes' memory. His relations with them had not always run smoothly, and he was well aware of their limitations and peccadilloes. 'Rossetti,' he told Benson, 'went off the lines a good deal', and no-one knew more about Burne-Jones's affair with Maria Zambaco. When he observed to Sydney Cockerell that Lady Burne-Jones's *Memorials* of her husband gave 'an incomplete impression ...from much being omitted, purposely of course', he knew what he was saying. He was not, however, being critical. For all his anxiety to hoard and preserve relics, Murray was as reticent as any Victorian when it came to intimate matters, arguing that no life of Swinburne could be written without 'a certain whitewashing', and admitting that he had 'destroyed an important letter of Morris's . . . because I found that its purpose was *absolutely misunderstood* by an outsider'. Graham Robertson, another great frequenter of Pre-Raphaelite studios, ended his reminiscences with the immortal words: 'A really interesting book could be compiled from my omissions, and I think I could promise that it would prove a Best Seller. I know I can promise that it will never be written'. Murray, who had died more than a decade earlier, would have approved.

Murray might not be our man if we were looking for salacious gossip, but who, penning a Pre-Raphaelite catalogue entry, has not yearned to have him at his elbow to guide him in the treacherous paths of connoisseurship? A classic case, not entirely hypothetical, would be a drawing attributed to Rossetti. On the evidence of the eye it might seem doubtful, but there is something in its history which suggests that no less an authority than William Michael Rossetti, the artist's brother, had once given it his blessing. Murray would have put us right in a trice, no doubt in trenchant terms. In any case, it is always worth recalling what he said about William Michael Rossettti. The man, he told Samuel Bancroft, had not 'an ounce of judgement', allowing 'daubs . . . to be sold in his brother's name simply because he found them in the studio'.

Connoisseurship, the cultivation of an 'eye' with a view to attributing works of art and appraising their quality, is the capacity *par excellence* that Murray embodies. 'You're a magician!', exclaimed Stuart Donaldson, Master of Magdalene College, Cambridge, when Murray re-attributed almost everything in his collection of early Italian pictures. Aware that his own artistic talent was limited, Murray turned increasingly to dealing in the late 1870s, living much of the time in Italy and acquiring an encyclopaedic knowledge of the Old Masters. The market was enjoying a golden age and he was quick to seize his opportunities, building up a network of contacts across Europe and establishing an unassailable reputation as *marchand amateur*, expert and man of taste. By the turn of the century, Agnew's were glad to take him into partnership, mega-rich collectors on both sides of the Atlantic vied for his services, and the record of his life becomes dotted with the biggest names in the business: Berenson, Morelli, von Bode, Frick, Morgan and many others. Not that Murray was a Duveen *avant la lettre*, making a personal fortune and raiding the British heritage to assuage American *nouveaux riches* hungry for ancestors. His lifestyle was never lavish and he remained intensely public-spirited, advising the South Kensington Museum for many years and making princely gifts to the National Gallery, the Fitzwilliam Museum, and Dulwich. 'Murray', wrote Charles Ricketts, himself no mean benefactor of museums, 'has often shown a generosity that might be studied by richer men.'

During the last three decades of his life, Murray moved out of the shadow of the Pre-Raphaelite heavyweights to whom he had so long ministered. As his sphere of activity expanded to embrace collecting, dealing, museology and art-historical scholarship, he became a heavyweight himself in a field only tangential to his work for Rossetti, Morris and his peers. At this late stage of his career it would be possible to have no particular feeling for Pre-Raphaelitism and yet still find Murray a figure of absorbing interest.

We should be wary, however, of seeing his world as in some way fractured. Spanton might lament a loss of 'freshness' and 'sentiment' once his friend took to the saleroom, but Murray never repudiated his Pre-Raphaelite connections, merely adding new interests to old; and the different aspects of his work remained closely interrelated. The implications are obvious. As a member of the Pre-Raphaelite circle, he invites us to explore the connection between the priorities of the artists and those of contemporary art-historians, a connection most vividly illustrated by the mania for Botticelli that prevailed in aesthetic circles in the later nineteenth century. Equally, any assessment of his role as a dealer must acknowledge that he saw works of art through the eyes of a practising artist. Murray and Ricketts were virtually the last of the artist-connoisseurs. Heirs to a great tradition going back to Rubens and Van Dyck via Eastlake, Lawrence, Reynolds, Lely and others, they represented an approach which has long since become a casualty of specialisation. When Benson visited Murray at the height of Murray's dealing activity, he found him at his easel and was told: *'That's* really my trade'. Who in a position even remotely analogous to Murray's would be discovered so employed today?

Given the complexity of Murray's career, the innumerable people he knew and the ramifications of his private life, it is hardly surprising that scholars have balked at the prospect of writing his biography. David Elliott has put us all in his debt by finally grasping the nettle. He was not the first to embark on the task, but he alone has carried it through to fruition. He brings to it the inestimable advantage of being Murray's grandson, with access to papers on both sides of the family; while an energy which must be inherited from his industrious forbear has led him to scour archives in Britain, Europe and America for the other primary sources which, in the nature of the case, are essential. The result, to say the least, is illuminating, a long overdue removing of the mask which Murray himself may have found psychologically necessary but which now merely serves to obscure his considerable achievements. For all his brusque bonhomie, his 'hearty, unaffected manner', Murray struck Benson as 'a man of moods and mysteries'. Never again will he seem quite so enigmatic.

John Christian
February 2000

Author's Acknowledgements

I should like to offer my profound thanks to the great many people who have enthusiastically given their time and expertise to helping make this record of Charles Fairfax Murray's life and work. The support and encouragement I have received is, I believe, a measure of the significance of this unusual and intriguing character, and of the interest of art historians and art lovers alike in the people he knew and his place in the late- Victorian art world.

A great number of the relevant papers are now in North America, and I am indebted to librarians, archivists and curators at the Houghton Library and the Fogg Museum of Art at Harvard, the Isabella Stewart Gardner Museum and the Museum of Fine Arts in Boston, the University of British Columbia, the Huntington Library in San Merino, the Pierpont Morgan Library, the Delaware Art Museum, the Cleveland Museum of Art and the Harry Ransom Library of the University of Texas (where a substantial part of Fairfax Murray's own hoard of Pre-Raphaelite papers now resides) for allowing me to use their collections. Among those to whom I owe a personal debt are Julie Codell, Cara Denison, Abby Smith, Mark Samuels Lasner, Patrick McMahon, Jeanette Toohey and Royal W Leith, whose knowledge of the American expatriate artist colony in Florence in the 1880s has proved invaluable.

In Europe I have been greatly assisted by access to collections and archives at the John Rylands Library of the University of Manchester (where another extensive collection of Fairfax Murray's papers is located). I am particularly indebted to the Trustees of Dulwich Picture Gallery, the Ruskin Library at Lancaster University, the Courtauld Institute, the Fitzwilliam Museum, the Ashmolean, the British Library, the National Library of Scotland, the National Gallery, the V&A and the National Art Library, to the Ruskin Literary Trustees, the Guild of St George, for permission to quote from unpublished letters from Ruskin to Fairfax Murray, and to Simon Howard for permission to use unpublished correspondence between Edward Burne-Jones and George Howard in the Castle Howard archive. The Collection Frits Lugt in Paris, the Bibliotheca Marciana in Venice and the Central Archive of the Berlin Museums have been particularly helpful. Personal acknowledgement of their help and advice is due to Peter Cormack, Jim Dearden, Robert Hewison, Christopher Ridgway, Duncan Robinson, Simon Taylor, Lucy Till, and to Richard Kingzett of Agnew's who gave me the run of their archives. I should like to extend my thanks to everyone who has lent me papers and given me their time. To those whom I have unwittingly failed to acknowledge go my apologies and thanks. This book would not have been written without all of them.

Fairfax Murray's Italian descendants, Liliana Murray, Daniela Dinozzi and Patrizia Baldini have been welcoming and hugely helpful in giving me access to family papers and suggesting avenues to explore. Their enthusiasm has been very important.

I should like especially to thank Paul Tucker whose knowledge of the Italian art world of the nineteenth century and extensive researches in to Charles Fairfax Murray's own works, the pictures he dealt in and his Italian connections have been invaluable to me; and, lastly, to record my deep gratitude for the encouragement and advice of John Christian and Stephen Wildman, two of the foremost authorities on the development of the English schools in the nineteenth century, who have generously shared their scholarship in to the context of Charles Fairfax Murray's career.

1. Early Days

Charles Fairfax Murray, aged 12, Manchester. *Carte de visite* photograph by H. Petschler & Co Charles Fairfax Murray, the draper's son who became one of the most influential figures of the late Victorian art world, was born on 30 September 1849 at 14 High Street, Bow, on the outskirts to the east of London. Before he was 17, Fairfax Murray would be John Ruskin's protégé, Edward Burne-Jones's first studio assistant, the eager disciple of Dante Gabriel Rossetti, and the close friend and associate of William Morris. In his mature years he would be their confidant and ambassador, an internationally successful art dealer, a distinguished collector and connoisseur who gave great collections to the nation anonymously, and the keeper of the Pre-Raphaelite flame. The circumstances of his birth into this middle-class shopkeeper's family were, by contrast, unremarkable.

Charles Fairfax Murray was the last of seven children of the marriage of James Dalton Murray and Elizabeth Scott. The first three, the oldest aged six, died from scarlet fever in one terrible week in June 1842, when James and Elizabeth Murray's surviving child, their daughter Lucy Maria, was little more than three months old. Lucy was born in Bow on 25 February 1842, when her mother was 26 years of age and her father was then 34. The family lived in the centre of the village above their shop. Two years later, a son, Arthur, was born, and another, John Dalton Murray, followed in April 1846. Charles Fairfax arrived three years later.

Epidemic outbreaks of cholera, transmitted by pollution of the water supply, were not uncommon; nevertheless, Bow in 1850 was a far cry from the Dickensian stews, the dank enclosed courtyards and the grinding poverty of the late-Victorian East End.[1] Until the 1820s Bow had been an outlying country village which prospered as the principal inland dock for unloading grain, brought down the River Lea in shallow-draught sailing barges from Hertfordshire for the capital's bakehouses. With its recently-built late-Georgian terraced High Street running to the north and south sides of the ancient church of St Mary's-atte-Bow on the road to Essex, the village was still very much as Samuel Pepys described it 200 years earlier, when he would take a ferry from the naval dockyard at Deptford across the Thames to visit the house of prosperous friends in rural Stepney. There he took long country walks along the Mile End Road past Bow to an inn at Stratford where he enjoyed a dish of strawberries and cast lingering glances at a pretty serving maid.

A stone's throw along Fairfield Road from the highway were the open meadows where a gaudy and notorious country fair came twice a year to the outer edge of the Great Wen and the itinerant traders, beer-sellers, prizefighters and showmen set out their stalls and attractions. Here the ragged populace of Bethnal Green and White-chapel, along with the pickpockets, whores and beggars, streamed out of the metropolis to enjoy a day in the country.

By the 1840s Bow was a rapidly growing new community, but the road from Mile End still lay over farm land and market gardens. The speculative neo-Georgian terraces of Tredegar and Albion Squares, intended for 'respectable' people who would keep servants and lead the comfortable life of the middle classes, were yet to be built, and as the suburbs extended east they took a growing proportion of the better-off seeking to escape the overcrowding and filth of London. Poplar, Bromley and Bow all enjoyed leafy open spaces in the 1850s.

The railway came to Bow through Stepney from Fenchurch Street only in the year of Charles Fairfax Murray's birth, with the construction of the North London Railway link. Two years later, 85,000 passengers used the line in six months and the outlying village began to be embraced by the eastward expansion of the capital; even so, Goade's *Plan for London* of 1867 described Bow as having 'the maximum concentration of shop-assistants, clerks, sub-officials and independent traders' in the east, 'the area at its most salubrious, where beautiful open squares ... witnessed the absence of poverty.' As London's population increased dramatically – there was a leap of more than one-fifth between 1841 and 1851 alone – shopkeepers, clerks, representatives and dressmakers benefited more than proportionately from the new prosperity. James Dalton Murray, the linen draper in this bustling suburban community (there was also a woollen draper), was a man of some standing and substance in the neighbourhood, typical of the aspiring middle classes of Victoria's reign. On the death of three of his four children in 1842, he was among the first to purchase a family burial plot in perpe-tuity in the City of London & Tower Hamlets Cemetery that had opened that year, a monument both to their memory and to his belief in the future.

James Dalton Murray was born in 1808. His marriage to Elizabeth at the age of 26 or 27 was relatively late for the times, and it seems that he was at sea in his earlier years. One of Fairfax Murray's early memories was of a visit to Portsmouth and of days spent on the Isle of Wight with his father. 'We went first to Ventnor I think, thence to Shanklin and Sandown ... my father knew it well. At Portsmouth we duly inspected Nelson's ship and the *Royal Sovereign*, a turret ship of the latest pattern of that time.'[2] Fairfax Murray at 17 had a repertoire of sea shanties which he sang quietly to himself when concentrating on a painting, and he loved the sea and travel all his life; they were in his blood. He was keenly patriotic though he abhorred jingoism, and his father's influence was greater than he later cared to admit. James Dalton Murray is known to have had some talent as a water colourist,[3] though his fiercely independent son once remarked that the only thing he could bless him for was his second given name, Fairfax. This he adopted into his surname at 16, not for aggrandisement although the flourish would have pleased him, for the wholly practical purpose of distinguishing himself from another half-dozen Murrays who were painting at the time.

The extraordinarily rapid growth of London in his earliest childhood years was achieved at a heavy price. Smoke from coal fires and open ranges hung in a deadly, grey cloud all year long, covering houses in soot. While Britain dominated world trade and the Great Exhibition of 1851 symbolised the nation's wealth and innovation, there was no London sewerage system until 1865. Public health was painfully slow to improve. There were successive cholera epidemics in 1849 and in 1854, when men, women and children from the workhouses were buried in batches of ten, until in August records could no longer be kept because grave-diggers and cemetery clerks alike were themselves victims of the disease. The Great Stink of 1858, when the House of Commons was forced to remove its deliberations away from the polluted Thames, heightened public concern over the consequences of overcrowding in the inner city areas, the lack of sanitation and the deadly state of the city's water supply; but the ever-present tubercular infections were still little understood.

When Charles Fairfax Murray was just two years old, his mother was found to be suffering from phthisis, pulmonary consumption. She lingered for two more years and died on 2 November 1853, four weeks after his fourth birthday. When his wife first became fatally ill James Murray sold his business to his assistant, Arthur Oliver, and the family moved to a house, close to the draper's shop where her seven children were born, in the quieter neighbourhood of Robert Terrace, Poplar, where Elizabeth Murray died aged just 37. It was a mundane tragedy, a commonplace of life and death in the middle years of Victoria's reign.

The young Fairfax Murray was in Sudbury in Suffolk four years later. In his twenties Murray recalled childhood memories of the annual Croft Fair in Sudbury, the 'try your strength' machine and the majestic merry-go-round with its brass poles and finely chiselled horses.[4] It appears that the children were sent to the country to escape cholera which again swept through London in 1854, the year after Elizabeth Murray died. Lucy Maria, nearly 12 years of age when her mother finally succumbed to consumption and close to the time when she would have gone out to work, was now the young woman of the family and she devoted herself to looking after her younger brothers. She never married; Charles Fairfax Murray and Lucy Maria remained close for the rest of her life.

The gregarious Dr Charles Murray of Friar Street, Sudbury, out all the hours in his pony and trap for a gossip or a confinement, was a much-loved figure in the Suffolk market town. He may have been an older cousin of James Dalton Murray. A Scotsman who qualified as an MRCS in Edinburgh, Charles Murray was in partnership as a surgeon and general practitioner in Sudbury, married to the daughter of the previous senior partner. Their own son was educated privately at home by his evangelical mother, but Dr Murray was also an elder of the Independent Chapel in Friar Street which was responsible for John Fenn's Charity School. That most individual of English portrait painters, Thomas Gainsborough, created an annuity by his Will for the school to educate deserving poor, and a life-long childhood influence from his Sudbury days was Fairfax Murray's admiration for Thomas Gainsborough, a painter he later collected in historical depth. Gainsborough's legacy remained strong in Sudbury almost a century after his death, and the young Fairfax Murray was animated by it. From an early age he was absorbed in the Old Masters and their pictures, and in the private world of his own drawing. Fifty years on, recounting a discussion of Gainsborough's technique with Sir W B Richmond – Gainsborough kept his studio almost completely dark, the only light falling on his subject, so that visitors would often stumble against the furniture – Fairfax Murray unexpectedly added 'I shouldn't at all mind going to Sudbury one day, not for the sake of the pictures but from old associations.'[5]

Charles Fairfax Murray was an avid reader with a wide vocabulary. He received a sound, middle-class schooling, though he did not enjoy the opportunity of higher education, a lack he felt keenly all his life. The 1840s saw a great widening of accessibility and popular interest in art and literature through the shilling magazines and monthly part-works, of which Charles Dickens's *Household Words* is an often-quoted example. It was a good time for a curious and creatively inclined child to travel in the realms of gold, and no moderately well-to-do home would have been without books and prints. Fairfax Murray subscribed to the *Autographic Mirror*, a publication devoted to the new process of printed reproductions of popular pictures. He was educated well beyond the basic accomplishments, but it was as a draughtsman that he had a shining natural talent. It is tempting to imagine a genius 'self-taught', but the truth is that Fairfax Murray's prodigious innate aptitude was carefully nurtured, although his mentor cannot be identified with certainty. The ageing Richard Gainsborough Dupont is one possibility, another his friend George Fulcher, publisher, print-seller, engraver and sometime Mayor of Sudbury, both of whom were well-acquainted with the genial Dr Murray.

The family was dispersed by 1861. Their father worked as an accountant after he sold the draper's business. The death of Elizabeth Murray signalled the decline of his Victorian confidence and courage in the face of adversity, and on 1 January 1868, the first New Year's Day following his 60th birthday, James Dalton Murray was admitted as a Brother to the Charterhouse, the ancient foundation for 'gentlemen by descent and in poverty,' nominated by the Duke of Buccleuch, a Governor of the charity. Charles Fairfax Murray at 12 was living in London, lodging with a family from Ipswich in a tenement building, long demolished, in Derby Street off the

Gray's Inn Road. Fairfax Murray's eldest brother Arthur, by then 17 years old, was in Manchester, working as a secretary. On 7 June next year, 1862, Arthur, who gave his age to the Registrar as 20, was married at St Saviour's Parish Church, Chorlton, Manchester, to Kate Elizabeth Tipton, 23, the daughter of a pattern-card maker with a substantial business at 24 Marble Street, Manchester. Neither the bride's nor the groom's parents signed the register, and it is likely that the bride's parents were unenthusiastic over her choice of husband. The earliest known photograph of Fairfax Murray was taken in Manchester at the time by the leading *carte-de-visite* photographers, H Petschler & Co. It captures the young Charles Fairfax Murray at the age of 12 in a confident pose leaning nonchalantly on a chair back, legs crossed, left hand in jacket pocket. He is wearing a well-tailored serge three-piece suit edged in petersham ribbon, with a single button at the neck. A silk cravat and pearl pin complete the ensemble, the middle-class 'Sunday best' of the mid-Victorian era. The gaze towards the camera is candid and assured, and the impression is of a young lad from a comfortable background on the verge of manhood.

It is a cleverly posed photograph. There is little sign of any constitutional defect. Fairfax Murray inherited a rheumatic tendency from his father, but the chief evidence of weakness was his seriously-bowed legs. His build was muscular and thick-set, but he was shorter than his strong physique might suggest. 'The words bandy-legged only faintly expressed the pronounced nature of this strange deformity – which had, however, nothing either disconcerting or repellent about it, except for the wonder as to how he supported himself at all.'[6] The cause of this disability has been variously ascribed to rheumatic fever and polio, but it is probable that he suffered early in childhood from rickets – the result of dietary deficiency leading to softening of the bone – exacerbated by his starving himself in his early teens to buy the art materials that were food and drink to him. Fairfax Murray appeared to be completely unaware of it, and not surprisingly he never mentioned it.

At the zenith of Victoria's reign 12 was considered to be a proper age for a young man of the middle classes to go out to work. Indeed, necessity demanded it; there was no money to spare Fairfax Murray the need to earn his living. More than that, he had the ambition to become an artist and to make his career in the studio, and to achieve that he must earn his keep. Childhood was at an end. Some time between September 1862, when he was just 13, and April 1866, when at the age of 16 he became John Ruskin's protégé, Fairfax Murray was 'taken up' by Sir Samuel Morton Peto, one of the foremost of the contractors in the great age of expansion of the world's railways. Morton Peto was a towering figure in the entrepreneurial and political worlds of Victoria's Empire in mid-reign. Articled as a young man to his uncle, a builder, he succeeded to half of his business on his uncle's death and, with his cousin Thomas Grissel, built the London section of the

Great Western Railway, Nelson's Column and Trafalgar Square, the greater part of the South Eastern Railways and the Woolwich Graving Dock before dissolving their partnership in 1846. He went on to build the railway contracting business in to an international enterprise in partnership with E L Betts (while Grissel was content to build the Houses of Parliament). Morton Peto was London's Deputy Commissioner for Sewers, a guarantor of the Great Exhibition of 1851, and MP for Norwich from 1847 to 1854, when he resigned in order to build, at cost, a much-needed railway to bring up munitions and supplies from the Black Sea port of Balaklava to the siege of Sebastopol which closed the last chapter of the Crimean War. He returned to the House as MP for Finsbury in 1859.

The 13-year-old Charles Fairfax Murray found employment in the Great George Street drawing office of Peto & Betts as a 'shop-boy' or office boy, the first step towards becoming an apprenticed draughtsman. It was in this flourishing environment that Fairfax Murray's 'uncommon appearance and his talent for drawing had attracted attention.'[7] Sometime before May 1866, when a devastating banking crisis caused by the failure of the City's leading secondary bank, Overend & Gurney, brought Peto down for a time, the young Charles Fairfax Murray – then little more than a boy with an extraordinary talent – had stayed in Sir Morton's house in Kensington Green. Charles Fairfax Murray's first known work as a professional artist was a group of portraits of the four younger Peto children. It was a remarkable commission for a 15-year-old, from one of the most prominent men of his day. Fairfax Murray spent his leisure time in his employer's library; books were to become as great a passion as paintings. Morton Peto was a notable philanthropist and his partner Betts a patron of the arts, and it is possible that he assisted Murray in other ways, allowing him time to study in the British Museum. Fairfax Murray remained on good terms with Peto and his family after he left their employ, returning to draw a portrait of Morton Peto's mother, Sophia Alloway, in 1868.

Fairfax Murray's diary for October 1874 records that he 'called on Sir Morton Peto, saw the brothers Harold and Hubert.' Sir Samuel's son, the landscape designer Harold Peto, whose enchanting water garden flows through woodland to the lake at Buscot House – Burne-Jones's 'Briar Rose' canvases decorate the dining room – was a visitor to Fairfax Murray's studio in 1888,[8] 25 years after they first met.

Throughout his life, Charles Fairfax Murray's decided personality and outspokenness attracted and irritated in equal measure the people he encountered. Despite his preference for staying in the background, Fairfax Murray was difficult to overlook. Having lost his mother at so early an age that he can scarcely have remembered her, if he remembered her at all, it was natural that he should have grown up self-sufficient, his own man from the beginning, wary of the outside world. Shy and content with his own company, thoughts and ambition, he was able to pursue his dreams undisturbed. He was strongly self-willed, inner-directed. Stemming perhaps from his physical weakness he was, from the outset, always on the look-out and fiercely resentful of any sign of his being patronised, confident in his opinions to the point of unwitting offence, outspoken and tenacious in their defence when crossed, traits which led him to be described as pugnacious: 'A favourite phrase was "on the contrary". It followed as a matter of course that he could not put up with contrariness in others.'[9] Despite strong opinions and a deep inner reserve, Charles Fairfax Murray was by nature no introvert. He was good company, cheerful, sociable and endlessly active. Quiet and easy-going, without any pretensions to formality, which he greatly disliked, blessed with a strong sense of the ridiculous, he was kind, generous and helpful. He loved children, and as many as found him antagonistic found him charming and sympathetic.

Charles Fairfax Murray was not a fluent conversationalist,[10] though he was described as an amusing raconteur with a certain dramatic talent to enliven his stories.[11] He was inhibited by a belief that he had neither the literary talent nor the intellectual rigour to construct an argument in writing, although his personal letters are flowing and spontaneous. It was a self-fulfilling impediment despite the encouragement of many who urged him to publish and who were glad to seek his advice. Long after he had achieved his high reputation as a *marchand amateur* he felt constrained by his lack of university education. It was something he was deeply aware of, and he was at great pains to ensure that his children were well-educated. His failure to publish anything of his pioneering work as a critic and connoisseur was symptomatic of this misgiving; he nevertheless set to achieve his goals with determination and considerable success. The uncertainties of his early life had taught him to confide in no-one, to rely on no-one but himself, to count on nothing: 'it may never happen – who can tell – I believe in nothing till all is complete' he once wrote.[12] He was fond of quoting St Matthew vi:3, 'Let not your left hand know what your right hand doeth', and he lived that advice to the limit. He was an intensely private man.

At 16 'his glance was direct, he had a baritone voice, a winning manner, an indescribable air of romance, shrewdness and ideality. His forehead was square, his eyes were brown, his nose slightly upturned, lips full, chin well-formed but not too prominent, rounded cheeks, olive complexion, a fine crop of curly hair, dark but with colour in it. Interested in the affairs of others without neglecting his own ... he regarded the world with an amused smile.'[13] Self-effacing though he was, one of Charles Fairfax Murray's great gifts was his capacity for making friends. He took people as he found them and never betrayed a confidence, and his amiable manner, except when roused, drew people towards him. Having no pretensions himself he was unimpressed by titles and status, weighing only the person; reverence was nowhere in his make-up. If he was crossed or patronised his independence quickly asserted itself. He was unforgiving and never changed his mind about anyone who angered him. Paradoxically, he was endlessly tolerant of those people he admired.

Among a multitude of cordial acquaintances and close relationships in Charles Fairfax Murray's 69 years, one or two names stand out as true personal friends. William J Stillman, the American journalist and diplomat, was one. Edward Robert Hughes, the painter of the gentle allegory of infant mortality, *Night with her Train of Stars* was another. Teddy was the nephew of Arthur Hughes, whose *The Long Engagement*, with its uplifting theme, its use of brilliant colour on a white ground, and its detailed, natural woodland setting is quintessentially Pre-Raphaelite. The closest of his friends was William Silas Spanton, a photographer and supplier of artists' materials of 16 Abbeygate, Bury St Edmunds. Spanton, four years his senior, had set his sights on a career as an artist – some childhood work had attracted favourable notice from Queen Victoria herself – but the untimely death of his father brought him back to Bury to take over the family business, and it was only after he retired that he was able to take up painting seriously once more. He later wrote his reminiscences, curiously entitled *An Art Student and his Teachers in the 60's and Other Rigmaroles*, about his days as a student at the Royal Academy Schools where he was sponsored by Sir Edwin Landseer. William Spanton and Fairfax Murray worked side by side in the summer of 1866 at the Venetian Room of the National Gallery and at the Dulwich Picture Gallery, where Spanton was finishing his copy of Veronese's *Saint Jerome Blessing a Venetian Nobleman*, for which he received the Academy's Silver Medal in December of that year. Fairfax Murray was dividing every spare moment between copying and studying drawings and engravings in the Print Room at the British Museum[14]; his burning ambition was to find a way in to the world of Dante Gabriel Rossetti and his circle, and he was close to achieving his goal.

William Spanton's memoir of Charles Fairfax Murray is a deeply felt tribute to his friend and they kept up a lively correspondence from 1870, shortly before Fairfax Murray went to Italy for the first time, until a few months before Murray died, a span of almost 50 years. Spanton came close to being Fairfax Murray's only real confidant, though Marie Spartali, William Stillman's wife, shared the most intimate secrets of his personal life and understood him. When he retired, William Spanton – encouraged by Fairfax Murray and Edward Hughes – returned to painting at exactly the point at which he left off, contentedly copying the great Gainsborough and Reynolds portraits he had worked at so diligently in his youth, and he died in 1930 in Blackheath at 85, run over by a motor car.

Charles Fairfax Murray was born into the most confident and prosperous era in British history, and he lived between the peak of Victorian influence and the abrupt end of a social and economic system that had evolved over 150 years. In 1849 the Punjab was annexed, Hong Kong had recently become a British colony, and Lord Palmerston sent a gunboat to Piraeus to ensure that the Greek Government compensated a British subject whose house had been burned down by an anti-Semitic mob. Austen Henry Layard, who would later figure in Fairfax Murray's story, was, aged 26, excavating the ancient Assyrian city of Nimrud to the great benefit of the British Museum. At home, as middle-class prosperity took hold, the Chartist riots were at last subsiding although troops had been mobilised to keep the peace in the previous April. There were 6,500 deaths from cholera in the London metropolitan area alone in September 1849, the month that Fairfax Murray was born. The Roman Catholic hierarchy was restored in England in the following year. The Great Exhibition of Art and Industry of All Nations in Hyde Park would not open for another two years.

The handful of years of Fairfax Murray's childhood were also times of profound change in the Victorian art world. At no other time in the story of art in Britain was the mood for change so intense and the outcome so far-reaching, in style and subject, in popularity and interest, in patronage and art dealing. The movement was fuelled by radical changes in the social structure of Victorian England, by the increasing availability and interest in art fostered by prints and monthly magazines, and by growing prosperity. Both the era and the art it supported were ripe for reform. Charles Fairfax Murray's career paralleled the changing social basis of the art market; art patronage moved inexorably during his lifetime from the aristos to merchants, contractors and manufacturers who wanted the work of living artists on the walls of their splendid, overdressed homes. These were men of energy and discrimination who were confident enough to buy the pictures that reflected their own tastes and times, men such as James Leathart, the Newcastle mining and shipping magnate, William Graham, a merchant in the India trade and MP for Glasgow, and Frederick Leyland, the Liverpool shipowner. Studio copies multiplied, and technical advances in colour lithography fed the mass market of middle-class home owners who decorated their parlours with the latest and best in modern art, though they could not afford the originals. Artists could now negotiate and assign the reproduction rights of their work to be published as prints; the dealer as middle-man and buyer for stock became increasingly important in developing the public's taste for art and stimulating rising prices in the market.

An awareness of the value of art as 'the means of giving the people ennobling enjoyment'[15] led to the foundation of the National Gallery, which moved into its building in Trafalgar Square only ten years before Fairfax Murray was born, and continued to share the premises with the Royal Academy until he was 20. The dispersal of many of the great collections formed by the nobility in the years of the Grand Tour a hundred years earlier, and the dramatic rise in the American market for the Old Masters, would not be widespread for another 30 years or more, but a subtle reappraisal of their grandiose attributions and values was already taking shape. Charles Fairfax Murray's career as one of the great pioneering connoisseurs of European art almost exactly paralleled the development of the collectors' skills and outlook in England.

With consummate timing for one whose career was to be so intimately bound up with the Pre-Raphaelites, Fairfax Murray was born in the year that Walter Deverell introduced Elizabeth Siddal to Dante Gabriel Rossetti, and that Rossetti completed *The Girlhood of Mary Virgin* and *Ecce Ancilla Domini*. Both the Pre-Raphaelite Brotherhood and the Arundel Society were one year old. John Ruskin, arbiter of the arts, was in Venice with his young wife Effie, at work on the Venetian gothic for his encyclopaedic study *The Stones of Venice*, much more than a survey of the styles and history of La Serenissima's buildings, which formed the basis of his historical theories of moral and social decay and the ills of English society. In the year that Charles Fairfax Murray first went out to work, Morris, Marshall, Faulkner & Co was founded.

Charles Fairfax Murray's awakening ambitions were still clamouring to be realised when, early in 1866, he took the step that was to shape his life. With the keen instinct for an opening that served him well in later life, Fairfax Murray wrote to the distinguished author of *Modern Painters,* John Ruskin. Including with his letter a parcel of his drawings, Fairfax Murray asked for his advice 'on becoming, or how to become, an artist.'[16] Among the many who wrote with similar appeals, he succeeded in attracting Ruskin's attention. Absorbed and tormented though he was by his agonised relationship with the 18-year-old Rose La Touche, John Ruskin found his interest aroused by the young lad's promise. He straight away sent the drawings to the coming young artist he supported, the 33-year-old Ned Jones – Sir Edward Coley Burne-Jones, Bt., was as yet a struggling painter with a young wife and two small children but without a regular income – asking him to make arrangements with Charles Augustus Howell, his 'man of affairs', for Fairfax Murray's further training and maintenance. In March Ruskin wrote again, this time to Howell: 'Did Ned speak to you about an Irish[17] boy I want to get boarded and lodged and put to some art schooling – and I don't know how?' and once more later the same month: 'All I want is a decent lodging – he is now a shopboy – I only want a bit of a garret in a decent house, and a means of getting him in to some school of art.'[18]

Supported by Howell, who found the young painter lodgings just off the Fulham Road and supervised his studies on Ruskin's behalf, Fairfax Murray divided his time during the summer between classes in figure drawing from classical casts at Heatherley's School in Newman Street, copying at the National Gallery and study in the British Museum, where the kindly poet Coventry Patmore – another of the Pre-Raphaelite circle – had granted him access to the Reading Room although he was under age. He began working too on the painting entitled *The Children in the Wood* that he would exhibit at the Royal Academy in the following May. John Ruskin returned to England at the end of the summer of 1866 from four months spent in Italy and northern France, and in September he wrote afresh to Howell: 'The boy's sketches are marvellous.'[19] He had scented a talent that he could foster and instruct, and with the imperious philanthropy typical of this contradictory and impulsive man, he was already impatient for the fruits. Curiously, John Ruskin and his protégé came face to face only in the autumn, almost by accident, in the National Gallery. William Spanton described the incident which took place when Ruskin was giving a lesson to a pupil copying Turner. 'He clapped his hands, and spoke with the greatest animation. As he was leaving, I emboldened Murray who was bashful and shy, to go up and speak to him. Murray had been recommended to Ruskin, who had expressed a wish to see him, but they had not met before.'[20] Spencer Stanhope, independently wealthy but a dedicated artist, a friend of Ned Jones and Dante Rossetti and one year Rossetti's junior, was another Heatherley's pupil and National Gallery copyist whom Fairfax Murray already knew when he met William Spanton there.[21]

Howell, 'the Owl' in Rossetti's circle, proved an illuminating and supportive mentor that summer, introducing his young charge in to the company of the outstanding creative personalities of the time, and to ideas, knowledge and accomplishments that he can only have dreamed about. During the autumn of 1866, Howell arranged with Ned Jones to take the lad into his studio, where help was sorely needed, as his first assistant.

2. 'On Becoming an Artist'

In August 1864, Edward and Georgiana Jones's second son, Christopher, died just three weeks old. While Georgiana awaited her baby in the country at the Red House with the Morrises, Ned had painted *Green Summer*, a pastoral allegory of fleeting innocence, the tranquillity blending with an air of quiet foreboding. Among the seven maidens pictured in this idyll are Georgiana, her sister, and Janey Morris. Now, the transient sunny days in the orchard at Bexleyheath, laden with promise, were over forever; bleaker reality ruled all their lives. The Morrises had forsaken the house that Philip Webb had built for them, and they now lived in Queen Square over the workshops of 'the Firm', Morris, Marshall, Faulkner & Co, that they had dreamed in to being five years before at the Red House. Georgiana, Ned and Philip Jones had moved to 41 Kensington Square so that Georgiana should never return to the house opposite the British Museum where her baby had died and she had herself lain for three weeks delirious with fever. Margaret, their consolation, was born in June 1866, but Ned's work did not flourish and the young couple faced the melancholy realisation that their youth was flown.

There is no start of any new painting noted in Ned Jones's recollected list of works[1] between August 1864 and the following March, although in 1865 he exhibited *Green Summer, Merlin and Nimuë, Astrologia* and *Blind Love* at the Old Watercolour Society – the Royal was now known as 'the Old' to distinguish it from the New Watercolour Society, which had been founded in protest at the fogeyism and exclusivity that continued to mark the OWS. Edward Burne-Jones, as he would later become known, had started an oil-painting of *Circe* intended for Ruskin (although it went to Leyland in the end) and had begun a portrait of Ruskin which was never finished. He was seriously behind with the commissions that were both his livelihood and his future as a painter, though he finished *St Theophilus and the Angel* and a watercolour version of *Chant d'Amour,* one of two which precede the intense, poignant oil painting he commenced in 1868; but at the beginning of 1866 he was overwhelmed by work for the Firm,[2] and by the no less demanding task of illustrating Morris's *Earthly Paradise*, for which he produced 70 subjects for *Cupid and Psyche* that year.

Seeing the danger that decorative work for the Firm might distract Burne-Jones from his calling as a painter, John Ruskin set about remedying the situation. He devoted much of his generous and perceptive sponsorship at this period to the development of his artistic career, and to tiding him over financially. Ruskin had once promoted Dante Gabriel Rossetti until, finding the wayward poet and painter contemptuous and intractable, he had transferred his bounty to Rossetti's fiancée Lizzie Siddal. After her death in 1862 Ruskin had turned to Edward and Georgiana, who were among the few close enough to share his disturbed confidences about Rose La Touche. Now a wealthy man on the death of his father in 1864, Ruskin subsidised and promoted Burne-Jones to the limit. Charles Augustus Howell, acting as Ruskin's 'man of affairs' (on a suggestion of Burne-Jones's that he would later deeply regret), told everyone within earshot of his confidences that he was buying up any of Burne-Jones's work that came on to the market, 'to be re-placed at Jones's disposal for resale, any profit to remain for Jones's use,'[3] and regaled dinner parties with tales of Ruskin's infatuation with the 18-year-old Rose. This was the period of Howell's greatest involvement with Ruskin and his closeness to the Burne-Joneses, literally, since when they moved once more next year, this time to The Grange in Fulham, Ruskin installed Howell in a house in North End, a stone's throw away, to watch over his new disciple.

The move to The Grange was still in the future when Charles Fairfax Murray met Burne-Jones for the first time in the summer of 1866. He was not yet 17. He enrolled for the autumn term at the Working Men's College in Queen Square – across the square from the Firm – where Ruskin, Rossetti, Madox Brown and Edward Jones had once taught, and on 19 November 1866 he joined Burne-Jones's studio, a week or two after his 17th birthday. Fairfax Murray was given a basic wage of 25 shillings a week when he was on duty – £65 a year – to cover his living expenses, and there were substantial additional sums for individual pieces of work. At a time when a cook or a living-in servant might have £10 to £20 a year, it was a good wage for a 17-year-old. The additional payments were generous recognition of Fairfax Murray's usefulness and skill. (One of his 1867 payments – for his copy of the figure of St Dorothy in the lost *St Theophilus and the Angel* – was £60, almost doubling his annual basic wage.)

Fairfax Murray met William Morris a week or two later. They became immediate and firm friends.[4] Howell had introduced him to Dante Gabriel Rossetti and his brother William earlier that year. In December there followed an anxious correspondence between 'the Owl' and Rossetti, the latter intent on establishing a level of basic and additional payments similar to, but no more than, that paid by Burne-Jones[5] for which Fairfax Murray could also work for him; Dante Gabriel Rossetti was perennially anxious to find assistants to produce studio copies and so multiply the 'tin'. In January 1867, Rossetti suggested that Fairfax Murray should attempt a copy of the *Beata Beatrix* and, almost predictably, he failed to capture the subtle and elusive quality of the work as W J Knewstub had failed the test before him. 'Altho' I was a constant visitor I did not undertake any work for him 'till 1869–70'[6] he later recalled, but Rossetti generously found other ways to encourage and inspire the impressionable Fairfax Murray, perceptively recognising a gift in search of a vocation. He made himself useful and agreeable in any way he could for the sheer joy of it, and in a matter only of a few weeks he had found his way to the heart of the circle of poets, painters and patrons that dominated the progressive trend in the mid-Victorian arts. He quickly became the mascot of the circle. Dante Rossetti dubbed him 'Little Murray' – amended on special occasions to 'Little Muffy' – and the name stuck to the curly-headed lad, 'little more than a boy' as William Michael Rossetti described him. In the last year of his life, Burne-Jones still addressed his letters to 'DLM', or sometimes Dear Little Murray.

There was employment in plenty for Fairfax Murray in Kensington Square. Myles Birket Foster was chafing at the delay in completing the St George murals he had commissioned from Morris, Marshall, Faulkner & Co, known always as 'the Firm,' to decorate the dining room of 'The Hill', his house at Witley. Fairfax Murray was set to work on these from Burne-Jones's exquisitely detailed pencil drawings. William Morris had also felt obliged to reject the 12 zodiac figure panels painted by the Firm's assistants from Burne-Jones's designs for Philip Webb's Green Dining Room at the South Kensington Museum (prompting Alphonse Warington Taylor, the newly-appointed General Manager, to write a sharp memorandum to the partners pointing out that the Firm lacked the necessary skills to undertake this kind of decorative work). Charles Fairfax Murray was quickly commissioned to repaint all but one of the panels.[7] An Old Etonian contemporary of Algernon Swinburne, Warington Taylor was recruited one evening while working as a cloak-check man at Her Majesty's Theatre: 'he had not yet found his place in life', as Georgiana delicately put it.[8] His appointment was a further example of the inspired improvisation that marked the Firm at this point, with their work in great demand but increasingly disorganised and unprofitable. It is probable that the Firm would have gone under without him.

When Morris, Marshall, Faulkner & Co had opened for business at 8 Red Lion Square on 11 April 1861 there were seven equal partners: Ford Madox Brown, his friend Peter Paul Marshall, a surveyor and engineer, and Charles Faulkner, together with Dante Rossetti, Ned Jones, Philip Webb and William Morris. Morris and Charley Faulkner, an Oxford mathematical don, were the only two salaried members, Faulkner as the Firm's part-time administrative General Manager and accountant, and Morris as Business Manager.[9] The others were to be paid for the work they contributed and to take an equal share of the annual profit. George Campfield, a glass painter by trade whom Morris had met at the Working Men's College, was recruited as foreman.

Despite shared enthusiasms there were deep undercurrents among the partners from the beginning. The original members were hugely assorted personalities, and all but William Morris had other work of equal or greater importance. Only Morris had money in the company. It was, however, in the personal relationship between William Morris and Dante Gabriel Rossetti that the greatest tension existed when Fairfax Murray came into their circle. The observant and unobtrusive Murray could not have remained long unaware of the situation. Ever since the Oxford Union days of 1857, and throughout Morris's year-long engagement, there had been a barely concealed closeness between Rossetti and Janey Morris, an edge to Rossetti's treatment of Morris who became the butt of his witty rhymes and cruel cartoons. Beneath the raillery lay a more corrosive struggle, a battle of strong wills between two talented poets for Morris's creative identity and Rossetti's dominance. Rossetti was accustomed to lead; Morris was unaccustomed to follow.

In retrospect the romantic Red House years were a short, carefree interlude before reality – parenthood and paying bills, and the dictates of running the Firm while following their own directions – took hold of their lives. By the time that William and Janey Morris moved to the two floors above the Firm in Queen Square in 1865 Janey, now the mother of two small girls, had already devised the rôle she played in public for the rest of Morris's life, the remote and unattainable *chatelaine* of Castle Morris, working at her embroidery and studying her books as she lay, decorative and semi-invalid, on her couch. Morris was dismayed, helpless to reach out to her, while Rossetti paid her court for all to see. His slighting description of William Morris as 'the Bard and Petty Tradesman' was deftly calculated to play on the change in their fortunes.

With Janey now more easily accessible, Rossetti again started to paint her, first as *La Pia de Tolomei* who was confined by her uncaring husband Nello della Pietra in a tower set in the marshes of Maremma, where she died by poisoning. The story comes from Dante's *Purgatorio* Canto V, and the painting occupied Rossetti fitfully until the middle of 1880. The choice of subject, a beautiful woman ensnared in a loveless marriage, could scarcely have been entirely innocent, while Janey once again found in Rossetti the awakening touch of admiration and pleasure in her emblematic beauty. They were never discreet. 'Gabriel ... I must say acts like a perfect fool if he wants to conceal his attachment'[10] William Bell Scott wrote to Alice Boyd, but, of course, Rossetti in love wanted no such thing. He painted Janey again in 1869 as *Pandora*, as *Mariana* in *Measure for Measure* – another tale of promised love neglected – and in 1870 once more as Beatrice in *Dante's Dream at the Time of the Death of Beatrice*.

These were difficult times too for Edward and Georgiana Burne-Jones, as Fairfax Murray could not help but be aware, if he was not already forewarned by the conspiratorial Howell. As well as Burne-Jones's deep involvement in the growing success of the Firm to the exclusion of his painting, there was a deeper cause of his inability to concentrate on his work that Autumn. Unaccountably, the shy and self-absorbed artist had fallen painfully and inextricably in love with Maria Cassavetti Zambaco, one of the three strikingly lovely younger members of Greek society in London – Maria Cassavetti, Marie Spartali and Aglaia Coronio – the Three Graces. Maria Zambaco was the wild and accessible daughter of the formidable Euphrosyne Cassavetti, the immensely wealthy widow of a prominent member of the Greek merchant community in Alexandria. Known to all as 'the Duchess' for her imperious ways, she was the sister of Alexander Constantine Ionides, doyen of the Greek community in London. The Ionideses were wealthy and influential collectors, the patrons of Dante Gabriel Rossetti, George Frederic Watts, William Morris and Edward Jones himself. Maria Cassavetti, elemental and compellingly beautiful, with long, glowing red hair, had defied her family to marry a vain and unimaginative specialist in venereal diseases,[11] the physician to the Greek community in Paris, Dr Demetrius Zambaco. Tiring of the relationship after five stormy years, she had returned to London. Her mother had brought her to Edward Jones to sit for her portrait in June of 1866. He was completely enthralled by this overtly sexual and tempestuous woman. Georgiana, bewildered and deeply hurt, coped stoically with her new baby daughter, the threat to her marriage and with her distracted husband. Matters were patched up for a time so that, when Charles Fairfax Murray joined the little circle in October, some muted semblance of the old ways had been re-established. The crisis was, however, far from passed.

While Fairfax Murray worked on the backlog of figure painting in the studio looking out over Kensington Square, Burne-Jones was listless, weary and unable to make any decisive move or new creative beginning. In July of 1867 he was back in digs in Oxford with the family, the Morrises and Charley Faulkner, still unable to get to grips with his work: 'Mention Mantegna to me: I am doing nothing – can't in lodgings with the noise of the children' he wrote to Fairfax Murray who was holding the fort, delightedly showing William Spanton around the studio in a proprietorial manner in the family's absence.[12] Charles Fairfax Murray exhibited his *Children in the Wood* at the Summer Royal Academy. 'Those babies – it's the sweetest picture I ever, ever saw & I hadn't seen it before & I didn't know of it at all, so well are you rewarded'[13] Burne-Jones wrote when he saw the picture. He was protective of his new assistant. In August, he wrote to Fairfax Murray to say that 'Mr Rossetti hearing of my absence has proposed to relieve me of you for a while... I have written to say that another fortnight will see me back and that you are busy on your own work. Write and tell me how it prospers.'[14] The family returned to Kensington Square from Oxford in September to learn that their landlord had sold the freehold while they were away. The new owner was not minded to renew their lease.

The Joneses and the studio moved west once more, to Fulham on the outskirts of London, in November 1867. They rented half of The Grange in the North End Road, a rambling, neglected late-Georgian house surrounded by orchards and market gardens, sharing it at first with

Wilfred Heeley in order to defray the cost. Burly Val Prinsep's dancing at the house-warming brought the ceiling down on the supper-room below. Life on the surface had resumed its routine, and Fairfax Murray was present at a dinner in the following May of 1869 for Charles Eliot Norton, the Professor of Fine Arts at Harvard. The others present were Dante Gabriel Rossetti, Georgiana and Edward Jones – host and hostess – William Morris, Mrs Norton, Philip Webb and Janey Morris, reclining as ever on the sofa. He made a sketch recording the occasion.[15] 'Gabriel came in the evening – I sang to him a long time while Ned worked and Murray – friend to us all by this time – made himself happy in the background' wrote Georgiana Burne-Jones[16] of those days, striving to rekindle happier times. Charles Fairfax Murray seemed always to be at hand throughout the crises of this period.

Not long after he had joined Burne-Jones, Dante Gabriel Rossetti wrote a letter of introduction to Isa Craig, the editor of *Argosy*, cordially recommending Fairfax Murray as an illustrator.[17] Now a note arrived from Rossetti, asking 'would you any time between 10.00 and 2.30 call on Mr F W Burton ... in Kensington. He mentioned to me a little thing he wanted done and it occurred to me that it might suit you to do it ... the work is to make an enlarged drawing from a photograph of a gothic statue.'[18] Rossetti's generosity in seeking patrons and promoting the talents of his circle was one of his most conspicuous and engaging characteristics, but even he cannot have foreseen the importance of this introduction to the young Fairfax Murray. Burton was later to become the Director of the National Gallery and one of Fairfax Murray's most valued clients. Murray in return 'was always ready to do any friendly and good-natured service to my brother,' wrote William Michael Rossetti, 'copying his poems from the original manuscripts or sending him photographs ... from Italian works of art interesting or useful to him.'[19] When in October 1868 Charles Augustus Howell arranged the recovery from Lizzie Siddal's grave of the notebook containing Rossetti's poems which he buried with her, a period of intense editing and expanding the collected poems ensued. While Swinburne assisted with the revisions, the publisher and drama critic Joseph Knight[20] and Fairfax Murray endlessly transferred Dante Gabriel Rossetti's alterations into fair copy for the typesetters: 'Do you mind my tearing up your mss. copies to give to the printer if necessary?' Rossetti enquired. 'I'll give you a set of the printed things.'[21]

1868 was another inauspicious year so far as Edward Jones's work was concerned. John Ruskin was still supporting him despite a deep and evident distaste for his continuing involvement with Maria Zambaco. Edward Jones continued defiantly to see Maria Zambaco in the spring; there were parties at the Ionideses and at Evans's supper club, where they met in public. In June he tried to break with his lover and there was a dreadful scene: 'a terrible day'[22] Ruskin confided to his diary. Work was out of the question, and Fairfax Murray was given time off in July to travel up to Leeds to visit the Fine Art exhibition of pictures from the Layard and Barker collections in the newly-built Leeds Infirmary. He still spent most of his spare time studying the Old Masters, learning brushstroke by stroke the style and techniques that distinguished the great from the first-rate, and weighing attributions with an increasingly expert eye. The *Chant d'Amour* which Murray was to copy was not yet ready, 'there is no hurry – stop and enjoy yourself – come home when you like, a week later if it's doing you good to be away and enjoy yourself – nothing has happened or is going to happen ... write again and tell me about the Mantegnas.'[23] Fairfax Murray later said that he thought that several paintings were 'school' pictures or even modern forgeries, but felt he was too young to express his doubts publicly.

Edward Jones at last steeled himself to tell Maria Zambaco that he could not leave Georgiana. On the night of 23 January 1869, walking with her lover in swirling fog between the Ionideses house in Holland Park and her own in Little Venice, she attempted to drown herself in the Paddington Basin of Regent's Canal. Next morning, William Morris arrived early at The Grange and the two friends departed for Rome; but at Dover, Ned Jones was too ill to make the crossing and they returned. He shut himself up in The Grange and Georgiana took the children away to the country once more. Rossetti made light of the incident, writing gleefully to Ford Madox Brown 'Poor old Ned's affairs have come to a smash altogether, and he and Topsy, after a most dreadful to-do started for Rome suddenly, leaving the Greek damsel beating up the quarters of all his friends for him and howling like Cassandra.'[24] In April a shaken Ned Jones pressed Rossetti to make a portrait of Maria, with 'a frame made that has a door in it that locks up, and that I may return an evasive answer to an inquisitive world.'[25] Both painter and patron were pleased with the result – 'I have made a good portrait of Mary Zambaco and Ned is greatly delighted with it... I enclose a note from the poor old dear as it shows how nice he is. I like her very much.'[26]

For the moment Maria Zambaco continued to sit for him. Unabashed by the scandal, 'the Duchess' commissioned the series of four small oil paintings of *Pygmalion and the Image* which were completed in 1870. As was by now their usual practice, Charles Fairfax Murray assisted Edward Jones with the preparatory work: 'come on over as soon as you can after (dinner) and bring your sheaves with you – bring the oil Pig as well – in a cab. You shall return with tin – the 2nd Pig is in a very luckless state and we must scheme out some other work to go on with. I should like to make a show of work at the OWS this next year, possibly you might help me.'[27] He completed the watercolour first version of *Phyllis and Demophöon* in which Maria is depicted as the rejected Phyllis imprisoned in the bough of an almond tree, reaching out to her naked lover. In August Edward Jones wrote to Fairfax Murray: '*King's Wedding* is ready for you to have – it needs a few hours more work... I sent it to Madame Zambaco to have for a day ... come here for instance for lunch, you might go there afterwards for it.'[28] Fairfax Murray would be more than a silent witness to the doomed affair. Ten years after their meeting he was still their trusted intermediary.

Fairfax Murray's red-chalk portrait of Janey, commissioned by Rossetti's publisher F S Ellis at Murray Marks's suggestion, dates from this time. Ellis also proposed that Fairfax Murray should draw the illustrations for Christina Rossetti's *Sing Song* nursery rhymes, a suggestion enthusiastically endorsed by the author: 'Mr Murray is everything I can wish if he can be persuaded to accept the commission.'[29] In the event he could not find time, and after Alice Boyd's illustrations were rejected Arthur Hughes completed the task. They all took a keen interest in his work despite the complications of their own lives. Edward Jones wrote on Christmas Eve 'Dear Little Murray, when will you come and see me? I want to tell you about things, but the week has been so horribly dissipated, no work, no anything that I wanted ... I saw the portrait[30] and thought it very promising – Mr Morris would tell you the things I said about it. *Love in the Ruins* not touched – nothing done – 2 days horrible headache.'[31] The strains of his affair with Maria Zambaco continued to take their toll. 'Thanks for remembering this bloody day'[32] he replied to Fairfax Murray's 38th birthday greetings in August 1871.

Charles Fairfax Murray too had an affair of the heart about this time, with 'a favourite model of Burne-Jones's I was once much smitten with' he told his client Samuel Bancroft[33] years later (a confidence quite out of character). The lady in question was probably the imposingly-named Reserva, a statuesque raven-haired beauty who was thought at first to have been of Romany blood but whom, it transpired, was so named because – an inspired lunacy – she was born close to the Camden Hill reservoir.[34] (Reserva, a dancer by profession, was later in the chorus of Gilbert and Sullivan's *Patience,* all of whom wore Lazenby Liberty's dresses, an idea suggested by Luke Ionides which led Gilbert to recast his plot from two rival curates to the rival aesthetes.) Fairfax Murray also cast a lingering glance at two pretty sisters, Clara[35] and Emma, the daughters of his landlady in Effingham Street. He took an appreciative interest in feminine beauty and kept a number of photographs of society beauties on the mantel in his bedroom; a young man in the highly charged atmosphere of Rossetti's circle, he was in every way imbued with the romantic Pre-Raphaelite pursuit of iconic beauty, quite distinct from everyday life.

When he arrived at Kensington Square, Fairfax Murray was already highly practised in pencil, chalks, sepia and watercolour, though less experienced in oils; he referred to 'Mr Jones, my master in painting'. Edward Jones's studio practice was similar to the Italian 'schools'. He would prepare finished pencil drawings which Murray would transfer to a prepared canvas in burnt sienna or terre-verte line and shading, and later assist with backgrounds and drapery. 'The years I spent with Mr Jones I regard as amongst the best spent of my life ... my work for him principally consisted in commencing pictures from sketches and studies, decidedly good work' Fairfax Murray wrote ten years later.[36]

At the time he was rather less enthusiastic about the way that Edward Jones worked. 'Masters should be content to let the pupil's work remain. Perugino paints the heads, his pupils the draperies and landscape and finish them minutely. The bane of modern art is the want of system which prevents this satisfactory union ... an artist like Mr Jones cannot be satisfied with any work but his own and has always destroyed anything I have done for him, however carefully, so that it is no pleasure to do it. He insists that it is useful to have it so prepared for him, but there is no pleasure in doing a little thing carefully and spending days over it (to have it) destroyed ruthlessly in a few minutes. It used not to be so; they had more the spirit of decorative contractors, they were not nearly so anxious about their works as we are. Mr Perugino contracted to paint the head, hands and feet in a picture – he was allowed gold and ultramarine (fancy such a clause in an agreement with a swell of the present day.) He took care not to do more than his share for the money – it (was) not like the great artist with an idea of his mission being to astonish the world with his works.'[37] Fairfax Murray's practical and historical approach to painters and painting was well-developed early in his career, and it served him well in his deep understanding of the Italian *trecento*.

When he was not working at The Grange or for the Firm in Queen Square, Fairfax Murray busied himself with buying and selling drawings at Christie's, and with commissions from Collinson & Lock, the cabinetmakers who rivalled Morris's work in quality. The company employed designers of the standing of T E Collcutt (the architect of Imperial College, South Kensington, the Savoy Theatre and the Palace Theatre) and E W Godwin. Fairfax Murray received a steady flow of decorative work from his friend George Lock; painted figure panels, a 'trademark' of Collinson & Lock furniture design, was work at which he excelled, and his surviving account records show that he painted 29 pieces in one year alone.[38]

Charles Fairfax Murray was beginning to prosper, and in September 1869 Henry Treffry Dunn told William Michael Rossetti that 'young Murray has now started as an artist on his own account.'[39] Leaving his full-time employment, Fairfax Murray now embarked on a career as a painter in his own right and as a connoisseur and expert, collaborating with William Morris on his manuscripts, assisting Edward Jones, and working for Dante Rossetti as a copyist. His new employer wrote regularly from Scalands, Barbara Bodichon's house near Hastings where he was staying with Janey Morris, to enquire anxiously about his progress. Studio copies were in demand, and that spelled much-needed money to Rossetti. His letters to Fairfax Murray in the spring of 1870 are gently pressing: 'Have you got on with the things in hand for me? I find I shall be needing the oil picture on Thursday to show to someone, but shall be able to let you have it again the same evening or next morning as you like,'[40] and in another later letter: 'I wd. be glad if you cd. get on with it as speedily as may be' (a commissioned copy of the *Sybilla Palmifera*).[41] The letters also cast light on Dante Gabriel Rossetti's technique. 'It strikes me that your best place with that picture would be to paint in all but the head area, only lay in the head in blue, with such brushwork as seeming desirable to work over. Then when all is in & the head dry, we would see whether it is best for you or for me to finish the head.'[42] An underpainted blue ground, in contrast to the more usual terre-verte, gave a particular translucency and life to Rossetti's voluptuous skin tones.

Fairfax Murray took rooms with William Spanton's landlady in Effingham Street, Pimlico, at this time. George Howard, an able amateur artist, later the 9th Earl of Carlisle and owner of Naworth Castle and Castle Howard, would call there on horseback to visit him.[43] There was an exemplary classlessness among the mid-Victorian artists, their friends and patrons, and George Howard was another of Fairfax Murray's gifted friendships across the divides of age and social standing which would remain important to him in years to come. Delighted by Rossetti's commission to copy the *Sybilla Palmifera*, and conscious of the gravity of his task, Fairfax Murray rented an additional room which he set up as his studio. As the appropriate setting for his work, he chose William Morris's new 'Pomegranate' design to cover the walls, and enquired of Mr Jones the price of this costly paper. He received in reply a letter informing him that 'the common price of that paper is 13d a yard. I have spoken to Mr Morris and you are to have it at the price to a member of the firm which is I think 5d a yard, he silent as to the outrageous profit' and continued 'Wardle has written to you re some work – if it promises to be at all remunerative, take it.'[44] The commission was to paint the miniatures to Edward Jones's designs for Morris's poems which he gave to Georgiana on her 30th birthday.

Throughout the spring of 1870, William Morris, Burne-Jones, George Wardle and Fairfax Murray worked on the beautiful illuminated *Book of Verse*, with Morris undertaking the calligraphy and the greater part of the decoration, Wardle completing the borders and the illuminated initials, Burne-Jones painting one illustration and Fairfax Murray doing the remaining miniatures for this exquisite volume. He went with William Morris on 14 June to John Parsons, the photographer, to obtain the profile image of Morris that he used for his portrait medallion on the cover, and all was completed for Georgiana's birthday on 26 August, though not before the ever-impatient Morris had written to Murray: 'I should be so much obliged if you could get on with the little pictures, for I have done all the ornament.'[45] When the *Book of Verse* was finished Morris tried for a while to take up painting once more, drawing from life at Fairfax Murray's little studio in Effingham Street.[46]

This was William Morris's lowest time. His marriage had become an agonised, tolerant friendship. His mentor of ten years before and his business partner, Dante Gabriel Rossetti, was openly in love with his wife, and the demands of the Firm – a measure of its success – were mounting. He turned for understanding to Georgiana Burne-Jones in burning affection; deeply hurt by her husband's affair, she nevertheless drew back from the brink, but the closeness and sympathy between them remained fresh throughout their lives. William Morris could not contain his despair. On the evening of 24 May 1869 he had dinner with Burne-Jones and Fairfax Murray at which he roundly condemned his great friend for his treatment of Georgiana in such forthright terms that he felt it necessary to write to both, apologising, next day.[47]

There were evenings to fill when the light failed in the studio. Fairfax Murray and William Spanton would spend evenings at the opera, often with the American painter, Francis Lathrop. His great love of music – Mozart and Verdi were favourite composers – distinguished him from many of the later Pre-Raphaelite circle, who seem collectively to have had little ear for music. The unfortunate Alfred Buxton Forman who sent William Morris his English text of *Die Walküre* in the expectation of praise, received a magisterial polemic for his pains: 'I wish to see Wagner uprooted. I look upon it as nothing short of desecration to bring such a tremendous and world-wide subject under the gaslights of an opera, the most degraded and rococo of all forms of art – the idea of a sandy-haired German tweedle-deeing over the unspeakable woes of Sigurd...'[48] Morris commenced his reply. Wagner was much admired both by Rossetti and Burne-Jones, but it was for the composer-librettist's mythic gods and the struggles of his Teutonic heroes against the forces of tyranny and evil rather than for his music.

Dante Gabriel Rossetti was tireless in creating new circles of friends from his own. He went to some pains to introduce Fairfax Murray to James Abott McNeill Whistler, and made a point of organising a dinner at Tudor House in order that he should meet Ford Madox Brown. Madox Brown, Rossetti's senior by seven years, was one of those who might have parted company with him on many occasions – he once accused Rossetti, not without reason, of 'venom and spite and delight in setting friends one against another' – but who recognised that his significance was greater than his weaknesses. In the self-inflicted decline towards the end of Rossetti's life Madox Brown remained a constant friend and support, and a good friend of the much younger Fairfax Murray.

Samuel Bergheim, a friend of Whistler, was another of Fairfax Murray's lifelong friendships formed in Cheyne Walk. He was an amateur mesmerist, one of the several mediums (including the washerwoman Mrs Marshall) who conducted weekly seances to contact the spirit of Elizabeth Siddal. The young Fairfax Murray also first encountered George Price Boyce, landscape

mental journey, a search for the truth, for the older man. When Morris later revisited Bruges once more, this time with Janey, he wrote to Aglaia Coronio from the Hotel du Commerce: 'I am in the same room as Janey and I had on our wedding trip. This morning we went to the Hospital of St John (where the Memling pictures are) and I looked in the book for my name and Murray's and found them, 3 October 1870.'[52] It was a generous 21st birthday present. Edward Jones wrote sourly to George Howard on his birthday: 'Morris is starting for a week in Bruges with little Murray who grows more pronounced and oracular daily... (he) has this advantage over anyone I know that he is only twenty one.'[53] There is an unmistakable air of resentment that the ambitious and youthfully-opinionated Fairfax Murray was confidently setting his own course, a hint of jealousy that he too should enjoy George Howard's friendship.

On their return there was a letter from Burne-Jones that offered no clue to his exasperation of the week before: 'Dear Little Murray, Will you paint some portraits? One of Mrs Ionides and one of Mrs Coronio and her daughter together – and if so arrange with me about them? Come over and grub on Wednesday at 7, I shall be going over to Holland Park afterwards and can take you with me ... they are for Mr Alecco.'[54] Charles Fairfax Murray had come of age as a draughtsman and portraitist as well as in years. Alecco Ionides, old Alexander's son, was one of the wealthiest and most judicious patrons of the arts in London. It was signal recognition; the twenty-one years old painter had worked alongide George Frederic Watts, who would paint five generations of the Ionides family and had hitherto received all of the family's commissions, as his studio assistant during that summer of 1870. The introduction by way of Burne-Jones can only have come from him.

In the Spring of 1871 Fairfax Murray worked with William Morris on a second illuminated manuscript book, *The Story of the Volsungs and Niblungs*, translated by Morris from the Icelandic, more sparingly decorated than the *Book of Verse*, to which he contributed the lightly drawn figures of the title page and the single historiated initial that opens the text. The Morrises were a family to the self-sufficient Murray: 'Will you come and dine tomorrow and have a bed? 7 o'clock to dinner, though I dare say the kids and Janey would be glad to see you earlier... I will take care you have a pudding.'[55] Fairfax Murray was an honorary uncle to the children and their particular friend; he was only eleven years older than Jenny, and he loved children. Morris and Murray went on wonderful expeditions together: 'Breakfasted with Mr Morris. Went with him to Faringdon, lunched at Lechlade and drove over to Kelmscott to look at a house and returned in the evening' Murray noted in his diary for 16 May 1871,[56] a wonderfully detached account of the day on which William Morris discovered the Cotswold manor that would be his greatest source of happiness for the remainder of his life.

By June, William Morris had arranged a joint tenancy of Kelmscott Manor with Rossetti so that he and Janey could legitimately be there together, distanced from the growing storm of scandal around their relationship. Pausing only to bid Janey be happy, Morris departed for Iceland. Fairfax Murray was among the small gathering of intimate friends that the Joneses assembled to welcome Morris back in September: 'Come and dine on Monday and drink to the most desirable return of the polar expedition.'[57]

Fairfax Murray was blessed from the outset of his career both with a singularly unprejudiced view of his abilities and with a robust and unromantic understanding of the market for any but the most celebrated painters of the day. Now 21 years of age, he was precisely aware of his talents, his strengths and weaknesses of skill, education and attitude, the chances of his becoming a celebrated artist and the struggle that lay ahead in realising his ambitions. Dante Gabriel Rossetti had long encouraged Fairfax Murray in his bent for scholarship. He employed him to index his extensive collection of photographs of the great masterpieces of European art and in researching references for his work. They mulled over Rossetti's prized *Portrait of Smeralda Bandinello*,[58] attributed to Botticelli, and studied the photographs of the *Primavera*, from which Rossetti thought he identified Smeralda as the model for 'Spring'. They pored together over old engravings. Most important of all, Dante Rossetti and Fairfax Murray talked for hours over his embryonic plan to go to Italy to study the masterpieces he knew only from photographs and engravings, Rossetti urging and encouraging him, full of confidence in his success. For as long as he had studied the great masters Charles Fairfax Murray had been fascinated by the characteristics of composition, by the subtleties of brushwork, by the nuances of style and the variations of technique that distinguished one artist from another, one school from its predecessors, the master from his pupils. He was confident of his wide-ranging knowledge of the painters he had been able to study at first hand, and he was possessed of a remarkable visual memory – a natural gift which he honed by hours of painstaking analysis. His way ahead led towards Italy.

In August of 1871 Rossetti wrote to Fairfax Murray about the attribution of a painting to Luini in the recently published *A History of Painting in North Italy*, which the latter had disputed. He urged that he should 'open (his) critical career by finding out all about the picture & writing to the Athenaeum to set Crowe & Cavalcaselle by the ears, as no doubt each will tell the other that it was his business to know.'[59] Later that month he wrote 'of course that Lucretzia is a Francia now you say so. It is just like the type and turn of his heads... I really do advise you to write a note on the subject to some paper – either the Athenaeum or the Academy. I would see to getting it inserted if you cared to do so.'[60] Rossetti later remembered that, significantly, Fairfax Murray had not done so.

By the autumn of 1871 Charles Fairfax Murray was busier than ever, having work in hand for Dante Gabriel Rossetti, William Morris and for Edward Jones as well as his own painting and research. He rushed from studio to studio, from Effingham Street to Queen Square and out to the edge of London at Fulham, back to Christie's and on to Morris, Marshall, Faulkner & Co. He worked with Burne-Jones on the Firm's commission for new decoration and stained glass for the chapel at Castle Howard. 'It has struck me that it would be a great gain if you were to do the bronze babies in the Castle Howard window, I don't see how they are to be rendered unless you do them for the knowledge of babies is not broadcast among workmen... I wish you had done the 8 Sibyls, but that seems impossible, do if you can seize those 8 babies, I have spoken to Mr Morris about it ... as soon as ever you have a studio we can plan some work for mutual help. I only want you to do them.'[61] The Castle Howard commission came at Burne-Jones's lowest time in his artistic career; he had resigned from the Old Watercolour Society in July 1870 over the disapproval of his nude male depiction of *Demophöon*. His personal relationships with Dante Gabriel Rossetti and even with William Morris were at a low ebb. Ruskin was sternly disapproving. Georgiana and the children were more often away from The Grange than at home. He inclined self-pityingly to anticipate the worst of everyone. 'I spoke to little Murray and strange to say that great soul unbent and was affable and we are to organise the wall pictures at once'[62] he wrote to George Howard.

The work fell behind and there was a confrontation in October: 'I began to suggest it would be a comfort to have the pictures begun' Jones wrote to George Howard '...he said pretty plainly that he repented the undertaking ... as I think because he wants to get away to Italy... I feel seriously angry about it....'[63] Thomas Matthews Rooke assisted in the studio now, and Georgiana was still in the country with the children. Fairfax Murray spent a happy week at Kelmscott Manor with William Morris. Dante Rossetti wrote 'I should be sorry to miss seeing you and having a chat.' In the third week of November, Charles Fairfax Murray slipped quietly away to Italy.

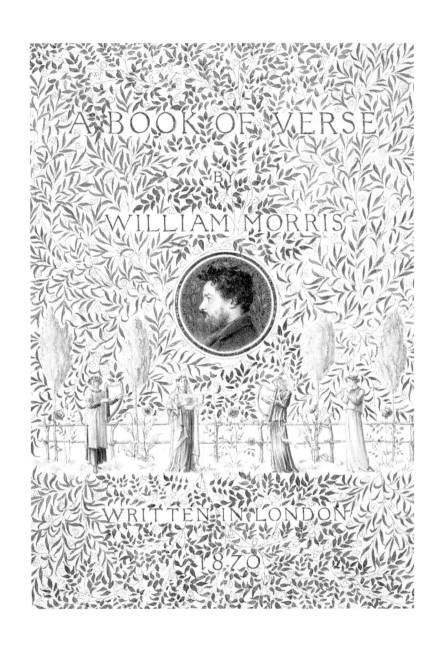

A BOOK OF VERSE
BY
WILLIAM MORRIS

WRITTEN IN LONDON
1870

3. A Visit to Italy

William Morris's
Book of Verse,
1870: ink,
watercolour and
gilding on
vellum. William
Morris, Edward
Burne-Jones,
George Wardle
and Charles
Fairfax Murray
contributed to
this, Morris's
first essay in
calligraphy; the
cover portrait
and all but one
illustration are
by Fairfax
Murray. *V&A
Picture Library*

Charles Fairfax Murray arrived in Pisa in a cold, wet winter. 'People here are seldom without green umbrellas' he noted. 'Today is such a day as is usually supposed peculiar to England – a regular even wall of dull sky and a continual steady downpour from it after a preparative two dull days out of three. You might imagine yourself in Hackney, Camberwell or any other suburban place where there are unfinished houses, heaps of bricks and rubbish, and a railway station.'[1] He spoke no Italian. He knew almost no-one in Italy and seems to have had few introductions in Pisa. He was in a strange country, surrounded by people yet completely alone, and it is small wonder that he found the contrast between the prospect as seen from Cheyne Walk and the chilly reality of Pisa daunting. The carefully planned adventure had been much discussed all summer, but nothing had prepared him for the homesickness and loneliness he felt.

Pisa had seemed the natural choice of a base. Burne-Jones had returned from there only a few weeks before and was able to describe the town and its sights, while Lasinio's engravings of the frescoes in the Campo Santo where Fairfax Murray wanted to work were a central theme in the mythology of the Brotherhood (though Rossetti had long since forgotten why). His only English friend in Tuscany at this moment was Spencer Stanhope, who was on the point of leaving Bellosguardo, some 70 miles away, where he had a studio, to return to England for Christmas. Fairfax Murray made two visits to Florence to study in the Uffizi and at Santa Maria Novella and to enjoy the company of Dante Rossetti's ebullient and carefree follower. The friendly face, and letters from home, heartened him. Philip Webb wrote to F S Ellis urging him to write to Fairfax Murray – 'he pines for letters and must be very lonely'[2] – and gradually he settled to life in Pisa. On Boxing Day, Edward Burne-Jones wrote to cheer him up: 'Stanhope told me about you, and I am afraid that from his account you have had rather a bad time of it – I don't see how it could be helped. You will have to look on Pisa as a kind of distant Hastings where you have gone to winter with Campo Santo thrown in – but I do wish your first sight of Italy could have been happier… keep up your heart, easy words to say but I am afraid you are very lonely unless you can make friends more easily than I do…'[3] Burne-Jones was never one to be outdone in burdens nobly borne.

As the days became weeks, Fairfax Murray found new resolve, immersed in painting and the intensive study of the art treasures that had brought him there. His early attempts to learn Italian gave rise to a rueful account in a letter to Dante Gabriel Rossetti: 'I have been studying Italian under a funny old priest (whose

English library includes *The Amours of a Friar*) but after making an awful mistake in speaking to a lady by which I intimated that I would draw her when she was asleep instead of her infant, I have given it up for a while, slightly discouraged.'[4] In February he was painting the view from the Academy in Pisa and settling to making notes of all the better paintings there. He planned further visits to Florence, where the sacristan of Santa Maria Novella was already a firm friend who left him to sketch the frescoes in the Spanish Chapel when he went home for the night.

Fairfax Murray was weighing and discussing the merits of Taddeo Gaddi's frescoes of the *Theological Virtues* against the restless and beautifully detailed figure from the *Church Militant* of Simone Memmi, the name by which Simone Martini was known at the time. He had already made a careful copy of another Memmi, a 'half-length figure of a Saint, I'm not sure who,' to be shown at the International in London in the spring. He had been to Prato to see the Fra Filippo Lippi frescoes in the Duomo there, and was planning a trip to Siena and San Gimignano. He also found time for a sardonic comment on Ruskin: 'the things that Mr Ruskin has been doing lately have not raised him in one's estimation – fancy his cutting up a beautiful illuminated book and presenting a few leaves to one place, a few leaves to another, and keeping a few for himself – the energetic preacher against vandalism! Mr Morris declares him to be a brilliant rhetorician ... without really caring much for art.'[5] Ruskin's diary mentions a 'busy morning cutting up manuscripts'.

The seeds of Charles Fairfax Murray's future career were sown in his first four months in Italy. Spending 'without exaggeration a fortnight copying the Memmi, I shall not make any more complete copies – I find I can make as good a remembrance of a picture in two hours as in two weeks,' he wrote to William Spanton: 'it is a pity that copying these beautiful things is so unsatisfactory (to me at least) that I lose my pleasure in the originals for the time being.'[6] At the time, Fairfax Murray had no thought of spending long hours copying, and he cherished the intention of making his way as a painter and as a connoisseur to rival the expertise of Crowe and Cavalcaselle, whose *History of Painting in North Italy*, published in 1871, soon became staple reading in Dante Gabriel Rossetti's circle.

Charles Fairfax Murray's youthful confidence was based not on book-learning, though he was well-read, but on the detailed and painstaking examination of hundreds of works of the great masters allied to an extraordinary visual memory, which he supplemented by an extensive collection of photographs. Letters to Spanton constantly reveal him at work. In Florence in March of 1872 he saw the Raphael portrait 'that used to be called *Madalena Doni* until that picture of her turned up in the Pitti. I suppose it certainly is a Raphael, the hands are like his work and the colour is like the finest Venetian pictures. I do not know whether the *Fornarina* is by him – this justifies its attribution so far as colour is concerned, Crowe energetically denounces it & declares it to be pure Venetian, most likely a Piombo in his first manner.' He filled page upon page with comparisons and comments. 'S M Novella is remarkable also for the chapel painted by Orcagna – there is also an altarpiece painted by one of the Orcagnas, very different from the frescoes, signed and dated – it is a great gain to find a certainly genuine work of his to go from; the pictures at the Campo Santo are not his work and should never have been attributed to him, fine though they are.'[7]

Home thoughts intruded from time to time. Fairfax Murray and William Morris had spent a few days at Kelmscott before he left, stopping off at Oxford for Morris to buy a punt to fish his reach of the Thames. 'I was reminded very forcibly of a delightful week spent at Kelmscott; I was much happier there than here, the result of delightful company I suppose' and '...who was that student Mr Ruskin was clapping his hands at? Was he studying Turner?'; but the memories did not deter him from writing 'If I can, some day I will come and live in Italy – if only one friend would migrate with me I would leave England and rove from city to city.'[8]

Twenty-five years later Charles Fairfax Murray told Arthur Benson, a housemaster at Eton at the time, later Master of Magdalene College, Cambridge, 'I never could do much on my own account – I have no invention.'[9] This modest aside of an unassuming man, by then internationally recognised both as art expert and collector, conjures up a vision of the young Fairfax Murray working in the long shadows cast by Rossetti and Burne-Jones, despairing and disillusioned as he wrestled with his painting. Rather, he was simply without illusion. He had already known artists of the magnitude of Ford Madox Brown, Holman Hunt and Burne-Jones struggling to make ends meet, and he held an uncompromisingly realistic view of his own chances of commercial success. He could freely accept Burne-Jones's self-deprecatory description of himself as only a fourth-rate Florentine painter, without admiring his technique any the less. Fairfax Murray was, moreover, content with the role in which he cast himself. 'I would sooner paint a design of Mr Jones's than one of my own if I was allowed a good deal of liberty in doing so & could make my reputation by doing it well. It is a great pity that people now do not understand the desirability of a great artist swallowing a host of smaller ones who in very little time could produce pictures relatively as good as the numerous old "school" pictures, many of which fall little below the master works.'[10] He was singularly unprejudiced about his work.

Above all else, he was deeply committed to the systematic study of attribution, and an early exponent of the identification of works through the study of sketches and drawings. There was a passionate delight in Fairfax Murray's study of the work of the Old Masters, engravers, sculptors and craftsmen. He never missed an opportunity to learn about style, about painters, about technique, about pigments and media. He had boundless curiosity, a retentive mind, unclouded judgement and an unerring eye for quality. He was, in short, a true connoisseur at a time when the art of critical study was still young, and science in the service of art scholarship was half a century away.

Charles Fairfax Murray was greatly excited by the apparently limitless opportunities he found for dealing in Pisa. Murray Marks, the dealer in antique bronzes and Nanking china, the friend of Rossetti, Morris and Burne-Jones, bought a picture on his recommendation, optioned a number of other pictures from the same collection and put up the purchase price for a picture Fairfax Murray wanted for himself. (He had also found a little Benozzo Gozzoli for which the owner wanted too much but would, he had little doubt, come down in price; and he had taken the first steps to acquiring a fine Venetian portrait said to be by Titian, another of Andrea del Sarto, an Il Sodoma, and a young lady erroneously attributed to Leonardo – all very fair pictures in good condition, he noted, at moderate prices.) 'There are numbers of beautiful things to be bought here yet, especially pictures, in spite of what is said... I could lay my hands on a dozen at least that would sell for double in England even if the price asked were given.'[11] Fairfax Murray was warming to life in Italy, and planning his return. 'I think I told you I found a little head by Moroni' he added as an afterthought. His own work was suffering a little, and he felt obliged to confess that his picture of the view over Pisa from the Accademia was lacking in interest 'and not very well painted either.'

By 28 March 1872, Charles Fairfax Murray was in Turin on his way back to London, having stopped off in Bologna, Ferrara, Parma and Milan en route. Delayed by having to wait for money to be sent, his acquisitions postponed for the moment, he passed the time making notes of the pictures he had seen. Ludovico's [Carracci's] works he found 'curious' and could not imagine why Sir Joshua Reynolds recommended them so strongly, being he thought demonstrably bad. The gallery at Turin disappointed: 'there is a decided dearth of first-rate works – the Botticellis save the gallery, little else particular but one of the best van Dycks I have seen.' In Milan he saw 'the remains of the *Last Supper*' in Santa Maria della Grazie, which shocked him deeply by its condition, the result of overcleaning and poor restoration. Attempts to correct misattributions to Leonardo da Vinci in Milan were haphazard or worse: 'they now simply select one of his principal scholars at random – the number of his drawings is not nearly so large as is generally supposed – I am confident that fully two-thirds are by his scholars. A good deal might be done by connecting drawings with pictures which has never yet been done.' This direct and practical approach to attribution was one of the cornerstones of his expertise.

Fairfax Murray was home in the first week of April. He had been away for four months, and in that time he had had more than sufficient of his own company to think about his future. He spent a few days calling on Burne-Jones and his many friends and acquaintances at the Firm in Queen

Square, and went off down to Bury St Edmunds to see William Spanton. On his return to Effingham Street he set about arranging for the exhibition of his pictures. That done, he put aside further thoughts of Italy for the time being and set himself to work.

Morris, Marshall, Faulkner & Co were now busier than ever before, the hectic improvisations of the late 1860s succeeded by a more orderly regime. Alphonse Warington Taylor was dead at 34, the victim of consumption, and George Wardle, who had joined the Firm around the time that Charles Fairfax Murray had first started work with Edward Burne-Jones, was now Business Manager. The Firm continued to work on the two great Cambridge projects, the decoration and stained glass for G F Bodley's restoration of Jesus College Chapel, which were falling behind the promised delivery date, and the decoration of the Hall and Combination Room at Peterhouse, which had been started in 1868 and would take another two years to complete. William Morris, back from his first visit to Iceland six months before, was immersed in a new epic poem, *Love is Enough*, but he did not neglect to re-establish good relations with E H Morgan, the impatient Dean of Jesus. In January he not only made proposals for the great south window of the south transept but succeeded with Bodley's pressing help in gaining the commission for the windows of the east and west walls, in the face of stiff competition.[12] Fairfax Murray's return was doubly welcomed, both as a friend and for his much-needed experience in glass-painting. In the next ten months that he stayed in London, Fairfax Murray worked almost wholly for the firm or with Burne-Jones on behalf of the Firm.

Fairfax Murray had great regard for Burne-Jones's instinctive and powerful sense of design and composition, his draughtsmanship and especially his handling of figures. Their relationship was particularly satisfying when they worked together in stained glass. Here the design requirements were particularly well-suited to Burne-Jones's talent for expressing figures in a restricted frame, while the techniques of glass-painting allowed for a clear distinction between the drawing and its translation in to the full-size cartoon and on to glass. Fairfax Murray was a skilful and creative glass-painter, 'the most brilliant stained-glass painter in the Firm's service,'[13] and he enjoyed the freedom of expression that the work allowed. The earliest identified stained glass by Fairfax Murray was done for the Chapel Royal, Savoy Hill, now demolished, for which Murray both drew the cartoon and painted the glass. This was a window depicting St James as Bishop of Jerusalem, based on a Burne-Jones design of 1862 for Christ Church, Southgate. The same hand can be traced in the cartoons for the *Ten Angels of the Heirarchy*[14] for the south transept windows of Jesus College Chapel, Cambridge, designed in 1873. The elaborately traceried window contains ten figures of angels, with ten figures of saints below, and eight minstrel angels above; seven of these were designed by Morris on lines similar to his minstrel angel tiles. The overall design of the window, and all but two of the twenty angels and saints are by Burne-Jones. The cartoons – enlargements for the glass-painter from the designer's smaller drawings – are probably the work of Charles Fairfax Murray, 'a crisper and more incisive touch than is usual in Burne-Jones's work, suggesting an executant accustomed to the strict economy of means required of a glass painter.'[15] He may well also have painted some of the glass that was being worked on during the summer months, but it was not Morris's usual practice to allow signed work – even the designers of the Firm's glass were intended to remain anonymous. A notable exception to this rule, and the best-known of Fairfax Murray's collaborations with Burne-Jones in stained glass, is the Vyner Memorial window in Christ Church, Oxford, erected in honour of an Oxford student murdered by bandits in Greece in 1870. This beautiful example of Burne-Jones stained-glass design illustrates *The Last Supper*; Charles Fairfax Murray painted the window, which is signed 'EBJ INV CFM PIN', in the summer of 1872.

Fairfax Murray also drew cartoons of *St Peter and St Paul* for Over Storey Church in Somerset, and for the window of *Mary, Wife of Cleophas* for St Mary's, Edge Hill, Liverpool, from William Morris's designs, late in 1872. Writing in 1876, when he was still very much involved with work for Morris & Co, Murray remarked that 'stained glass ... has other pleasures than those of absolute copying... I received great praise for my Oxford window when it was finished and it is still to me one of the most pleasant pieces of work I ever did. I was responsible only for the execution of the designs and I think I fairly succeeded so I felt like a workman who had done a piece of good work and had unalloyed pleasure therein, no regret or dissatisfaction from an incompletely carried out ideal because the designs were not mine.'[16]

A number of the Firm's domestic decorative contracts called for tiles, and Fairfax Murray also undertook a considerable amount of the design work from William Morris's original sketches about this period. There is a number of Murray's original drawings and hand-painted tiles from Morris's early designs of *Minstrels*.[17] In these particularly, and in a group of the *Four Seasons*, Fairfax Murray's incisive line has simplified and strengthened the original concepts to suit the medium.[18] William Morris was himself working that summer on two beautifully decorated and illuminated manuscript editions of *The Rubaiyat of Omar Khayyam* in his own translation. Fairfax Murray collaborated with him on the more elaborate of the two versions prepared, a gift from Morris to Georgiana Burne-Jones, invested with profound thought and all of the creative energy of which he was capable. It is written in a Roman minuscule with a crow quill on vellum, lavishly decorated, with illustrations made by Fairfax Murray after designs of Burne-Jones.[19] It is the richest and most densely ornamented of all William Morris's manuscripts. By contrast, the most carefully sustained example of

William Morris's calligraphy is *The Story of Frithiof the Bold*, which is quite sparingly decorated. Graily Hewitt contributed the initials, Louise Powell the decoration and Fairfax Murray painted the two important historiated initials.

He did not see Rossetti in 1872. By the time that he had returned to England in April, Dante Gabriel Rossetti was in poor mental and physical health, his mind having given way, never to recover fully, under the strain of his guilt over Lizzie Siddal and the increasingly widespread speculation about his relationship with Janey. The crisis was magnified by Buchanan's celebrated, and not altogether unjustified, attack on the 'Fleshly School of Poetry'. The possibility that the coincidence of the private life and the idealised, but sexually explicit, relationships of the poems might become public was very real. With his mind and body weakened by chloral and alcohol, this was sufficient to push Rossetti in to paranoia and hallucinations. On 8 June, the anniversary of Lizzie Siddal's stillbirth of their daughter, he attempted suicide, and it was not until the end of September that he was sufficiently recovered, though still in a most fragile state of mind, to return to Kelmscott and 'the one necessary person' almost a year after he was last there with Janey.

As Fairfax Murray was returning to London in April, John Ruskin had been travelling to Italy once more, the visit overshadowed and eventually disrupted by his relationship with Rose La Touche. He returned from Venice at her request at the end of July and once again proposed marriage. Rejected, Ruskin shut himself away at Brantwood in Coniston; but by November he was seeking a copyist to work in Rome for the Arundel Society, which existed to publish chromolithographic reproductions, mainly of the early Italian masters of fresco, for its subscribers and to exhibit examples painted by copyists commissioned by the Society. John Ruskin and his fellow Council member Austen Henry Layard were particularly interested in the techniques of narrative fresco painting and many of the Arundel Society's prints were copied from the best examples of these works. Edward Burne-Jones was consulted as to whom they might send, and he cordially recommended Fairfax Murray, with whom Ruskin had no more than occasional contact since they exchanged a few formal words at the National Gallery six years before. Accepting Burne-Jones's judgement without further discussion, Ruskin asked him to arrange for them to meet; it was a decision of crucial importance to Charles Fairfax Murray.

Fairfax Murray had talked of his intention to return to Italy when the opportunity arose almost from the hour he got back, intending to return to Pisa where, by now, he felt at least a little more at home. Ruskin's assignment to work in Rome for the Arundel Society was unbelievable good fortune for Fairfax Murray, for whom Rome was a distant dream. On 3 December Georgiana Burne-Jones wrote to Murray, commanding him to come to The Grange for lunch next day, and by 6 December Burne-Jones was writing 'now try to get rid as fast as you can of all impending work and work 12 hours a day for you can be off as soon as you like – come here on Thursday to meet Mr Ruskin, I'll tell you what hour, and perhaps you could by then get the copy you made in Pisa, not that it is essential but it might be as well – I have puffed you up tremendously.'

Burne-Jones's alacrity in dealing with Ruskin's request is one measure of the anxiety he still felt over his patron's dismay at his affair with Maria Zambaco; he had painted her once more during the summer, this time as *Temperance Dousing the Flames of Passion*, an insensitive choice of allegory at best, and again as *Venus Epithalamia* for 'the Duchess'. She had commissioned this poignant, idealised nude portrait of her daughter as a wedding present to Marie Spartali and William Stillman. It is the most like of all Burne-Jones's portrayals of Maria Zambaco. When the time came to part with it 'the Duchess' commissioned Fairfax Murray to make a replica which hung in her lifetime in her Kensington drawing-room, and afterwards it remained with Maria Zambaco until she too died, in Paris in 1914. The tempestuous Maria, who still nursed the hope that she might carry her lover away (the embers of the relationship still glowed fiercely in the late 1880s[20]), was instead afflicted by a serious mental and physical breakdown. In December she put her children in the care of her mother and left for Paris.

John Ruskin had been deeply perturbed by the affair, his earnest determination to support the work of the young artist he so greatly admired being much at odds with his moral disapproval of the liaison and his heartfelt sympathy for Georgiana's plight. He lectured Burne-Jones; his discourse on the 'carnality' of Michelangelo's work contrasted with the purity of Tintoretto was conceived as a serious critical essay which he went on to deliver in his Slade lectures at Oxford, but his manner of reading it to Burne-Jones was clearly understood, as it was intended to be, as a rebuke. Ruskin's well-intentioned concern for Georgiana led to awkward moments: 'Georgie came to dinner and Mother spoke of what she should not in the evening' he confided to his diary.

Along the way, Charles Augustus Howell was dismissed from Ruskin's service. He had meddled unhelpfully in the affair (though the authority for this lies in Howell's own account, and he was an imaginative story-teller. It is possible that he wished to divert attention from the true reason). The immediate cause is carefully obscured, the exchange of letters elaborately imprecise, but it seems that Howell attempted to defraud George Howard. Burne-Jones, having once commended him to Ruskin, now pursued Howell relentlessly. When Howell left the house in North End, Fulham, where he had lived at Ruskin's expense to watch over affairs at The Grange, a procession of 12 hansom cabs wound endlessly back and forth between North End and Chelsea for a week, removing his furniture and effects. William Michael Rossetti's diary in November 1870 recorded the break between Ruskin and Howell in his characteristically opaque manner: 'I am not qualified to enter into an account ... my impression is that a highly distinguished friend of Rossetti's, and one who liked Howell enormously at first and disliked him intensely afterwards, had something to do with this result.'[21]

A cloud, nevertheless, still hung over Burne-Jones; conscious both of the hazards of recommending anyone to undertake Ruskin's bidding and of an opportunity to restore himself in Ruskin's favour, he continued his letter to Fairfax Murray: 'I trust you think of me much when you are in Italy so as to redeem me from shame – because I recommended a secretary to him in glowing terms and you have it in your power to wipe that disgrace out of my life.'[22] Fairfax Murray's success must atone for Howell's failure. Burne-Jones was to remain anxious until he saw Murray's first copies arrive from Siena in the following April.

Ruskin's generous praise of Murray's skills – 'a heaven-born copyist, the most skilful of the artists thus employed was, beyond comparison, Mr Charles Fairfax Murray, and the sketches we possess by his hand are among the principal treasures we can boast' – was contained in his Master's Report to the Guild of St George in 1884, the year after he and Murray had finally fallen out.[23] Fairfax Murray would paint many fine copies for Ruskin between 1874 and 1883, some 40 for the Guild of St George and half as many again for the Arundel Society and Oxford. Copying was a necessary and honourable occupation before the universal availability of lithographic colour reproduction, and accurate copyists with the ability to convey the qualities and feeling of a painting as well as its colour and composition were much in demand; to Fairfax Murray it was simply the means to earn the living that enabled him to develop first as connoisseur and collector, and later as dealer. He worked at his copies with diligence and pride in his work, striving to capture every nuance of brushwork and texture, deeply unhappy when he failed to reach the standard he set himself. But it was without joy.

Ruskin's first public recognition of Fairfax Murray's skills was, however, not in praise of his copying but of his knowledge of Italian art: 'a young painter, Charles Fairfax Murray, working with me, who already knows the secrets of Italian art better than I ...'[24] he wrote. Ruskin's affectations of speech and mannerism were precisely calculated to bring out the worst in his protégé, who had not yet subdued the impatient authority of youth; the veiled sparring apparent in many of their letters, warmly absent when they were together, continued over the years. 'Murray,' Ruskin wrote, 'whose help is given much in the form of antagonism – informs me of various critical discoveries lately made, both by himself and industrious Germans, of points respecting the authenticity of this and that ... the picture in the Uffizi that I had accepted the ordinary attribution to Giotto is in fact by Lorenzo Monaco.'[25] Philip Webb, who knew at first hand that Fairfax

Murray was a stout defender of his opinions, was vastly amused by Murray's 'antagonism', and it remained a running joke between them for the next ten years.

As 1872 ended Charles Fairfax Murray was winding up his affairs in London. He gave up his rooms in Effingham Street, and on New Year's Day 1873 he was staying at Brantwood with John Ruskin, his patron once more, who wrote on 3 January to Joan Severn: 'Murray who is staying here leaves tomorrow bringing a caricature by Albrecht Dürer, the first I ever saw by him, of a *Lord and his Attendants*...'[26] In addition to the Dürer, Murray also interested Ruskin in some coins he had bought. 'I am heartily obliged to you for letting me see those coins – how we have degenerated since George II. I have written letters for you to the Arundel,' he wrote, and added, 'of course the painting [apparently a work discussed over the New Year at Brantwood] should be attributed to Filippino Lippi and not Sandro [Botticelli, another common usage of the day].' Charles Fairfax Murray, copyist to Mr Ruskin, had lost no time in establishing his credentials.

4. Return to Italy

'Murray is about to go to Italy, for a somewhat lengthened stay in Rome and elsewhere, at Ruskin's expense. He is to make copies of the Botticelli frescoes in the Sistine Chapel' William Michael Rossetti recorded in his diary for 7 January 1873: '(he) also thinks of examining the Old Master drawings in the various galleries, and drawing up a catalogue of them, correcting errors of attribution, tracing the connection between drawings and pictures, etc, etc. He is under the impression that nothing (or next to nothing) of the kind has yet been done in any Italian gallery.' The first task was a matter of 'bread and cheese', the second lay at the heart of his future career.

The administrative detail needed to secure his admission to the Vatican delayed his departure. The Secretary of the Arundel Society, Mr Maynard, wrote to Ruskin on 10 January to inform him that 'the Council think that the best way they can assist Mr Murray is to ask Mr Layard to give him a letter of introduction to Cardinal Antonelli', the powerful head of the Curia, whose brooding presence – the dark, piercing eyes overshadowed by a heavy brow, the aquiline nose and Oriental appearance – left no doubt that his word was law in the Vatican. Ruskin passed the letter on to Fairfax Murray: 'it is not my fault that this letter is for James instead of Charles... I have written to the Archbishop of Westminster's secretary.'[1] Cardinal Manning's secretary, James Knowles, replied by return to tell Ruskin that 'the Archbishop has instructed the Rector of the English College to do all in his power for your friend Murray.'

Charles Fairfax Murray painted his well-known portrait of Philip Webb[2] before he left, a wonderful likeness that conveys the warmth and wit of this outwardly rather reserved man. 'You brought me last evening the most graceful, as well as the most delightful gift you could have made me – namely a portrait of my life's friend' Webb wrote. Enclosing £10, he said 'my present shall cost me something, to show my gladness, but I cannot in any way represent the value of the gift.'[3]

Then it was time to leave. 'I think you had better get south and write me a letter every week, not long but saying where you are & what about & where I can write to you' wrote his patron: 'Off did you say, really off? No! How to see you – it's too late for you to come tonight, else you might kill three birds with one stone – Mr Morris and Mr Webb being here ... driven frantic with work but come over and see me and receive my blessing' wrote Burne-Jones.[4] Fairfax Murray was forgiven his offences and his friends crowded round to wish him well. George Price Boyce wrote, wishing him an enjoyable and prosperous sojourn in Italy and

His faithfully rendered body-colour copy of Ambrogio Lorenzetti's *Allegory of Good Government*[12] in the Salla della Pace was still incomplete when he set off for Rome once again in the middle of May to examine more closely the Botticelli frescoes of the *Trials of Moses* that he was to copy during the winter, and to measure the spaces in order to have his stretchers ready beforehand. That accomplished, he returned to Siena by way of Assisi and stayed to finish the Lorenzetti fresco by the third week of June.

On his return from Rome there was a letter waiting from Edward Burne-Jones which foreshadowed Fairfax Murray's rôle of arbiter and authenticator of the work of the Pre-Raphaelites in later years. 'I want you to tell me if you can remember how many copies of any chalk heads of mine you made for Howell, they go about the world and turn up to worry me and I should like to know for a certain purpose how many there are and all you can remember about them – a disagreeable affair has happened about one of them lately and I want the history of it.'[13] Charles Augustus Howell had been offering Fairfax Murray's exercises as original. 'Murray Burne-Joneses' turned up at auction regularly in the next few years.[14] Howell had also acquired some Burne-Jones drawings intended as a gift for Alecco Ionides which he offered him instead for sale, murmuring discreetly that Burne-Jones was extremely short of 'tin' and would be glad to have the money.

On 2 August Burne-Jones wrote again: 'I hear Mr Ruskin is like to be in Assisi in September ... all you tell me about your work is very satisfactory. I shall be glad of any photographs you have – you share in every way what I like ... were you disappointed in Rome, take an old man's advice and be silent on that first impression – it isn't possible not to be disappointed ... one has made up an image of something out of hearsays ... have you learned to speak Italian yet?'

Next, John Ruskin wrote to say: 'I want you to go to Pisa and make a sketch for me of the cornice of the Baptistery outer door with its 13 half-length figures and tell me what you think of the date of the stone below and of its style – it puzzles me.'[15] Ruskin relied greatly on the 22-year-old Fairfax Murray's comprehensive knowledge of the Italian *trecento*. Copyists he could employ without difficulty, but Fairfax Murray's exceptional ability, Ruskin recognised, lay in his expertise '... I counted more on your scholarship than on your drawing from the first.' In the next few weeks Murray made three trips from Siena to Pisa and a trip to Florence, where he spent several hours 'which I made such good use of I could scarcely stand next day.' Florence in high summer was almost deserted, but the 'horrible old lady who belongs to Angelico's *Madonna del Tabernacolo* was still at her easel in the Uffizi, working at a picture – I trust unique – she was adding the body of one of Angelico's angels on to the head of a young lady with a black chignon of enormous size – poor Angelico!'

Fairfax Murray had now been in Italy for six months of hard work and exhausting, uncomfortable travel, almost alone. He was momentarily disenchanted with his work, his prospects and with Italy. 'My work here is very troublesome to me – I found it very different on getting it into a strong light a few days ago – and since have scarcely cared to go on with it, I am so much disheartened. I am duller here also than I could have imagined. Italy used to be such a land of promise to me'[16] he wrote to William Spanton. He was probably hungry. Burne-Jones and Philip Webb had sent him money in July, and Ruskin was exhibiting early signs of the cavalier approach to payment for his commissions which would lead in the end to the rift between them. He was also a little in love.

In Pisa in July, he had met the girl who would be his wife, a pretty 16-year-old country girl from Volterra whom he had encountered by chance, standing in the gateway of the house where she worked as a servant to the family of relatives there. This Botticelli Cinderella immediately aroused the romantic and passionate side of Fairfax Murray's nature. He was greatly attracted by her beauty and from that moment he set his cap at her, but it was not until October that he was able to return to Pisa for more than a few hours at a time. The young girl was constantly on his mind, and separated from her by distance and language he was more lonely than had he been simply alone. The mood passed.

Years later, Charles Fairfax Murray told Dante Gabriel Rossetti (who lost no time in embroidering the tale for Janey Morris) of his first few months in Siena: 'Little Murray looks in now and again. He told me an extraordinary story which seems to show both how he learned Italian and how he became a dealer. When at Siena, as yet unmarried and ignorant of Italian, he heard a man and woman go by talking English ... the man was Italian and his wife English. He had worked in England where he found the language very difficult, but managed to get a fellow worker to help him. He read through the whole of Walker's pronouncing dictionary and eventually (Murray says) spoke like a native. This man, seeing that Murray cared for nothing but pictures used, while Murray was painting in the galleries, to hang about on street corners and talk to passers-by, managing to turn the conversation to pictures. Thus he used to hear of wonderful bargains in corners and induced Murray to go and see some which generally resulted in some old woman ushering him in to her bedroom and showing him some vile daub; but eventually treasures began to turn up and he was the gainer by them.'[17]

His commission in Siena for John Ruskin completed, Charles Fairfax Murray spent most of the last three months of the year and the first three weeks of the New Year in Pisa, making encouraging progress with his Italian and working on various small projects for Ruskin which filled the days until he could go to Rome. He saw his aptly-named Angelica – Angelica Albina Isolina Colivicchi – every evening and they played the age-old lovers' game of deceiving the chaperone: 'seminole and tombola after her mother came in' he remarked to his diary on 2 January. Philip Webb showed how well he understood the younger man: 'Thank you for your letter – like parliamentary eloquence it was so artistically inconclusive that I could not make out whether you had really been idle or not – at the moment you seemed to be about telling me you smiled and withdrew your pen.'[18]

Too soon it was time for Fairfax Murray to be on his way to Rome, though not before Philip Webb was moved to enquire: 'Are you gone to Rome? Or, do you think that by some diligent waiting Rome will come to you?'[19] Murray noted 'lots of kisses' in his diary and Ruskin resumed his barrage of instructions: 'Form the most careful opinion you can of the Luca Signorelli with the *Death of Moses* at the end[20] – it seems so much more beautiful than anything he could have done' he ordered, before he had so much as left Pisa. Another, undoubtedly welcome, letter arrived: 'I neglect you horribly and cannot think how you get on without money...'[21] enclosing £50. Once in Rome, Fairfax Murray rented a studio in the via San Nicola da Tolentino, close to the Piazza Barberina. He started work in the Vatican in mid-February, alone with his canvases, pencils, paints and brushes and his thoughts of Angelica, at the top of a swaying scaffold. Philip Webb, the practising architect, could never resist a jesting comment on his dislike of heights: 'Don't mind scaffolding ... only one architect in modern times has broken his neck, and what is that among so many?'[22] he enquired.

Before he left Pisa, Fairfax Murray had packed and shipped the *Pax* that he had copied in Siena during the summer back to Burne-Jones to hold for Ruskin until he could get to London to see it. He was in Rome when he heard from Burne-Jones that his copy from Lorenzetti's *Good Government* had arrived safely. 'The other day the magnum opus came upon which I entirely congratulate you – I have never seen such a copy in my life for fidelity & I think Ruskin will be very pleased... I want to add personal thanks too because I felt a bit responsible to Ruskin (though I need not have done) and now I feel as if I have done him a good turn.' The old anxieties about his patron's reactions remained. 'There's a bit of news that will interest you, Boxall has resigned at the Nat. Gallery and Burton has the place.'[23]

Maria Zambaco was still much on his mind; during his trip to Italy over the Easter holiday of 1873, Edward Burne-Jones had quietly commissioned Fairfax Murray to paint a picture for her as a keepsake, and now he could write to tell him how much it had been appreciated: 'the copy of the small Siena picture you did for Madame Zambaco was in every way delightful and satisfactory and it is now in a big gold frame, so wide that it is astonishing ... the fever Madame Zambaco caught in Italy still clings to her and I have to spend many anxious days on her account still – I get old with worry my dear, if I drop down from my perch some day I shall look – that is my ghost will look – to you not to let people say too much evil of me.'[24] It was an injunction that Fairfax Murray carried out scrupulously to the end of his life. Edward Burne-Jones had not parted finally with his tempestuous muse, a confidence he shared with Fairfax Murray. Burne-Jones too had returned from his visit to Italy with a fever, and it seems not unlikely that the two lovers had been together for a while.[25]

William Morris was devoting his huge creative energies to the crafts of calligraphy and illumination at this period, studying styles of penmanship and trying out different mediaeval recipes for inks. He wrote to Fairfax Murray in Rome as soon as he arrived there, asking him to obtain an estimate of the cost of 100 skins of the finest grade and hardness of vellum from the Vatican, the only source of skins of the size and quality he sought; but William Morris's letter was not all business and he kept him informed of the children's progress as they grew up: 'Jenny is certainly big, has long coats now and looks quite a grown-up young lady ... nevertheless she is not beyond a romp – to judge at any rate by the infernal row she & Phil & Margaret made last Saturday... May is the more grown up and writes quite like a young lady, Jenny rather appearing to dread the pen.'[26] Fairfax Murray was very fond of them and, despite his long absences in Italy, remained close to the family long after William Morris died; only May outlived him.

Fairfax Murray still thought of England as his native land as he would all his days, but the attractions of Italy grew more apparent every day, along with his confidence in the language and his growing closeness to his beautiful tutor. He wrote a carefully worded letter to William Spanton to prepare him for an announcement: 'I think of travelling homewards ... preparatory to a longer absence ... possibly of important changes'[27] and four days later, unable to contain himself any longer, adding: 'a few weeks after I arrived I attached myself to a young Italian girl who has divided all my thoughts, since for nearly six months I was unable to say a word to her. Away from her in Siena I could not turn my attention to Italian at all. I passed my evenings in absolute sadness doing nothing. I produced there however in the daytime a fair quantity of work, my unrest relieving itself somewhat that way. With great patience and some misery I finished a copy which Mr Jones has or had and was to retain until Mr Ruskin came to London. After I left Siena I was in Pisa again as you know for some time, about three months. During this time I began for the first time to learn a little of circumstances, in which I became involved, through my desire to remove her from all intercourse with some people to whom she had been a sort of foster-child for some years. It brought me in to closer contact with her; I succeeded not without immense difficulty and afterwards with one interruption saw her every evening at her mother's. I now correspond with her constantly and am getting along rapidly – still without any regular plan of study – but the effort of writing and her letters take such a hold on my memory I get on in spite of all these disadvantages.'[28]

Despite his first impressions of Rome, the treasures of art and architecture that he saw all around him slowly fired his imagination, and his initial disenchantment gave way to delight as Burne-Jones had predicted. He became better acquainted with the city, 'a place I once dreamed of but scarcely ever thought of getting to ... hitherto I have been exceptionally fortunate, certain physical weaknesses however trouble me and I am one day miserable and another happy, for the rest I am somewhat overworked – that is, I want to do more than I can, but I do not always have the strength...' He starved himself for months on end, living on three cups of coffee a day in order to save money to buy drawings[29] and materials. Notwithstanding his newly-found pleasure in Rome, Fairfax Murray spent Easter in Pisa ... 'look at the distance on the map and imagine what a powerful magnet it requires to drag my weary body that distance. I will send you a photo of the magnet presently.'

He was back in Rome at work when Ruskin joined him on 16 April. They worked amicably together side by side in the Sistine Chapel. 'A delightful day yesterday at Sistine and pleasant evening with Murray' Ruskin recorded in his diary on the 23rd, and almost immediately travelled south to Sicily for a few days. Once there he wrote on the 29th 'I shall come to you in the Sistine on Monday. Then, if you bequeath me your scaffolding, you may take your holiday as soon as my group of Midianites is done. I merely send you this line to warn you that I have not fallen into Etna.'[30] Fairfax Murray, who had been looking forward to a return to London for the summer months, promptly wrote to Spanton to ask him to find him rooms: 'I expect I shall be seized by intolerable restlessness as soon as I reach London and be back in Italy before the summer is over but that is another matter altogether.'[31] On 5 May Ruskin noted in his diary 'Yesterday began sheep in Sistine Chapel' [beside the figure of Zipporah in Botticelli's *Life of Moses*], and the same day he despatched a note to Fairfax Murray to enquire: 'can you come down yourself any time today and clear away your colours and slops which I'm always dropping my pencils in ... you might tell me a thing or two about my sheep.'[32] During the week, Fairfax Murray again broached the subject of his return to London. Ruskin had other views: 'Mr Ruskin finds me useful here so I have consented to remain, not very unwillingly I must admit, as I find much pleasure in going about with him to see things... Mr Ruskin thought I only intended to return home for two or three weeks and was rather taken aback when I mentioned three months' he wrote once again, this time to cancel his request for rooms.[33]

They went together to San Clemente to see the fifteenth-century Masolino frescoes of the *Life of St Catherine*, and to San Giovanni in the Lateran, with its magnificent Gothic papal altar and Giotto's fresco of Pope Boniface VIII announcing the Holy Year of 1300. They visited the Angelico Chapel and Santa Maria in Aracoeli, the sixth century church on the Aracoeli steps that is decorated in frescoes depicting scenes from the *Life of San Bernadino of Siena* by Pinturicchio. There is something attractive in this glimpse of the two, the older man a national figure in the arts, the younger just 24 years of age and unknown, slipping away together when they should have been working on a scaffold in the Sistine Chapel to discuss the finer points of a late *trecento* fresco. Although they would later fall out, as Fairfax Murray became less dependent on his erratic income from copying and Ruskin became more undependable, it is clear that the two very different personalities found great pleasure in their pursuit of knowledge and beauty together.

Halfway through the month 'Ruskin came and took possession of the scaffolding.'[34] Fairfax Murray continued to work in his studio in the via San Nicola da Tolentino, superintending the casting of various pieces of architectural moulding that Ruskin had discovered, 'which he says he never would have been able to look after himself', and painting on his own account. He also made a drawing of part of the mosaic pavement of the Sistine 'which he declares all sorts of things about – and is immensely set up with.' Then, almost as suddenly as he had appeared, Ruskin was about to leave: 'I send you a generous present of six sheets of paper I can't use myself.'[35] One week later he wrote once more, from Assisi: 'As I see there's a bank in Siena I send you £80 in circular notes – all I have by me – and a cheque for £60. I shall want you here for a day or two to hear what you have to say about Giotto, it's not my field at all.' Ruskin had travelled to Assisi to supervise the work of another of his copyists for the Arundel Society, Edward Kaiser, whose work in the Basilica di San Francesco he later criticised for 'too much rather than too little pains.'

Fairfax Murray was now free to make his own plans. He returned to Siena during the third week of June in time to follow the procession that accompanied the removal of the central panels of the Duccio *Maestà* to the Casa del Opera: 'The Rector ... is inclined to keep the picture and not put it back in its place ... it seems to me to be worthy of all praise, but yet far from Giotto, Duccio (is) rather to be compared with Cimabue than his great follower'[36] he wrote that night to Ruskin, who was still in Assisi. 'I am more than ever delighted with the city, and think of making it my residence for some time on my return from England', he added. 'Still there... you'll be better in Pisa'[37] Ruskin replied; Giotto forgotten, Ruskin was working on a Cimabue *Madonna* in the lower basilica, 'a discovery to me, wholly unexpected, (that) upset Giotto from his pedestal in a minute or two's close look'[38] he wrote to Charles Eliot Norton, enclosing Fairfax Murray's letter. Two weeks later, Ruskin wrote again to Murray, this time from Lucca. 'Please send an a/c note of the expense you have been at for me and funds you have had to meet them as I must stop for this year', and then he was gone, although he did not arrive back in England until late September.

Fairfax Murray set out immediately for Pisa to see Angelica. From Pisa he made the short trip to the dealer Alinari in Florence, where he bought the painting of *St Sabinus before the Governor of Tuscany*, attributed to Pietro Lorenzetti, which he later gave to the National Gallery. Back once more, he next set out again for Colle Salveti, 'found coach full, walked to Volterra'[39] to obtain a copy of Angelica's birth certificate, and returned to Pisa to spend a few stolen days with the girl he was to marry, before travelling home by way of Paris. Leaving Italy on 8 August, Fairfax Murray spent some hours in the Louvre, and he was in London by 10 August. He had been away for 17 months.

He found old alliances severely strained. Goaded beyond further dissimulation, in April 1874 William Morris wrote to Dante Gabriel Rossetti, who remained entrenched at Kelmscott Manor, to relinquish his share of the lease 'since,' he said, 'you have fairly taken to living at Kelmscott, which I suppose neither of us thought the other would do when we first began the joint possession of the house.'[40] To Aglaia Coronio he wrote with less restraint that it really was a farce that he and Rossetti should meet. Dante Gabriel Rossetti himself was increasingly paranoid: in July, walking beside the river, he had hurled abuse at an innocent group of anglers whom he believed were taunting him with the murder of Lizzie Siddal. He could not remain at Kelmscott, and he left forever the house that meant so much to William Morris. The break between the two founding members of Morris, Marshall, Faulkner & Co was final. Two of Fairfax Murray's early heroes had gone their different ways. Despite this he retained the friendship of both, Rossetti becoming increasingly erratic and rancorous, William Morris and Fairfax Murray sharing a fellowship of respect and mutual interests that ended only with Morris's death.

The liquidation of the Firm had become inevitable. William Morris could no longer afford so many sleeping partners and he was already in negotiation with Theodore Watts,[41] the lawyer and literary man representing Ford Madox Brown, who held that the assets of the Firm should be equally divisible between the founding members. His argument was that the agreed system of payments item by item to individual members for their work for the Firm was equitable, but that the goodwill and assets built up in the partnership were the equal property of all of the founders who had shared an equal risk, electing to ignore the fact that William Morris had financed the Firm almost solely from his own pocket. Rossetti, eager for 'tin', supported Madox Brown and in a malicious twist at the end insisted on settling the monies he received on Janey. Peter Paul Marshall, so Morris suspected, 'smelt the advent of the golden shower and was preparing to put his hat under the spout.' Splendid Philip Webb and Charley Faulkner waived their financial interest, and the discussions dragged on inconclusively all through the summer of 1874.

Edward Burne-Jones's part in the break-up of the Firm was carefully suppressed in the authorised accounts of his life, and became known to a limited circle only when May Morris was editing her father's works in 1905. Charles Fairfax Murray lent her letters that set out clearly the story that he had seen unfold, 30 years before.[42] Desperate for money, and fearing that wrangling over the future of the Firm would lead to its failure, Burne-Jones pressed Morris to dissolve the partnership and let him out. Three years earlier, in 1871 he had written in his Accounts Book that he 'felt indifferent to the reputation of the Firm at the time.'[43] Fairfax Murray, by buying the letters at Theodore Watts-Dunton's sale, kept them out of the public domain during Burne-Jones's and William Morris's lifetimes.

Burne-Jones was well aware that the break-up of the Firm would impose a heavy financial burden on Morris, who could by now ill afford it, but he was undeterred. 'I don't think you one bit understand the footing we are on legally in this business – my wanting to leave the firm has of course nothing to do with driving other members out of it, but I must have my fair share and for this purpose the property of the firm has to be realised' he told Dante Gabriel Rossetti.[44] The last meeting of the Firm was held on 4 November 1874. When the public announcement was made of the change to William Morris's sole ownership, and of the name of the Firm to Morris & Co, the circular made it clear that while Webb and Burne-Jones were no longer partners they would continue to design for the new concern. It was a measure of William Morris's stature that he mentioned Burne-Jones's betrayal of their friendship to no-one; the hurt Morris felt for Georgiana over Maria Zambaco and his own dismay over Janey were put aside in his concern over Burne-Jones's febrile state of mind.

In May 1874, Edward Burne-Jones was very close to a nervous break-down, the consequence of his continuing attachment to Maria Zambaco and the wilderness time of his artistic isolation. So tangible was the crisis that it was decided to send Philip Burne-Jones away to school, not for the benefit of his education so much as to distance him from the tensions that could no longer be kept hidden from him at home. (William Morris briskly recommended his old school, Marlborough, where he had 'learned very little, because they taught very little,' and hauled the lad off down there to see the place in June.)

Fairfax Murray was not immune from his former master's imaginary grievances: 'Murray is here waiting for me to finish this before snubbing me again – he is infinitely more haughty & glorious than ever ... but he's a good little thing & has brought me photographs of the Sistine Botticellis – the Zipporah one – which feed and fatten me for weeks to come'[45] he wrote to George Howard. Fairfax Murray had been back in England just 12 hours, and had called at The Grange as soon as he reached London.

He lodged with his sister Lucy at her rooms in Hugh Street, Pimlico, and he set to work once again on a manuscript of Morris's, this time of *The Odes of Horace* in 4 books and 183 pages. This fine example of Morris's Renaissance italic hand on vellum is complete other than a small part of the decoration, and the illuminations are some of the most elaborate he undertook. The opening pages of the three books were designed by Burne-Jones, and Fairfax Murray painted the decoration in watercolour and gilding in the next few weeks. William Morris had already moved on to work on the manuscript that was to be the high-water mark of his illuminated books, Virgil's *Aeneid*. This supremely beautiful volume was destined never to be completed by William Morris, whose attention was now diverted by a new, consuming interest in the techniques of indigo dyeing, which rendered his hands and arms deep blue above the elbow and precluded penmanship. Six of the seven books were, however, written and decorated, a total of 177 vellum pages, and years later William Morris sold the unfinished masterpiece to Charles Fairfax Murray, who commissioned Graily Hewitt and Louise Powell to complete it after his death. That September of 1874, however, the goal was a finished *Aeneid*: 'Yes, come tomorrow, but I shall be engaged with Mr Morris designing for his Virgil'[46] Burne-Jones wrote to Fairfax Murray. He never quite adjusted to the change in their relationship. 'The great – the very great Murray is in town – taking it out of us generally and having magnificent airs'[47] he told George Howard. It is difficult to account for this petulance; perhaps it lingered from the Castle Howard undertaking which Fairfax Murray had abandoned two years before. Burne-Jones admitted to George Howard at the time that 'Murray is a loss, for I need not have given one tenth of the time to it if he had executed it.'[48] For a while he remained alert, unsuccessfully, to mar a friendship that lasted until Howard's death in 1911.

In the first few days of his visit to London Fairfax Murray contrived to fit in a call on his former landlady, Mrs Sentance, a visit to Philip Webb, a meeting with George Wardle at the Firm, to have tea with William Spanton and take in an exhibition of William Blake drawings at Bain's in the Haymarket, to pay his respects to Georgiana Burne-Jones's mother Mrs Macdonald, lunch with George Price Boyce, spend a morning with Burne-Jones at The Grange, dine with Murray Marks, and spend a day with George Lock of Collinson & Lock, the cabinetmakers. It was the kind of feverish schedule he delighted in throughout his life. He called on Sir Samuel Morton Peto, and had tea with his father in the Charterhouse. He dined and spent a day with Morris as well as visiting Queen Square. John Ruskin was still in Italy during most of his visit, but he wrote.

Much of the next eight weeks were spent at The Grange, at the easel in the garden studio which Burne-Jones let friends use, and he worked hard at preliminary sketches for *The Music Party*, a picture entitled *Duet*, and a panel of *Winter* for Lock. Burne-Jones had eventually to ask him to return the key so that Spencer Stanhope could use the studio. While he was in London, Fairfax Murray also visited Whistler and Dante Gabriel Rossetti, whom he had not seen since leaving for Italy in November 1870; he found the man he had last encountered four years before, brimming with renewed confidence then and defying convention by flaunting his passionate attachment to Janey Morris, now much diminished by chloral and whisky, paranoid and dreadfully aged. It is evident, too, that Burne-Jones's relationship with Maria Zambaco was still an open wound; his birthday that August was a subdued occasion and on 16 October, due to meet Fairfax Murray two days before his return to Italy, he wrote what he could not bring himself to discuss: 'I haven't said a word to you about that miserable affair Mr Morris told you of – because I want to help myself to forget it and because there are no words for it really in any known tongue ... tomorrow when I go to you we won't allude to it but talk of pleasant things; ever yours affectionately, EBJ.'[49] Only William Morris had the strength of character to triumph over the pain of their tangled relationships; many cruelly mistook his dignity for a lack of humanity.

5. Siena

late 1840's Cavalcaselle had been exiled to London for his revolutionary political activities during the *Risorgimento*, the fateful period of Italian history that led eventually to the unification of the northern provinces of Parma, Piedmont, Lombardy, Modena, Romagna, Lucca and Tuscany with the kingdom of the Two Sicilies in the south under Victor Emmanuel II in 1861. Old Gabriele Pasquale Rossetti was himself a political exile, and Giovanni Cavalcaselle would have been welcome in the circle of would-be revolutionaries who met regularly at the house in Charlotte Street to argue over Italian politics and discuss with equal passion the poet Dante. Alberto Mario, Garibaldi's chief of staff and an associate of Cavalcaselle in the movement, was close to Christina Rossetti's friend Barbara Leigh Smith Bodichon during a similarly enforced visit to England. Calling so soon after his arrival, it is probable that Fairfax Murray had obtained some form of introduction from the Rossetti family during his visit to London. In Rome, formally correct visits were exchanged, Fairfax Murray leaving his card before noon, Cavalcaselle returning the call that very afternoon; from this sprung a cordial relationship which lasted until the older man's death in 1897.

Fairfax Murray also carried with him an order from William Morris for vellum from the Vatican. In March a letter arrived from Queen Square enclosing £5 for 'further disbursements on vellum – I would send more but for scraping everything together to pay my thieves of partners who have come to some kind of agreement with me.'[4] There was no disguising the relief and satisfaction with which he wrote two weeks later to Murray: 'I have got my partnership settled at last and I am sole lord and master here now, and never a Jorkins to refer unpleasant words to.'[5]

It was an unsettled time in Fairfax Murray's relationship with John Ruskin, who had returned to England on Murray's birthday to a period of emotional extremes. Two days after he got back he saw Rose La Touche once more, but she was desperately ill and he knew she was dying. Despair over her condition weighed heavily against his joy at seeing her again, and Ruskin's uncertain temperamental balance was seriously disturbed. Prompted only by a solicitous remark, he had written to William Stillman '... I have more friends than I know what to do with.. I am encumbered with affection which I cannot answer or use...'[6] At Christmas, however, he wrote to Stillman to express his sympathy over the illness of his young son, Russie, and of his own state of mind he said 'there are many of them (friends) who say pleasant things to me and when I am gone, pity me for a madman.'[7] He wrote also to Charles Fairfax Murray: 'No, I have not forgotten you, but I am so unwell and so busy... I am writing to say that I must give up work in Italy it being too exciting and too sorrowful...'[8] He had seen Rose La Touche for the last time a few days earlier.

It was apparent that Fairfax Murray would enter married life with Angelica with his longer financial future more uncertain than of late, but weighing up his situation he concluded that there was still much to be grateful for. William Spanton received an account of the prospects for the year ahead: 'I have had a disagreement with Mr Lock, but I doubt it will make much difference to the amount of work I do for him... I have no more work to do for Mr Ruskin who has bid adieu to Italy forever as you may have guessed after reading the note from his Florentine diary in "Fors" but he has promised to help me if it should be ever necessary... I have a new commission from Mr Morris for six furniture panels which will find me in bread and cheese for the summer and with this I begin the world afresh after my marriage, which I hope will take place in less than a month's time...'[9] Murray was also at pains to warn his friend: 'Better not say nothing to nobody about Mr R, William, if you are a man of the world; no man living I think has so many enemies.'

Angelica returned home to her mother at the beginning of March to prepare for her wedding: 'my little girl has returned to her birthplace, sudden increase in affection (parental) hence removal of my sister home'; her father, Leopoldo, died. Fairfax Murray attended to the registration of his death, and early in April returned briefly to Rome to close the studio. The couple were married in Pisa at 10 p.m. in the evening of 18 April 1875 in a civil ceremony. An announcement of the marriage in *The Times* stated simply 'On 18th at Pisa, Charles Fairfax, youngest son of James Murray, Esq., of London, to Angelica Albina Isolina, third daughter of Leopoldo de Giusto Colivicchi, of Volterra. No cards.' Next morning they left for Florence, Arezzo and Rome. 'We left Pisa the next day for Florence – no marriage breakfast or any of that nonsense – I could only be married civilly being a Protestant so the ecclesiastical ceremony was entirely done away with' he wrote in high spirits to William Spanton. 'We managed to slip the crowd and nobody knew but the witnesses ... we stayed in Florence for a few days and I revisited the Pitti and the Uffizi Galleries... the Titian portrait remains as ever in my mind as one of the most wonderful pictures I have ever seen – I sometimes think I should choose it before all else if such a thing were possible, it is so entirely satisfactory – I feel German and voluminous on the subject...'[10] There follow four more pages of minutely detailed commentary on Titian's *Portrait of a Young Man* and several more pages of vivid description of Raphael's portrait of *Leo X* and a Velasquez in the Pamphili Doria gallery in Rome. Fairfax Murray thoroughly enjoyed the leisure to study pictures afforded by his honeymoon, and one can only conjecture what Angelica thought of this baptism by total immersion in the galleries of Florence and Rome. During their stay in Rome, he took his 'little girl' to meet Giovanni Cavalcaselle and his wife,[11] and to the Vatican where he now had many influential friends, and they started married life in Siena a week later.

'I have taken a villa belonging to the above photographer [Paolo Lombardi] who is a very fine fellow – I could give you a bed for the whole summer. If we could only get two or three good fellows out here we could be as jolly as sandboys. I have one friend staying here now, but there are two spare bedrooms as we have four…' he wrote to William Spanton. Married life appealed to the gregarious side of his nature, and he enjoyed the bustle of a full house, even relenting so far as to welcome his mother-in-law and Angelica's younger sister, whom he brought from Pisa in August on his way back from Florence, where he had been to make some sketches from life for his own paintings, models in Siena being few and unsatisfactory. Despite his new-found domesticity he clearly did not envisage any change in his way of life, confiding in the same letter: 'I have also been thinking of returning for a little while alone [underlined] leaving my wife with her mother.'[12]

For the time being he had work on hand. His own pictures aside, William Morris had asked him if he would undertake the figures for the *Aeneids of Virgil*, which was now taking shape. 'I have got my partnership business sorted out at last; so I am asking you to do some of the figures and what it would be worth your while to do it for. I am up to my neck in turning out designs for paper chintzes and carpets and trying to get the manufacturers to do them…'[13], a reminder that Morris was no longer independently wealthy, with a business to enlarge and a wages bill to meet. In addition to the furniture panels which Morris & Co had commissioned, there were still three major undertakings for John Ruskin in hand that year, copies of a *Madonna and Child* by Filippo Lippi, and two Botticellis, *The Adoration of the Magi* and a *Nativity*.

Rose La Touche died in Dublin in May, and the relationship with Ruskin continued on its uneven course without much contact between them, Fairfax Murray taking his time (the Botticelli copies were not completed until 1882) and Ruskin struggling to maintain some degree of normality by immersing himself in his writing, not only for *Fors* but also *Ariadne Florentina, Proserpina, Deucalion,* and the first two parts of *Mornings in Florence*, as well as producing a new edition of the *The Elements of Drawing*. Although there were tensions between them, Fairfax Murray did not find Ruskin's critiques of some work for the Oxford lectures wholly unconstructive. Deference was nowhere in his make-up, but neither he did resent his patron's criticisms when he thought they were valid. He had expressed his own dissatisfaction with some drawings he had made in Pistoia to which Ruskin replied promptly in March: 'I am greatly delighted by your present letter – I cannot say how glad I am you feel the want of chiaroscuro. I believe it can only be remedied by making sketches in chiaroscuro only. It is quite immaterial whether you make them from Carpaccio, Titian, Botticelli or nature. In painting one should never darken to full chiaroscuro – the use of chiaroscuro study is to enable one to see what are the facts before we modify them' – the dictum that had marked his early teaching at the Working Men's College and which so clearly distinguished his approach from that of the Government Schools, where outline was considered to be fundamental to the study of drawing. 'No one could be more charming and interesting than Ruskin so long as you were in the looking-up attitude.'[14]

Ruskin's melancholy, however, brought out once again the admonitory and arbitrary elements in his unstable nature. Indeed, the steady decline in Fairfax Murray's hitherto reasonable relations with Ruskin over the next eight years closely parallels the rise and fall of Ruskin's periodic mental disturbance. In a letter to Fairfax Murray in November, grudging praise was larded with heavy-handed criticism: 'I am heartily obliged by yr. letter but a great deal of the use you might be to me is lost by yr. careless writing. Never mind saying little to me – it will exercise yr. language – (why do you spell Botticelli with one 't' by the way?) but write round and slow...'[15] Fairfax Murray was becoming inured to these outbursts. Nevertheless, he made a tacit effort to improve his hand, and the result was widely welcomed. 'The calligraphy of your letter was wonderful, to say nothing of being easy to read', Philip Webb wrote around this time. 'You had better write to Mr Morris at once before this style has worn out and your third period begins.'[16]

Fairfax Murray was, however, dismayed and irritated by Ruskin's erratic and didactic pronouncements on works of art, and critical of his increasingly wild conclusions. 'I bought the first two numbers of *Mornings in Florence* on the spot and didn't care much for them', he wrote to Spanton. 'It is extraordinary that amongst all the pictures in Florence he should select the Golden Gate and companion frescoes to write about, everything he says is true or nearly true in principle but what he sees is not there. The frescoes are nearly worthless – originally in no way remarkable for the time in which they were painted, they have been almost completely overpainted... I believe that the attribution of them to Giotto rests on no authority but his own and the custode's[17] ... he dubs a picture Leonardo da Vinci which nobody has yet been able satisfactorily to settle the authorship and which is less like Leonardo than most of his fellow scholars in that wonderful school of Verrocchio. If he had ever looked at the early pictures of Credi for instance he might have had more doubt about it. With the same perversion he persists against clear proof to the contrary in asserting the Spanish Chapel in S. Maria Novella to be by Simone Martini whose pictures bear no resemblance to the ones in question and whose identity is clearly established.[18] Isn't it extraordinary? Mr Ruskin always lays it down so peremptorily that people ought not to have "opinions" about things they know nothing of ... but it is useless talking, you know him, or at least that side of him, as well as I do...'[19]

The summer passed merrily. Angelica was pregnant for the first time. Fairfax Murray sketched her and worked at his picture of *The Violin Player and Listener* – one figure was completed by the end of June – and he made sketches of the six figures for Morris's cabinet panels. A *Concert* in waterco-

people's feet hurrying to chapel will lighten our hearts...'[27] Burne-Jones wrote on one occasion. The short visit to London can only have sharpened his awareness that for all the promise of Italy and a happy marriage there was little work in prospect that would pay for his dreams. He was back in Siena five weeks after he had left.

'I got back here on the 26th January, my wife gave birth to a daughter in the morning – I got here in the afternoon about 4 hours after and so was saved from the attendant misery – both are doing well and so I hope will all continue, the baby appears healthy and strong.'[28] Charles Fairfax Murray fathered 12 children, seven of whom survived to adulthood, apparently never doubting that childbirth and the rearing of children were in some way subject to immutable natural laws in which he might not properly inter-vene. He was profoundly imbued with those most conventional of Victorian values, that children were the province and responsibility of the womenfolk, that a woman's place was in the home, and that sons should be given every educational opportunity to achieve in life for themselves while daughters should be taught the social graces. He was caring and attentive to the education and well-being of his brood all his life, but singularly detached from day-to-day domestic distractions, fond of Angelica but not in the least way uxorious. Fairfax Murray's flinty refusal to enthuse over good times or to weep over the bad concealed a gentler nature, but he seldom lowered his guard; nor would he ever give a hostage to fortune or count on the future. He hated being in debt, morally or financially.

Angelica Maria Elizabetta's birth was registered with the British Consul in Leghorn on 2 February 1876. Ten days later she lay dead; on 12 February Murray recorded simply in his diary 'Baby died suddenly at 7 o'clock', and on the next day he made a drawing of her before she was taken to the church and afterwards to the Campo Santo Monumentale della Miseri-cordia, in the part dedicated to S Andrea Corsini. A simple marble tablet marks the burial. The promise of his marriage, after years of unremitting struggle to pursue the only career he was prepared to follow, was clouded for a while by this tragedy, but slowly he and Angelica put it behind them and life continued. John Ruskin wrote immediately with warmth and sincerity: 'I am grieved at hearing of the death of your child. I should be glad to know of your wife's health when you have time to write.' The practical and friendly Spencer Stanhope, whose ebullience belied the precarious state of his own health, offered Fairfax Murray his studio in Bellosguardo for the summer. He went with Angelica to Florence for the next four months, remaining there until the end of July when they travelled together to London.

There they stayed with his old friend Edward Hughes in Beaufort Street, remaining in London until the end of November. Edward and Georgiana Burne-Jones, and George Price Boyce and his wife, were among those to whom Angelica was introduced. At Boyce's Chelsea home the talk had turned to Fairfax Murray's acquaintance with Cavalcaselle, who was working with Joseph Archer Crowe on the third of their great collaborations in art history, *Titian, His Life and Times*, and Boyce extended an invitation through Fairfax Murray to visit him. They visited the Burne-Joneses at The Grange. Neither Janey Morris nor Dante Gabriel Rossetti seems to have met Angelica; spending a fortnight at Scalands with George Hake in attendance, sitting to Rossetti for the dramatic, curiously deranged *Astarte Syriacus*, Janey had discovered the extent of his chloral dependency and realised that the liaison must end for the sake of her children.

James Dalton Murray, his father, died on 2 September in the Charter-house, aged 68, while they were still in London. He had lived there eight years in comfort and fellowship with the 70 or so privileged gentlemen of middle-class background who were no longer able to support their style of living as before. He was buried at the City of London & Tower Hamlets Cemetery Company's South Grove Cemetery in Bow, in the grave which he had purchased 33 years earlier, when three of his children died in one week. 'I could have done more for him', his son reflected.

On their return to Siena, Charles Fairfax Murray and Angelica did not go back to the Casa Lombardi which had held such promise and witnessed so much sadness in the space of less than a year. They moved instead to 110 via del Casato, a few steps from the Piazza del Campo at the heart of the ancient city, dominated by the tower of the Palazzo Popolo, where Burne-Jones had left his former assistant working at Lorenzetti's *Pax* barely four years before. Fairfax Murray and Angelica, her health somewhat restored after the shock of losing her first-born daughter, settled back in to the routine of life in Siena. At Christmas, Fairfax Murray sent Georgiana Burne-Jones the gift of a book of Armenian music, and with her thanks, in the time-honoured custom, came news of the weather at home: 'We are having the mildest winter ever, I think your wife could stand it tho' perhaps the rain that comes with it would be bad for her. I trust you and your wife are well – give her my love and don't let her forget me. My husband sends his love and asks me to say he has your letter.'[29] Angelica's fear of London and her horror of the climate was apparent to all.

For the moment he was busy painting for William Morris, and finding time to play a part in the cultural life of Siena at the Accademia – the Instituto di Belle Arti di Siena – where he sometimes taught (he was also on the jury for the award of prizes in a competitive examination in painting in 1877). He met there regularly with his Sienese contemporaries – Luigi Mussini, an important painter of the time and Director of the Instituto, Giuseppe Partini, the architect and tactful restorer of many of Siena's mediaeval buildings, Gaetano Marinelli who taught there, the friend and follower of Alessandro Franchi, and Franchi's pupil Ricciardo Meacci. Meacci, 'a gentle soul of extraordinary modesty', the most notable of all the Italian painters of the period, was considerably influenced by Fairfax

Murray. He adopted a style that faithfully reproduced that of Burne-Jones, and it was natural that Fairfax Murray – the direct link with his inspiration – should be an important source of encouragement.[30] The Instituto was also Fairfax Murray's meeting place with those acquaintances who knew the owners of a wealth of pictures, and who could help him with the necessary introductions: 'I tried 4 years since to get in there without success & the man who was to have introduced me came to a tragic end shortly after – being assassinated – with him perished my chance for the time being – I hear that he has amongst other things a big altarpiece by Duccio'[31] Murray reported on one occasion. With fellow artists and *marchands amateurs* at the Instituto he added to his expert knowledge of the Sienese school and gained first-hand experience of the labyrinthine complexities of the Italian art market, dealing on his own behalf and for a number of collectors in England, who included John Ruskin.

His earliest close connection as agent and dealer was with Frederick Burton,[32] the Irish painter recently appointed Director of the National Gallery. Fairfax Murray had known Burton since Rossetti introduced them in 1870. They had met again when Burton came for a few days' stay in Siena with Paolo Lombardi. Fairfax Murray had acquired a Pietro Lorenzetti painting that Burton saw in Siena and wanted for the gallery. Though the purchase was not completed – funding then as now was a perennial problem – it seems that this was the picture of *St Sabinus before the Governor of Tuscany* attributed to Pietro Lorenzetti which Murray gave to the Gallery in 1882. He had by then conducted several difficult negotiations as agent for the gallery with notable success. When George Howard, who was later appointed a Trustee of the National Gallery, had visited Fairfax Murray in Siena in June 1875, he had shown him a fragment of a fresco by the Sienese Ambrogio Lorenzetti, Pietro's brother. Two years passed before Burton was able to inform him that the Trustees had given their sanction to his entering in to negotiations to purchase the fresco *A Group of Poor Clares*[33] for the Gallery, acting on George Howard's description.

The letter arrived as Angelica was giving birth to their second daughter, Beatrice Christina, on 12 August. 'Although somewhat tied to the house on account of a late event (the birth of a daughter) I nevertheless found time to get out & providentially met the owner of the picture which saved me a journey to the Seminary. There is no immediate hurry I find as he wishes to be clear as to his right to dispose of it before doing so – I imagine otherwise the matter would have been all over... I have meanwhile left the matter in such a condition that he is not likely to sell it without letting me know. I hope to have enough money in hand at the time to come to a settlement – delay is dangerous in these money matters ... there are no less than three competitors for this fragment... Lombardi the photographer negotiated for Mr Howard who unwisely made him his agent. He ascertained that it was to be had for 100 fr: or less & coolly offered it to Mr

Howard for double ... the Russian minister is here this summer & buys early pictures, he entered into the matter & made an offer less than 100 frs: I don't know how much less & I think from what I heard it would have been accepted... Lombardi might at any time cut in if he knew I intended to buy it as he would be sure to sell it at a considerable profit... I saw the priest also today & saluted him, nothing has transpired up to the present date...'[34] It was typical of the negotiating tactics of rival dealers; the owner's representative was the priest in charge of the Basilica of San Francesco, who was bemused by the pressures but alert to the possibilities.

By November, Fairfax Murray was reporting that one Peter Krohn had entered the negotiations on behalf of the Danish Government, and the price had suddenly leapt to a ridiculous 3000 francs. A few days later, Fairfax Murray added: '...I am afraid that nothing is to be done about the Lorenzetti fragment. The owner ... wishes to treat through Lombardi. This is impossible as he has an idea of pocketing a thousand francs at least for his share so that he is interested in the opposite way to myself.' Frederick Burton gave up hope at this point, and he must have been pleasantly surprised to receive a letter from Fairfax Murray, dated Christmas Day 1877, to say: 'I have another small item of news – Lombardi came here yesterday & asked if it was I who had made an offer for the Lorenzetti fresco & I said yes – & told him what I had offered. He said that for 1300 francs I could have it. I said I was not sure that I could renew my former offer as I had made it on the part of a friend and, disgusted with the conduct of the affair & the unreasonable demand, I had advised my correspondent that it was not to be had & regard the affair as finished.'[35]

Fairfax Murray arrived in London for a short visit at the beginning of April 1878 to discuss the developing situation with Frederick Burton; they decided that their best course was to wait. He also made a point of visiting Rossetti in Cheyne Walk: 'as modestly oracular as ever' Rossetti remarked afterwards. Dante Gabriel Rossetti had always known the secret fear that Italy was not the land of his springing imagination and that to go there would shatter the illusion. Still, he wrote to Janey Morris, who was wintering in Italy, that 'when he went away I remembered that I had failed to ask him, as I had long wished to do, respecting the particulars of his Italian home and the facilities for settling agreeably in the neighbourhood.'[36] He clung to his dream of Italy, the fancy now embracing a life with Janey. With reckless insensitivity, he asked William Morris to pass this message to Fairfax Murray. It is a wonderful instance of Morris's pained tolerance of Janey's affair that he did so.

On 19 April Murray set out from London on his return journey to Siena, in the company of William Morris who was travelling to Italy to meet Janey and the children, who had spent the winter nearby the Howards' villa in Oneglia. They reached Turin overnight on 21 April, having spent the previous day, Easter Sunday, in Paris with Edward Burne-Jones, Philip his son, Sidney Colvin and Crom Price, who were staying there. Burne-Jones was making another surreptitious visit to see Maria Zambaco: 'Bye the bye,' Rossetti had told Janey Morris, 'Mrs Stillman told me of her calling on poor Mary Zambaco who it seems must be dying of consumption. She was very pale, very ill-dressed and (added Mrs Stillman) she must be very ill, her hair was quite black.'[37] (Maria Zambaco was notable for her glowing auburn hair.) William Morris and Fairfax Murray were met at Oneglia by Rosalind Howard, Janey, Jenny and May, and the party travelled on to Genoa. Morris, who was plagued by a serious attack of the 'toe-devil', his recurrent gout, was so unwell that he fainted at the railway station and had to be carried bodily, not without difficulty, to a nearby hotel. Murray delayed his start for home for a few more days to help look after the children and took them walking around the sights of Genoa. 'Fairfax Murray turned up like a good fairy,' May Morris recalled. While he was still there with the Morrises, he received a letter from Dante Rossetti asking him to look for a house he could take with Janey; perhaps on reflection he thought that Morris might baulk at delivering his message. If nothing else, it showed the trust they all placed in Fairfax Murray's discretion.

The Morrises reached Venice on 28 April. William Morris, who was as determined as ever that Italy was greatly inferior to Iceland, wrote to Fairfax Murray next day to confess that he had been wonderfully surprised by the beauty of Lake Garda, and the Doge's Palace was quite different from what he had imagined: 'People paint it white & red, but I see the red is the faintest pink; this looks better than I had expected,' he admitted. He wrote again on 4 May, reporting the progress of his gout from the right foot to his left. He was clearly out of sympathy with Italy, and although he found something to admire in Verona, he was truly happy only when he reached the Channel coast once more. Angelica and Beatrice welcomed Fairfax Murray on his return home at the beginning of May, and with Angelica now in the seventh month of her third pregnancy, they set off immediately for a holiday, accompanied by Angelica's mother, her sister Philomena and the baby Beatrice's nurse.

They stayed in a rented house inside the walls of San Gimignano, the beautiful mediaeval hill town that overlooks the sweeping Tuscan countryside to the north of Siena, the skyline dominated by 13 spectacular towers built by rival noble and merchant families in the twelfth and thirteenth centuries, when San Gimignano's situation on the pilgrim route to Rome was the source of the town's great prosperity. The wealth of the trade that the pilgrims brought was displayed in the religious art in the town's many churches and public buildings – the Collegiata is decorated by a remarkable series of frescoes of Old Testament stories by Bartolo di Fredi, the Barna da Siena scenes from *The Life of Christ*, a Ghirlandaio *Annunciation* and others by Lippo Memmi. Sant'Agostino has a cycle of frescoes of *The Life of St Augustine* by Benozzo Gozzoli; and the Palazzo del Popolo has the vast

Maestà fresco by Lippo Memmi (the equal of his brother-in-law Simone Martini's *Maestà* in Siena) and the spirited *Wedding Scenes* by Memmo di Filipucci. Fairfax Murray filled his notebooks with sketches of details from this treasure-house of masterpieces, while the ladies cooked, read and sewed until they took their *passaggiata* in the cool of evening. At the end of the month it was time to return once more to Siena to prepare for Angelica's confinement. Emma Maria, Angelica and Fairfax Murray's third child and last daughter, was born just after midnight on 27 July 1878 and she was christened on 5 September.

Negotiations over the Lorenzetti had lain dormant for eight months when in August 1878 Murray wrote once again: 'I find I have another rival purchaser for the Lorenzetti. I am nearly sure it is a Mr. Keyser, a copyist employed by the Arundel Society at present working in the Seminary of S Francesco, he buys I know for some German [museum]. The matter has been referred to the Art Commission ... the owner will not name any price at present in haste.' It was becoming a contest of wills, and Burton replied immediately that he had 'prepared the way to procure the Lorenzetti.' He arrived in Siena on 20 September and set about making arrangements for payment with the Keeper, Charles Lock Eastlake, adding: 'I believe the affair will all go smoothly now – but hardly need say that it is as well to say nothing about it – £5 over will I hope more than suffice to pay the expenses of extracting the fresco from the wall ... [Murray] has presented an almost unique book to the National Gallery Library,[38] & a small picture ... Mr Murray,' Burton added, 'has great opportunities in Italy of picking up rare books on Art at a cheap rate.'

When the Lorenzetti fragment arrived in London, Burton wrote a memorandum to Keeper Eastlake: 'the acquisition of this work is due to the watchfulness of Mr C Murray ... (he) has been of the greatest use in conducting the negotiations. It will be proper to recognise his services in a more substantial way than by thanks.'[39] It had taken Fairfax Murray three years and five months to beat his way through the thicket. On Monday 25 November 1878, the Director reported that with the sanction of the Trustees he had recently purchased at Siena a fresco painting, 'being portion of one executed by Ambrogio Lorenzetti ... also that ... he had remissed out of petty cash the sum of £15.5.0 to Mr C.F. Murray at Siena for agency in connection with this and other matters.' The Lorenzetti negotiation was the beginning of a long and successful professional collaboration.

Fairfax Murray was busy during the late summer of 1878 with copies for Ruskin and at work on two paintings of his own, *The Garland Makers* and *A Pastoral*. He had contributed to a fund to purchase J M W Turner's *Splügen*, which Ruskin had been prevented by his collapse from buying himself. Now he received two sad letters within days of each other from the recuperating Ruskin, part apology, part encouragement, and part the pedagogue: 'My love to your wife – I hope she loves me a little', and the next day: 'You must allow for illness in my impressions of things. All mental disease shows itself in seeing faults and ugliness and in languor of enjoyment and beauty ... your Lippi drawing is not up to your usual mark in getting expression ... you cannot think how much I value the little procession of minstrels you gave up in disgust ... better times will come to both of us yet, I trust.'[40]

The day after Beatrice Christina had come into the world, Fairfax Murray had ended a letter to Frederick Burton with a simple hope: 'My wife & child are both doing well but I mustn't say "Te Deum". This time I hope however this one may be spared to me ... my wife was somewhat in danger on Saturday last but the danger has passed for the present.'[41] Just ten days before Burton met the Trustees to tell them of Murray's successful negotiation for the Lorenzetti fresco, Beatrice died suddenly, aged 15 months. 'I am sorry to learn of your new affliction...'[42] he wrote.

6. Partings; Ruskin and Rossetti

While Charles Fairfax Murray fenced with Paolo Lombardi over the Lorenzetti fragment in the closing weeks of 1876, John Ruskin remained in Venice with his close-knit team of artists – John Wharlton Bunney and Angelo Alessandri – who were copying for the Guild of St George. He was in a state of acute melancholy, suffering delusions and seeing in Carpaccio's *Dream of St Ursula* a manifestation of the dead Rose La Touche's presence beside him. In December, Fairfax Murray was urgently summoned to Venice, to copy the *Princess and her Father*. Ruskin had been deeply disturbed by an encounter with a gondolier who pressed him to take his craft as thick fog descended on the lagoon, seeing in him the Devil incarnate. Happier incidents such as the coincidence of a gift of some flowers that he found also in Carpaccio's painting represented for him the forces of light; so that he passed Christmas 1876 in a profoundly unbalanced mental state.

Wrapped in the friendly concern of his team of helpers including James Reddie Anderson, who was there to assist with his research into Carpaccio, Ruskin once again struggled back from the abyss, and by February 1877 he had so greatly extended his programme that he needed additional help. Charles Moore, the first Director of the Fogg Art Museum at Harvard, had joined Ruskin in Venice and was now copying from the *St Ursula* cycle in the Accademia.[1] His planned four-week stay lengthened to four months and they found themselves, in Ruskin's words, to be 'in perfect sympathy in all art matters.'[2] Fairfax Murray was called upon once again: 'I wish you could come here and make some drawings for me – any time between now and the 1st May but the sooner the better. I have presented [your drawing of the King] to the Sheffield museum and want more such, probably as many as you care to do … there are things at the Schiavoni I greatly need…'[3] Ruskin wrote. Four days later he wrote again: 'I am greatly pleased that you are coming – your drawing is producing great and good effect at Sheffield and if we can get more good records of the Pope picture it will enlighten their Protestant minds greatly.'[4] On 3 March James Bunney learned that he would come to Venice shortly. He was rather less enthusiastic at the prospect of a rival for Ruskin's attention, regarding himself with some justice as Ruskin's principal helper in Venice, and he sought reassurance: 'I refer everybody to you now as my agent for Venetian affairs' the Professor declared soothingly.

Charles Fairfax Murray returned to Venice before the end of the month, accompanied by Angelica, who was pregnant once more. He rented an apartment on the Fondamenta Bollani and was soon at work on the Carpaccio. 'I wanted to ask if you think you could do another St Ursula and her Maids for Oxford, working again from the original to the same point of finish'[5] Ruskin wrote at the beginning of April. At the end of the month Fairfax Murray began Ruskin's portrait.[6] Together with Angelica they enjoyed the beauties of La Serenissima, making a visit to St Alvise and watching the last golden rays of the setting sun reaching across the lagoon to the cemetery island of San Michele from the gardens of the Madonna dell'Orto; Ruskin was enchanted by Angelica: 'whenever you and your wife want to come in the evening I'll give you coffee and leave you to do what you like ... you won't disturb me,' he wrote, and 'I want to read you a bit of a new guide that I have some confidence will amuse you, ask Mr Bunney ... if you both can come and yr. sweet little wife doesn't mind hearing unintelligible foreign read and will grace the conclave, you both know I shall be pleased.'[7] There was work to be done: 'can you meet me on St Mark's Place tomorrow at half past nine. I am going up in to the gallery behind the organ at St Mark's to study a mosaic plainly visible and of extreme beauty and importance. A sketch of it such as you have done of St Simeon's robe details will be the most important work you or I have done in Venice.'[8]

John Ruskin returned to England at the end of May 1877, and almost as soon as he had left Venice, Fairfax Murray also moved on, renting an apartment at No 6 Volpini House on the Borgo San Frediano as a base in Florence for the first time. Angelica returned to Siena while he set out once more for London. Ruskin wrote with renewed goodwill to his testy collaborator: 'I hope this line may congratulate you on your safe arrival [in London] after having done most precious service in Venice to the St George's Company and to me ... for which sincere thanks.'[9] Two weeks later Ruskin wrote once more, enclosing payment for Fairfax Murray's work in Venice, unprecedented promptitude: 'I send guineas because it looks prettier – do you ever condescend to a bit of Paul Veronese?' Once again, the tensions between them had been dispelled in a few weeks of each other's company, working together; it was a partnership of opposites that only truly functioned when they were focussed on a single venture.

Fairfax Murray plunged in to a whirl of meetings and renewed friendships. As soon as he arrived in London he went to see William Morris and 'looked at leaves of Horace for illumination.'[10] He called on George Lock, Philip Webb, Charley Faulkner, Edward Burne-Jones, John Spencer Stanhope, Samuel Bergheim, F S Ellis (Rossetti's publisher), Murray Marks, Frederick Burton, Teddy Hughes, the sculptor Alfred Gilbert, George Wardle and George Price Boyce. In July, Edward Burne-Jones introduced him to Frederic Leighton. Then he returned to Siena, having worked for three days on the miniatures for William Morris's *Horace*,[11] arriving back three weeks after he had left Italy.

While they had been together in Venice, Fairfax Murray had discussed with Ruskin the opportunity to buy a fresco of Andrea del Verrocchio from the Palazzo Manfrin (which he had recognised, misattributed to Filippino Lippi), offered together with a painting by Bissolo. Ruskin immediately commissioned him to negotiate the purchase: 'You will be pleased to hear that the Verrocchio is safely lodged with Mr Bunney. Botti[12] saw it on Wednesday and approved what I had done to save detached gesso from falling... I had the Bissolo down and was rather disappointed ... it is not too late to withdraw from the negotiation...' Fairfax Murray next wrote. A further letter urged patience while he negotiated the purchase of the fresco alone. It was June before Ruskin, back in England, was able to write to Bunney: 'I was very glad to hear that Murray had got the Verrocchio without the Bissolo.' It was probably Ruskin's most important purchase, a *Madonna and Child* now in the National Gallery of Scotland.[13] In *Fors LXXIX* that July, Ruskin publicly commended both Fairfax Murray's expertise and his honesty: 'If you look at No VI of my "Mornings in Florence" you will see that I speak with somewhat mortified respect of my friend Charles F. Murray as knowing more in many ways of Italian painting than I do myself. You may give him any sum you like to spend in Italian pictures, you will find that none of it sticks to his fingers; that every picture he buys for you is a good one, and that he will charge you simply for his time'[14] and of his precious Verrocchio he said '...for £100... I have secured with his assistance a picture of extreme value that has hitherto been overlooked in the Manfrini Gallery ... it is a Madonna by Verrocchio, the master of Leonardo da Vinci, of Lorenzo de Credi and of Perugino.'

Buying for John Ruskin was not without hazard. Following the successful acquisition of the Verrocchio, which was now being restored under his supervision in Florence, Fairfax Murray had discussed other works that might interest the Slade Professor, among them a Botticelli *Madonna and Child* of which he sent him photographs. Ruskin soon instructed him to negotiate, and in mid-November Fairfax Murray 'wrote to Sagliani and offered 7500f for his Botticelli.'[15] At the end of the month Ruskin instructed Murray to acquire it, writing: 'I authorise you to spend £5000 for the Botticelli. I do very much think that I shall be able to get you in to position of doing great good for us here. I have been lecturing on your drawings for the last fortnight, 3 times a day.' The painting was bought and despatched to Oxford, where it arrived in the third week of December. A confused and despairing letter arrived in Siena from Ruskin within days: 'I have been ill and unable for all things. But alas what a strange fellow you are ... the Botticelli, it is one ... is so ugly that I've not dared show it to a human soul. Your buying such an ugly thing has shaken my very trust in you for my purposes... I must stop spending in this way for it entirely puts me off with anxiety and vexation. But I'll do what I can to get others to refer to you...'[16] he added.

Having acted on Ruskin's explicit instructions, Fairfax Murray was first angry and then perplexed. He responded by writing first to Frederick

Burton at the National Gallery for advice: 'Mr Ruskin is dissatisfied with the Botticelli I bought for him although I sent him a photograph such as I now send you ... he says it is ugly and coarse tho' he does not deny that it is a Botticelli or that he thinks it is... I am very much put out by this as I thought he had sufficient eye-sight to see through a little dirt and roughness whether a thing is good or not. The Madonna is full of sentiment and the Child is no uglier than usual ... it is certainly weak compared to his finest work, I consider it to be a work of his old age... I don't intend under the circumstances letting (Ruskin) have the other pictures I have here,'[17] a Vivarini among them, purchased on Ruskin's behalf with funds he had provided. Burton replied that the Botticelli was one of several versions, differing only slightly in detail, citing examples in the Louvre, in Frankfurt and in the Fitzmaurice and Barker collections; the question of another buyer remained unanswered.

John Ruskin spent the lonely Christmas of 1878 at Oxford in an uncertain frame of mind, relieved by the services at his old college, Christ Church, and in response to a coaxing letter from Fairfax Murray replied at the end of January: 'Thank you for your nice letter... I am sure you will do well for me in the long run ... it's just my usual ill luck about the Botticelli – I do hope you will get the Verrocchio over safe for me – it's worth a million.' They were bound together by their shared passion for the *trecento* and *quattrocento*, and by their capacity to irritate one another. John Ruskin's dogmatic and contradictory strictures, and his characteristic tendency to patronise him, angered Fairfax Murray as they had Dante Gabriel Rossetti before him. Fairfax Murray's refusal to defer was no less an irritant to his patron.

Less than a month later John Ruskin suffered a serious physical and mental collapse and although he recovered by April his breakdown was to prove only the first of the periods of madness that would eventually silence him.

Differences put aside, Fairfax Murray was greatly concerned to learn of Ruskin's illness. 'I have no news of Mr Ruskin, and I have written to Edward Hughes to make enquiries... Mrs Severn is no doubt with him at Coniston... I do not like to write direct to her' he told Spanton';[18] ten days later he had 'no news of Mr Ruskin, but the last was that he was no worse if no better, so there is hope yet.' A full year passed before Ruskin, still shaken by his illness, wrote at last from Brantwood: 'I can't criticise ... and I fear you would not care if I did,'[19] a succinct summary of the level to which their relationship had again fallen. Fairfax Murray was, nevertheless, concerned about Ruskin's continuing frailty: 'in my present languid state I am less eager in praise of even the best work than I used to be.'[20] A sympathetic enquiry while Fairfax Murray was in London in August elicited an outburst and an apology in the same letter. 'You need not be anxious about me,' Ruskin replied '... nor attend to gossip or newspaper passages. I am quite able still to do my own work, but not my own and other people's too, which – having been at their beck and call – astonishes them unpleasantly. But I shall always be glad to help with any possible encouragement to workers on Botticelli and Giotto,' followed by a second letter on the same day to say 'you will think my wits are gone really, but this was all written without understanding your kind letter and its feelings.'[21] On the following day John Ruskin wrote again: 'the only thing that I really want is that you should become all the things that you might be as a painter and a judge of painting.'[22]

The year ended on a better note with a long letter in which Ruskin said that he was busy on the catalogue for the Sheffield museum: 'your name is six times on the first page' and, no doubt of greater immediate interest to Fairfax Murray, 'I am writing to Mr Burton saying I am heartily glad that the President should have the picture.'[23] He referred to the Vivarini. The Botticelli *Madonna and Child*, now regarded as a school picture, continued to languish in Ruskin's possession until his death, but the Vivarini went in to the collection of Sir Frederic Leighton; it was, he said, 'a wreck; nevertheless it is a noble work, and if Ruskin not liking it would pass it on to me I should be delighted to call it mine at the price he gave.'[24]

'Let us from this date begin a quite clear a/c, your sending me priced sketches of anything you think likely to suit me, on approval, and I taking or leaving without disagreements,' John Ruskin continued. 'I hope to carry on things a little more pleasantly with you now,' he added. The basis was now to move from Ruskin's commissioning work to Fairfax Murray's producing copies speculatively, a particularly risky way of doing business with the Professor. There is no doubting the sincerity of Ruskin's intentions, but the relationship never regained its earlier intimacy; Fairfax Murray had outgrown it. Sadly, and more importantly, Ruskin would never entirely recover from his first madness, slipping periodically into periods of ever-deeper despair, confusion and mental illness.

In spite of the coolness between them, which they both now acknowledged, Ruskin remained anxious to make use of Fairfax Murray's presence in Italy. A recurrent cause of friction between Ruskin and his copyists – Murray was far from the only one to suffer this way – was Ruskin's repeated failure to acknowledge receipt of work he had commissioned and, worse, his increasing tendency to send work back or simply to refuse to pay for it. His relationships with the copyists were frequently confounded by imprecise instructions, and he always delayed approval. There were a number of reasons: the Council of the Arundel Society might decide not to publish a drawing Ruskin had commissioned, leaving him to bear the cost, he was increasingly short of funds personally having lavished so much of his inheritance on the Guild of St George and, as his health declined, he was less able to manage the volume of work he had always on hand. (The loyal Thomas Rooke languished a whole year in Venice at his own expense awaiting

Ruskin's further instructions.) Fairfax Murray's relations with John Ruskin resumed on a precarious basis, but the emphasis was shifting from copyist to advisor and agent. Fairfax Murray responded amiably enough, and he whetted Ruskin's appetite with a photograph and a description of a Luca della Robbia relief[25] which delighted Ruskin greatly. 'I beg you to secure the Luca – which I understand you can get for about £180'[26] he wrote excitedly from Brantwood on Christmas Day 1879. For the next six weeks he lived in an agony of apprehension: 'Clear rosy dawn and sunrise after starry night, at last. I very sleepless or dreaming of business – that Murray was dead and my cheque returned, and the Luca lost...'[27] until at last it arrived in February.

By June 1880 Fairfax Murray had completed the first of two Botticelli fresco copies, *Venus and the Graces*. The truce had seemed destined to collapse a few days before when, in reply to a letter from Murray about payment for work commissioned in Venice three years before, Ruskin airily replied that 'the reason I didn't write was I didn't quite like the Prato drawing. I was entirely delighted with 4 Carpaccio sketches, I will take all.'[28] Pressed for payment, the next letter said simply 'I send you cheque for £25 ... sorry you were bothered – my head's on yet and that is all I can say of it.' Their fragile relations trembled and then steadied once again, and Ruskin's next letter was unusually congratulatory. 'The Botticelli is here and it is entirely admirable. It is the first finished drawing of yours with which I have been entirely satisfied – and with this I am much more than satisfied. It is a most wonderful piece of drawing – greatly honourable to you – just and true to its utterly divine original. Tell me what will perfectly satisfy you for it – I send £50 on account.'[29]

A few weeks later the correspondence suddenly took a bitter turn: 'Please note in future I will not advance money; and I cannot have you dependent on my instant answer even when drawings are sent ... don't make this relationship between us uncomfortable by trespassing on its terms. Now, be a good boy and remember that advanced money is always a curse to the person who gets it, whatever it may be to the person who – so often – loses it.'[30] Peace was restored only because Ruskin now left Brantwood for the first time since his breakdown in February 1878 on a visit to Northern France, and apart from a brief visit to Canterbury he was out of the country until November.

Ruskin returned to Brantwood somewhat refreshed and set to work on *The Bible of Amiens*. He sorted through accumulated correspondence relating to the Guild of St George, and found some of Fairfax Murray's drawings that had been at the centre of the last exchange about payment. 'I am ashamed at finding that *Bacchus and the Fates* had not been returned as I said. I will now keep them,' to be followed the next day by a further letter: 'I am ashamed to say I have now found all your drawings.'[31] He wrote again in friendly terms twice more in January in praise of Fairfax

Murray's 'most precious talent for expression', sending him payment and promising him more work for Sheffield. Whatever might have come of this, the matter was postponed; on 21 February, Laurence Hilliard, Ruskin's secretary and companion, wrote to say that Ruskin was extremely ill once more, three years almost to the day from his first dreadful bout of paranoia.

Ruskin's salvation was that he recognised the nature of his illness when he recovered, and was able to discuss it without embarrassment. He was back to work at the end of March 1881, but it was only in the following September that he was well enough to return to his business with Fairfax Murray. On 3 September he wrote for the first time in eight months: 'I am entirely delighted to hear from you again. When *St Jerome* came I was still badly ill, and it chanced to be the first thing I opened when I came downstairs and I took it for part of the diabolism that had been possessing me and didn't know whether to keep it or not... I like *St Jerome* greatly – I think you said it was to be 15? – I send £20 for it and the Carpaccio, and I shall be glad to see the fresco copy when it comes... I think you can safely go on sketching for me when you have nothing better to do.'[32]

Work was warily resumed. 'Two sketches arrived... I am happy to pay £10 for each. The Botticelli frescoes also I am extremely glad to have at £100; I have positive and instant directions to give you and will you please stay where you are quietly, that is to say in Pisa or in Florence, until you get my intended letter tomorrow. Remember I must know where my men are or everything will get into a tangle again, and you may depend on it, you will have more final profit, if not more satisfaction, from work done for me than for anyone else.' But by the next day, matters were at a very low ebb once more. 'It is not my memory that slips for I never trust it,' Ruskin raged. 'It is your own confused and ill written letters [which] you must mend the manner of ... number your sketches, continuously. Keep your own list and refer to them by number. The Bellini on looking at it more carefully I do not care for and I return it with a Botticelli *St Catherine* which you must mend or make another for me. It is unworthy of the picture or of you ... square the head properly and accurately to begin with. There are many bad mistakes in the drapery ... you must not send me pictures painted with stick-liquorice.'[33] He was not an easily predictable man to deal with. Silence prevailed between them for a further six months until, in April 1882, he wrote from Herne Hill to Fairfax Murray, who was then in London, to tell him that 'since I saw you I have had another attack of violent delirium leaving me after 3 weeks of it gravely shaken and stunned; I only got in at the National Gallery on Friday last but I'll meet you there this week – Thursday? – and have another look and talk.'[34] Fairfax Murray had proposed that he should undertake a series of Turner copies, but Ruskin was lukewarm, or simply too weary to take on another ambitious project. Two days later he wrote again: 'I have been thinking over the

Turner business but can't see my way until you show me how much you could do on a given work.'[35]

Ruskin reached Italy in August, visiting various of his copyists in Lucca, Pisa and Florence, where he met up with Fairfax Murray once more: 'the Benozzo drawing will I have no fear be a valuable addition to the museum.'[36] Fairfax Murray took advantage of this acknowledgement to set out a balance sheet of work commissioned, delivered and paid for, and in October Ruskin acknowledged that the list was correct, adding that 'your summary of the sketches puts me right about them all... I had entirely forgotten about the Benozzo in the press of almost unsupportably various business which I am now managing or trying to manage.'[37] Murray was in Perugia doing 'some Perugino frescoes for Mr Ruskin' when he next wrote to say 'I must pause for a while in purchases for Sheffield as the subscriptions are too low to admit of the rate at which I have been going on lately.'[38]

It was Fairfax Murray's last attempt to work with Ruskin. In January, John Ruskin dismissively informed him that 'I can't find the Benozzo and I can't make up my mind about this Perugino... I have not time to see to their packing or I should settle the question by sending them back ... £60 a head is high pay to what I give other copyists. I am quite well in general health so you must not mind waiting a week or two till I'm able to turn round...'[39] Fairfax Murray's dignified response marked the end of the relationship: 'I would willingly wait not a week but a year without troubling you on a question of money but unfortunately so little of my work is paid for that the want of any amount due disturbs my economy... I know that by comparison my prices are at least a third less than those of such Italian copyists as the two Rocchis, Galeotti and others who, without overvaluing myself, I think I am equal to... I remember but one case in which you made any objection and that was to the price of a drawing you had not seen, promising that you would pay later if you found it worth the money. I believe you liked the drawing but I have never claimed the money again. You can pay me £60 or £100 as you please ... it is the last time there will be any money question between us.'[40]

Even now, Ruskin sought the last word: '... as a member of the Council of the Arundel Society before you were born I am perfectly well aware of the price of thorough work both in Italy and Germany. I have nothing to reply to what you tell me of distress for immediate payment... I send you £60 and will submit the work to the Council without saying what I have paid for it for their estimate; if they value it more you shall have the excess. If this is to be the last business transaction between us I feel it proper to tell you, it is more on your account than mine.'[41] When T J Wise published *Ruskin, Art & Literature* Fairfax Murray refused him permission to include this letter: there is 'no earthly connection with art or literature – moreover I never asked him to lend me any money, I asked for an advance on the large water-colour I had in hand for him and as far from his paying at once on completion it was not uncommon to have to wait for months to know if he had even received the work. This caused the final breach between us.'[42]

In the ten or eleven years between 1872 and 1883 Charles Fairfax Murray had painted some three score copies for John Ruskin, to his own exacting standards, 40 or so for the Guild of St George, and half as many again for the Arundel Society and the Oxford lectures. Copying is self-denial, and Fairfax Murray took this work seriously, though it gave him little pleasure. He had not yet achieved the financial security that would follow in the late 1880s, and he was grateful for, at times dependent on, his income from Ruskin. Despite constant problems over payment it was, on Fairfax Murray's part, his weariness of Ruskin's capricious assessments of work commissioned and then neglected, and of his dogmatic pronouncements, that lay at the heart of it. For Ruskin, their rupture was a tacit admission of failure; for despite the impact of Ruskin's patronage on Fairfax Murray's career, he had achieved nothing by way of influence. Once more a protégé, his own creation, had moved beyond his control, as Dante Gabriel Rossetti, John Everett Millais and Lizzie Siddal had done before him.

It was John Ruskin who saw in Fairfax Murray's early drawings the talent that led to his life's work in the art world, and who paid for its development out of his own pocket. It is plain that John Ruskin placed Fairfax Murray far higher than his many other copyists. Fairfax Murray's bitter epitaph is all the sadder: 'All those whom Ruskin has advised have turned round and cursed him' he wrote to William Spanton.[43] He had been tried beyond endurance.

By the end of 1877, Dante Gabriel Rossetti was already in the grip of a self-induced paranoia, and dependent on the great draughts of chloral he washed down with generous quantities of neat Scotch whisky. From then on, he seldom left 16 Cheyne Walk and James Whistler, Alphonse Legros, Frederick Shields, Frederick Sandys and the Hakes were now the only regular visitors to keep him company.[44] Rossetti's letters to Janey Morris, who no longer shared Rossetti's company though they maintained a close and uninhibited correspondence, show that from 1878 to 1880 Fairfax Murray was as frequent a visitor to Rossetti as his visits to London permitted; neither distance nor Rossetti's progressively more erratic behaviour loosened the bonds of awe and respect in which Fairfax Murray held him.

Little Beatrice Murray had lived just 15 months. She died only weeks after their third child Emma was born. It was a second bitter blow to Murray and his young wife, following so soon on the death of their first child. In London the news was passed around, the scant details embellished in the telling. 'I must say I am sorry to hear about poor Murray,' Janey Morris wrote to Rossetti. 'I heard that the second baby was doing quite well some time ago. His wife appears quite incapable of taking care of either herself or her children – soon after the last baby was born, Murray wrote to some lady friend of Ned's in Florence to beg them to come to him for his baby was dying, and his poor wife could do nothing for it. When they got there they found the poor little creature apparently dying of cold and wrapped it in flannel, and in a very short time it began to recover and took its food vigorously. I suppose it succumbed again when left to the sole care of its mother – but after all, I think it is a great charm in Murray's eyes, this total incapacity on the part of his wife, she loves him and that is all he cares about, and they can make more babies.'[45] Rossetti replied in kind: 'You give a very sad account of poor Murray and the chances of maintaining his character in the teeth of so shiftless a partner. Surely the woman must be an idiot.'[46] It is difficult to imagine a less feeling account, or to conjure up a more vivid picture of the consuming inwardness of the ties between Dante Gabriel Rossetti and Janey Morris. Angelica Murray was prone to post-natal depression. She had been pregnant almost from the day she married and for more than half of her first three years of married life, something of a burden for an unworldly young girl who was still less than 20 years old. Happily, the three further children she bore – all sons – survived without further alarms.

Marie Stillman painted a more kindly picture of the Murray home to Rossetti who lost no time in elaborating it for Janey Morris. '[Marie Stillman] told funny stories of Little Murray, his dignity and independence and complete refusal to be patronised or patted on the back. It seems he is going to sport a tailcoat for parties in which he will be great. She says his family look on him in silent awe and never speak much in his presence.'[47] 'The other evening [Murray] declared his wife to be the most like Botticelli that he ever saw in womankind and produced from near his heart several photos of her, but I must say she seemed to me an ordinary little wench. She however is another of Mary Stillman's beauties, who told me she is quite lovely.'[48] Rossetti, the compelling leader, had always been possessed by the need to put people down. He relished their coming back for more because it confirmed his authority. Now the friends were few indeed, and Fairfax Murray remained one of a faithful but diminishing band.

Never a man to resist exaggeration, Rossetti's occasional malicious comments on Little Murray – it was as though he could not bring himself to countenance a friendship – nevertheless often contained a kernel of truth. 'Murray is painting a picture,' he wrote to Janey, 'for which he expects to get £1000, and 2000 for a Palma he picked up. I am sure he has the gift for getting on, if only for the unutterable scorn of everyone else who makes the mistake of being alive and not dead – a sure sign of a successful destiny. There is a sort of superficial good nature about him, but depths of cynicism, perhaps grown with the growth of his legs. Crowe and Cavalcaselle he already waves aside as infants, and is the only man who knows the arcana of art history. I fancy he does know a great deal but seems not to have the slightest faculty for writing it down.'[49] Rossetti had marked the lack of any literary bent in Murray's make-up in 1870 when he urged him to write a piece for the *Athenaeum*. He was right, too, on the want of a painter's imagination: 'Murray said the picture of his own had more subject than any he had hitherto done – I asked what it was and was answered – *Two Lovers Playing at Chess*. I did not tell him that it hardly seemed to exhaust the Shakespearian cycle of humanity and that he had a subject or two to fall back on.'[50]

There were lighter moments. 'That wonderful little man passed yesterday evening with me and astounded me by poking fun at the legs of a costume figure of a Turk in a book he looked through. I didn't know what to say, they were much better legs than his own.' Before he left London, Fairfax Murray visited Cheyne Walk once more and again provided the subject of Rossetti's next letter to Janey. 'Little Murray was here again yesterday and brought with him one of Keats's sophistical, rarified letters which he had bought and he read it over to me as I worked, in the most practical tone imaginable. I am sure he must succeed, having no fancies of any kind, except a great fancy for fruit tart and I think babies so long as they are his own. He showed me the photos which I declared superior to those of all other Bambini.'[51]

In the last two years of Rossetti's life, Fairfax Murray continued to perform small services for him, obtaining photographs of Sienese street scenes, and on another occasion sending him 'some wonderful photos from Italy, especially two Botticellis: 'isn't Ned Jones's *Phyllis & Demophöon* plain as a pikestaff in one corner, isn't it just!' He made drawings with detailed colour notes of the misty Maremma, the Tuscan marshes that lie between Pisa and Livorno, for Rossetti to use as the authentic background for *La Pia de Tolomei*. 'Do you remember telling me that you would look up for my benefit [in the Maremma subject] some photos of desolate places which you had once collected ... they would be of great use to me, I doubt not, in the picture in question.'[52] In the end he settled for a third request: 'the Florence photos were on the whole rather disappointing, but the Siena ones are simply invaluable – I only wish I had always had them.'[53] Fairfax Murray continued to visit Rossetti whenever he was in London, when almost all his friends had long ceased to call. They talked of pictures and the past, of Rossetti's work, and of Ruskin: 'At any rate, you seem to have got the cheque cashed. This is something at a time when checks in one's career seem quite to have superseded the cheques that used to come plenti-fully through the post.'[54] Fairfax Murray was unfailing in his loyalty to the genius of Rossetti and wonderfully forgiving of his final years.

Dante Gabriel Rossetti's last letter, six months before he died, was an authentic voice from the past. 'It is centuries since I heard from you in any shape, though I have had occasion more than once to feel grateful to you when working on the 2 pictures for which you furnished me background photos; Ellis … tells me you are expected in London … things have gone better with the Arts for some time past. The good folk of Liverpool have just bought my big picture (3rd time of sale!)[55] and I am beginning to wonder whether increasing age will admit of my tackling another big canvas… What do you think of the unfinished M. Angelo *Entombment* being declared by Robinson to be a Bandinelli? Let me hear from you when you come.' Charles Fairfax Murray did not see Dante Rossetti again. He next returned to London on 12 December 1881, the day that Rossetti suffered the stroke that marked the beginning of his final decline and death in Birchington on 9 April 1882.

Seven years later, Fairfax Murray was drawn by his memories to pay a last respectful visit to his mentor. Taking the coach from Dover after a rough night-time Channel crossing, he paused by Dante Gabriel Rossetti's grave in Birchington churchyard. Fairfax Murray hurried on to London.

7. Florence

you can – and I wonder whether it wouldn't be best to come over and seek some work – I don't know – but for a year or two we may be all of us in more or less difficulty...'[3] There is an entry in Burne-Jones's account with the Firm 'Cash for C. F. Murray, £5.'[4] What little money Fairfax Murray had was spent on pictures in the next five years as he built up his collection and his portfolio of clients. Competition between dealers, private buyers and curators demanded the immediate availability of funds if pictures were to be secured, and having never enjoyed the luxury of capital, his financial difficulties were never far from the surface as his dealing opportunities increased. Moreover, he took a patriotic pride in his relationship with the National Gallery, and he would accept only half the usual commissions on his purchases on their behalf.

The deprivations of his childhood had developed in Fairfax Murray an acquisitive zeal, moderated only by an insistence on excellence. When he had built a collection of distinction in a school, or an artist's early work, or in majolica, he might sell it and move on. Charles Fairfax Murray, collector and connoisseur, was still the young man of huge talent and an uncertain future, whose dreams were filled with the history of art and technique, of the masters and their schools. Fairfax Murray the dealer was his *alter ego*, the man who made the possession of beautiful things a possibility.

Armed only with his gifts as an artist and a student of art, he had at the age of 30 achieved a host of friends and acquaintances in the art world both of London and Italy, a remarkable collection of paintings that would have done credit to the connoisseurship of any collector, a beautiful wife and two small children. Reflecting, after a gap in correspondence of several months, on the difficulty of combining married life with writing letters, he crammed all the news of his family in to one page before turning, as usual, to pictures. 'I have a number of new acquaintances,' he wrote to William Spanton, 'and might have many more if I chose, but one grows more crustaceous, armadillo-ish and hedge-hoggy as time rolls on ... how interested you would be if you could see the collection of pictures by the Old Masters I have here...'[5] followed by four pages listing the more important items in his collection in the via de Serragli.

His pictures included at the time an *Ecce Homo* by Paris Bordone, the follower of Giorgione, a *Buonconsiglio* of the school of Bellini, a self-portrait by Palma Giovane, the nephew of Palma il Vecchio, a portrait of an unknown man and a *Madonna and Saints* by the Venetian Lorenzo Lotto, an altarpiece of the School of Signorelli, a bust of Mary Magdalene attributed to Basaiti, the follower of Bellini, a Spagnaletto *St Jerome*, two Duccios, a *Fair* scene by the Tuscan Jacopo da Empoli, a *Madonna* which he believed to be by Gaddo Gaddi, three *Crucifixions*, one attributed to Andrea del Castagno and the others by Ambrogio Lorenzetti and Lorenzo Monaco. He had a fourteenth century tabernacle, the Madonna and Child in marble and the gilt wooden doors around this divided into 16 compartments, painted with scenes from the life of St Francis, the Adoration and individual saints, 'a fair collection added to those I have in London, which I hope to be able to remove this summer.'

The development of the American taste for early Italian painting owes much to Fairfax Murray's encounters at this time with the pioneers of the Boston collections. Charles Eliot Norton's influence, and his close friendship with John Ruskin, whose critical works were then read as gospel, had set a seed in Boston. The Association for the Advancement of Truth in Art was a typically Ruskinian concept, and among the early members were Thomas Farrer, Charles Herbert Moore and Henry Roderick Newman. Their 'naturalist' inspiration came from Holman Hunt, Inchbold and Brett – Rossetti was rigorously excluded – and of course from Ruskin himself. Farrer had studied with Ruskin at the Working Men's College, and he in turn taught Moore and Newman.

Charles Moore had played a leading part in the metamorphosis of the Fogg Museum from a cast collection and drawing school at Harvard to become one of America's great public collections, and under Norton's aegis he became the Fogg's first Director in 1875. He first took a year's leave of absence to study in Europe and he set out with a letter of introduction to Ruskin at Oxford. In July 1876, Charles Moore was reunited with his old friend Henry Newman in Florence, and by mid-September he had reached Venice, where he spent the next four months in Ruskin's company. Fairfax Murray joined them in December and again for three months in the following spring, and he and Moore there and then struck up a relationship. They talked of pictures for the Fogg: 'I shall soon have other appropriations'[6] Charles Moore wrote on his return to Boston.

Henry Roderick Newman, six years Fairfax Murray's senior, settled in Florence in 1874. He was a New Yorker by birth, a quiet man of distinctly Anglophile leanings with an English wife, and he soon numbered among the friends he made the Brownings, the Spencer Stanhopes and the De Morgans, whom Fairfax Murray knew well from Cheyne Walk and the Morris circle, and the Alexanders, an American family who became close friends of Ruskin. In Venice, Charles Moore had shown some of Newman's drawings to Ruskin who urged him – very much in his own mould as an architectural painter – to make a record of a number of threatened buildings in Florence. Although Newman undertook few commissions for Ruskin, he made this something of a personal mission, and he maintained a steady correspondence with Ruskin in which Fairfax Murray acted as an occasional intermediary, until they too fell out over Ruskin's ill-natured criticisms of Newman's admittedly curious palette; views that he pointedly passed on to another American pupil of Charles Moore, Joseph Lindon Smith, who was jealous of Newman's growing reputation.

When Fairfax Murray and Angelica moved to Florence in the autumn of 1879, Fairfax Murray and Henry Newman quickly found shared interests as well as friends in common. They 'spent many hours scouring the small Florence antique and bric-a-brac shops where one might still find hidden treasures... and with Murray's assistance Newman gathered a choice collection of primitive Italian masters which adorned his studio walls for many years, and an important group of 135 fourteenth-century illustrated books...'[7]

Another mutual acquaintance and occasional visitor to Florence was Harry Buxton Forman; senior official of Her Majesty's Royal Mail in St Martin's le Grand, bibliophile and forger who, with Thomas Wise, was responsible for a considerable number of literary fakes. Henry Newman had first met him in Venice in 1872, where they had formed an unlikely friendship. Buxton Forman, whom Fairfax Murray already knew as a fellow collector and associate of William Morris, had for some time been anxious to procure the correspondence between the poet Percy Bysshe Shelley, who had drowned at La Spezia in 1822 and Byron's lover, Claire Clairmont, for an edition of Shelley's prose works. Thomas Wise was Secretary to the Shelley Society, and this would be the crowning *coup* of their partnership. Henry Roderick Newman was commissioned to paint a picture of the fatal bay as a frontispiece. Claire Clairmont lived on quietly in Florence with her maiden niece, Pauline. On Claire's death in 1879 Harry Buxton Forman quickly appointed Henry Newman his agent to seize the prize, at the lowest price possible, from under the nose of a rival bidder, Edward Silsbee, who had long laid siege to Pauline for much the same reason and lived in the house. With Henry Newman anxious to return to La Spezia, it fell to Fairfax Murray to pursue terms. He put his personal stamp on the bidding by first securing the letters in a locked chest to which he kept the only key before he diligently resumed negotiations with Pauline Clairmont. Silsbee proved no match for the experienced intermediary, and the prize passed to Buxton Forman soon after.

Henry Newman distanced himself a little from the captious American expatriate circle that included James Jackson Jarves, the Stillmans and the sculptors William Couper and Preston Powers; indeed, the gentlemanly Newman achieved the dubious distinction of uniting James Jackson Jarves and William Stillman (who had in *The Crayon*, with surprising lack of judgement, perhaps arising from personal acquaintance, strenuously opposed the sale of Jarves's collection in the States) in an onslaught on his technique,[8] his subjects and his patrons. Willard Fiske, a distinguished American professor of linguistics and bibliophile who retired to Florence for his health, was another, less acerbic member of the circle. Fairfax Murray gave Fiske three Petrarch volumes for his collection and sold him pictures. Many pictures and early books from Newman's and Fiske's collections are now in American public galleries and university archives, but the greater result of Fairfax Murray's American friendships in the early 1880s is seen in the next generation of connoisseurs and curators who were introduced to Fairfax

Murray by friends from his days in Florence, in particular Edward Waldo Forbes, who succeeded Charles Moore as Director of the Fogg Museum of Art.

John Ruskin's deep concern for the threatened works of *trecento* and early Renaissance Italian art was expressed in his own wonderfully evocative, accurately detailed architectural watercolours, in his indefatigable researches and through his educational work for the Arundel Society. William Morris, so often the realistic mirror to Ruskin's rhetoric, was no less appalled by the damage wrought by architects and 'improvers' in the name of restoration in England's ancient churches. The work of his former employer George Street at the graceful Norman and early Gothic church at Burford enraged him to the point that he felt he must act to protect the country's heritage of ancient buildings. In March of 1877, while Fairfax Murray was working with Ruskin in Venice, William Morris founded the Society for the Preservation of Ancient Buildings, familiarly known in the Morris circle as 'Anti-Scrape'. Philip Webb, Spencer Stanhope, George Price Boyce, William De Morgan, Edward Poynter and George Wardle formed the first Committee with Morris. Arthur Mackmurdo was a founder-member.

Aware that the peril was not confined to England, William Morris next devised an elaborate structure of European correspondents to keep Anti-Scrape in touch with threatening developments elsewhere. Charles Fairfax Murray, a hitherto reliable member of the Morris circle, was appointed to the imposing position of Italian Correspondent as part of the grand design, apparently without his first being invited to accept either the office or the responsibility. When William Morris visited Venice next year, he was so infuriated by the work he saw in the Baptistery of San Marco that he squashed George Howard's hat in rage, mistaking it for his own. Work was started on replacing the marble facings to the great west front in the following year, and an Anti-Scrape campaign of vehemence and scorching rhetoric was launched in academic centres throughout England. Public meetings were held to publicise the issue. Ruskin was a vigorous supporter of SPAB from public platforms, while William Morris wrote a letter to the *Daily News*, accusing the Italians of vandalism and 'headlong rashness.'[9]

Italian reaction to criticism from abroad was understandably indignant. The patronising suggestion that they were insensitive to the danger of damaging an irreplaceable work of art in the course of restoration was furiously rejected. They pointed out angrily that the works had been in progress at intervals over a period of 40 years. The commotion that Morris stirred up was largely counter-productive. Fairfax Murray remained silent, pleased with having thereby avoided conflict with his Italian friends and colleagues. Giovanni Cavalcaselle from his influential official position in Rome told him of the reaction produced by the English agitation over St Mark's: 'the fact is the work has been suspended for 6 months and the

(Italian) government think we might have taken the trouble to inform ourselves of the fact before making such a noise. They object also to the form of some of the memorials which can only be characterised as impertinent and insulting, and were not calculated to do otherwise than they have done, viz. cause no notice to be taken of them... I have no doubt the whole thing has been badly managed.'[10] In the event, the final stages of the scheme were postponed and then abandoned for lack of funding. Next year, Morris was writing to Janey: 'I am just off to Anti-Scrape and will speak of the Campo Santo; what the deuce is Murray about, to let such things go on without a row?'[11] His unsought appointment as Anti-Scrape's Italian Correspondent was foreign to his temperament and beliefs. He was unsentimental about architecture and landscape: '...cultivated land is very much the same all over the world & I find it difficult to agree with Mr Morris that a field under cultivation is a beautiful object,'[12] he once remarked. Before long, a St Mark's Sub-Committee of Anti-Scrape was formed under Henry Wallis[13] to monitor the situation in Venice.

Despite his reluctance to become involved in the counterproductive dispute over the works in Venice, Fairfax Murray made a substantial contribution to Anti-Scrape's work in Italy once the San Marco debate had cooled. In the following five years, with the support of Bella Duffy and Spencer Stanhope in Florence, his was an isolated restraining voice, the committee in London in outrage on every issue before them to the detriment of their aims, while Italians of all shades of opinion united in their determination to resist outside interference. 'I am convinced from experience that public foreign protest & interference with Italian restoration is in no way beneficial & that on the contrary it irritates the national susceptibility to the point of making enemies of those inclined to be friendly or neutral. Whatever is done should I think be private,'[14] he urged. It was not until Philip Webb visited Venice with Fairfax Murray in 1885 that Anti-Scrape finally conceded the error of attempting to force their views on the restorers by pressure of public opinion and developed a less confrontational stance.

Charles Fairfax Murray had in the meantime to make such progress as he could by cultivating the acquaintance of those influential Italians whom he thought might be receptive to the arguments of Anti-Scrape. He mediated in three important projects in the early 1880s, the first no less than the renovation of Giotto's canonical fresco cycles in the Arena Chapel in Padua under the direction of Antonio Tolomei. Here the work involved both substantial architectural works to the fabric which included removing the loggia on the west facade, and inside the stabilisation and restoration of fresco depicting episodes in the Life of Christ that had been seriously damaged by damp. It was fortunate that Tolomei was a supporter of SPAB principles; the official record shows only that 'Mr Charles Fairfax Murray saw (Bertolli) at work in the oratory and was impressed,[15] an indication that Fairfax Murray was regarded by the Italians as the representative of Anti-

Scrape. Fairfax Murray's efforts to recruit Tolomei as a member of SPAB seem not to have succeeded, but a bridge had at last been built.

In May 1881, Fairfax Murray received a pamphlet from Tito Vespasiano Paravicini, campaigning against wholesale reconstruction of the Basilica of S Eustorgio in Milan, drawing attention to alterations carried out under the name of restoration in Pavia, and protesting that no notice was taken of any dissenting view. The author set out the failings of a system which allowed the same architects who carried out restorations to be appointed to the supervisory bodies overseeing their work. The problems were no worse than those experienced by Anti-Scrape in England, but Fairfax Murray made some practical suggestions for founding an Italian society, and put him in touch with William Morris. Henry Wallis meanwhile recruited Paravicini to the San Marco committee, where he became a valuable ally.

His support was soon needed in San Gimignano, where Fairfax Murray had been approached by a local artist, Niccolo Cannici, who found himself a lone dissenting voice on the Town Council in opposing plans to rebuild the front of the Palazzo Pubblico. The work designed to 'restore to its former splendour' this graceful, colonnaded building included added armorial bearings and battlements 'on the supposed mediaeval plan.' Fairfax Murray once again advised SPAB that a respectful and temperate letter would carry much greater weight than sweeping condemnation, and it may be that it was because of this advice that William Morris refused to sign the letter prepared by the Secretary until he had seen photographs of the threatened building. The architect directing these works was none other than Cav. Prof. Architetto Signor Guiseppe Partini, Fairfax Murray's long-time colleague at the Instituto di Belle Arte in Siena. Murray had left Florence for San Gimignano the day after he received Cannini's appeal for help, and in his letter to SPAB he mentioned as an aside that he would travel to Pisa in the next few days to report on the Campo Santo fresco restorations. The same letter shows that he was also supporting a failing campaign to halt works in Florence which Spencer Stanhope had publicised in the *Gazzetta d'Italia*. 'They have commenced the demolition of the tower above the roof of the Bigallo,' he wrote. Despite his reservations over tactics, he was an active representative of Morris, Webb and their colleagues in London.

Fairfax Murray's unpredictable appearances and disappearances in the restless pursuit of his livelihood were a source of great anxiety to Angelica. He had been in London for some weeks in May 1879 to arrange for two his pictures – *The Garland Makers* and *A Pastoral*, painted in Siena – to be shown at the Grosvenor Gallery, where they attracted some favourable attention. 'Your pictures look very good at the Grosvenor and many people like them … that little book of sketches for pictures you gave me is about the greatest delight I have – and anything of the kind you can send me will be greatly valued,'[16] Burne-Jones wrote. A letter from Frederick Burton in June brought Fairfax Murray news that Angelica had written in great affliction to Miss Lombardi begging her to ask if he was in London, having not heard from him for some weeks, and apprehensive that some misfortune may have befallen him. The letter reached him in Hugh Street as he prepared to return. 'Murray has gone back having shot amongst us like a meteor for a brief time,'[17] Burne-Jones reported to George Howard in a more friendly tone than of late. Chastened, he once more moved his sister Lucy to Florence to keep Angelica company during his long absences. 'Little Murray looks in from time to time,' Rossetti wrote to Janey Morris. 'He seems to have housed his sister with his wife in Italy and is really a meritorious though cocky little cove.'[18]

Marie and William Stillman had settled in Florence from Rome in the summer of 1878 with Bella and Lisa, the daughters of William Stillman's first wife Laura, and Euphrosyne – Effie – her own daughter. Michael, their son, was born in Florence in October 1878. Charles Fairfax Murray was glad to welcome their arrival in Italy, and when he moved his family to Florence the following year they resumed a close friendship that was unbroken in their lifetime. At the Stillman's house in the via Alfieri he gave Lisa and Effie drawing lessons, and he followed their development as closely as if they were his own children. The Stillman family stayed annually with Angelica at the Murray's holiday villa in Poggiarello. Lisa became a talented painter and Effie a considerable sculptress whose late work included the memorial to Thomas F Bayard – the United States's first Ambassador to the Court of St James – commissioned by Samuel Bancroft, the ardent collector of the Pre-Raphaelites and one of Fairfax Murray's most valued American clients whom he had introduced to the Stillmans. His travels still took him wherever paintings might be seen or sold. He was in London again in May 1880, exhibiting at the Grosvenor Gallery once more, this year his *Last Meeting of Helga and Gunnlaug* after William Morris's translation of an Icelandic legend and *Madonna Laura*. On 26 June 1880 the first of three sons, John Edward Leopold, was born, and in July Fairfax Murray wrote to Rossetti from Venice that 'my wife has presented me with a son, upon which I immediately fled to earn some bread and his milk.' He was copying again for Ruskin. Their third child, his daughter Emma, fell ill around this time; she survived, but was in poor health for the greater part of her life. By October he was back in London: 'did you ever by any chance see my cartoon of a 6 light paradise window – I have lost them & you know 10 times more about my works than I do – come and dine on Saturday will you?'[19] Burne-Jones enquired.

Janey Morris spent much of the winter of 1880 in Italy. 'I suppose that if I go to Florence I must have a look at Little Murray. I thought him more conceited than ever when in London last, and insufferably dirty'[20] she wrote to Rossetti. For his part he never lost his awe of Dante Rossetti, nor his love of William Morris, but his unbridled admiration did not extend uncritically to Janey Morris. There is no doubt that he felt strongly for her husband; it probably showed. Although his emphasis moved perceptibly towards dealing, Fairfax Murray worked hard at his easel during the early years of his residence in Florence. He exhibited two pictures at the May show at the Grosvenor in 1881, *Pharamond and Azalais* and a portrait of *Michael Darazs, Hungarian Violinist*. By August he had stayed some weeks in Bucharest as the guest of the Russian Minister, painting three portraits there, and spent a further week in Vienna on his way back to Italy. Frederic Leighton and Giovanni Costa visited him in Florence in October. Next April he was briefly in London once more to meet John Ruskin, who was again recovering from a bout of delirium, and to make arrangements for showing his *Portrait of Mary Collcutt* – the daughter of the architect who would later be his executor – and another *Pastoral*. He painted *The Violin Player*[21] and *The Wanderers*,[22] two major undertakings, in this period. Both are fine works of the second rank, accomplished but derivative.

Despite his occasional ironic comments about Giovanni Cavalcaselle's cautious attributions, and Dante Rossetti's fanciful claim that 'he waves him aside', Fairfax Murray had both affection and respect for the older art historian whom he had first made a point of visiting in Rome in 1875. They exchanged information and photographs over a period of 15 years – in particular on the Lorenzettis and other masters of the Sienese school, on which he was especially expert – and they went together on forays to study lesser known works: 'Cavalcaselle is staying with me till the day after tomorrow,' he wrote to Dante Gabriel Rossetti not long after he moved to Florence, 'when we go to Siena, and perhaps to Orvieto and Gubbio ... he is an easy, good-natured choleric & melancholy old chap – I like him very much – convinced that his end was near not long since he ordered his coffin and had it sent home. He wanted to keep it under his bed but his wife wouldn't have it; so after trying it to see if it fitted properly it was sent back to the maker to wait for him.' Cavalcaselle, who would remain the foremost art historian in Europe for another 20 years, for his part had considerable regard for Murray's connoisseurship. Both men were scrupulously honest in their attributions, based only on study of known examples, as with Fairfax Murray's identification of a panel painting of *Christ Bearing the Cross* by Barna da Siena.[23] Even now, little is certain about this important mid-fourteenth century Sienese painter, whom Vasari said to have been a pupil or *chompagna* of Simone Martini, and whose only other identified work is the fresco series of *The Life of Christ* in the Collegiata in San Gimignano. Fairfax Murray observed the stylistic parallels between this tiny panel and the *Way to Calvary* in the Collegiata, an attribution that has stood the test of time. He sold the painting to Frederic Leighton, and at Leighton's sale bought it back for his own collection, later passing it to R H Benson.

As Charles Fairfax Murray the connoisseur was also Fairfax Murray the dealer, so Giovanni Cavalcaselle the connoisseur was also Cavalcaselle the patriot, which gave rise to an uncomfortable difference of opinion in 1885. Fairfax Murray told him of his discovery of a picture by Naddo Cecchar- elli[24] who, as he later described to Wilhelm von Bode, was a scholar of Simone Martini, 'probably with him in Avignon. He is unknown in Italy, but a few panels have been attributed to him in Siena for want of a better name ... the picture seen (in Paris) by Cavalcaselle and this are the only two authentic pictures... Cavalcaselle immediately proposed to the owner to offer it to one of the Italian galleries although he knew how much I wished to purchase it. C hasn't behaved well towards me in the matter as he would never have known about it but for me.'[25]

Settled in Florence, Charles Fairfax Murray devoted much of his time to searching out works of art that might come onto the market, gaining the confidence of vendors, and defending his interests from his many rivals. As an unofficial agent of the National Gallery, Fairfax Murray proposed no fewer than 18 museum-quality Old Master pictures to Frederick Burton between 1877 and 1887. Eight of them – including a Buonaccorso, an Andrea del Castagno, two Duccios, a Bazzi (the painter better known, for personal reasons, as 'Il Sodoma') and a Bellini – he sold to the Gallery, mainly from his own collection; and he acted as their agent and negotiator for at least three further important pictures.[26]

Early in 1883, Burton instructed Fairfax Murray to resume negotiations for the Matteo di Giovanni da Siena *Assumption of the Virgin*, which Murray had first mentioned in 1878. This tempera painting, commissioned in 1474, was originally the central panel of an altarpiece for the church of S Agostino at Asciano near Siena. It had been rediscovered in 1800 in the convent's woodshed, and had passed in to the Griccioli family. News of the National Gallery's interest spread in Siena within hours, and by the end of January Frederick Burton was replying to Fairfax Murray that 'it is surely unlikely that Lombardi should not have guessed upon circumstantial evidence that you are acting for me', adding next day that 'under the circumstances I should not mind going to between 30,000–40,000 francs, say 35,000 francs if the owners continue to hold out firmly – this I do not hesitate to say knowing whom I am addressing.'[27] Fairfax Murray's erstwhile friend and landlord, the photographer Paolo Lombardi, was endeavouring to lever himself into the negotiation, and his opportunity came when in April Dr Wilhelm von Bode[28] entered the bidding: 'it will be a pity if we can't balk him there too,' Burton said. Von Bode, however, soon dropped out as it became clear that Lombardi was attempting to negotiate a price higher than Frederick Burton and Fairfax Murray were willing to pay. Neither gallery was overburdened with funds. Burton's refusal to deal except through Fairfax Murray reflected his trust: 'I have no fear of your not doing a good turn to the NG when you can...' and they let the offer lie for the time being. 'I have great hopes we shall get the Matteo in the long run. It is no harm that it should remain cooking for a while,' Burton wrote.

Eight months passed, and in January Burton told Fairfax Murray: 'I have had a letter from the Contessa Ermilia Griccioli Bandini-Piccolamini begging me to deal with her directly through her son-in-law, or authorise you to increase your offer of 45,000 as they are quite decided not to accept that sum. I shall reply that any offer made by you is authorised and if you state that offer to be final they may rely upon it, it is so. The lady's letter is in very good English and I suspect that it is written as well as constructed by Miss Lombardi.'[29] Agreement was reached on Fairfax Murray's offer before the end of the month, but difficulties still lay ahead. 'I hoped – expected – they would come to terms,' Burton wrote, thanking Murray but expressing some foreboding about difficulties of finding a source of ready money. 'I trust soon to hear from you whether Mr Howard was able to suggest any mode of getting the ready money required. As my acquaintance with Mr Butler is slight I could not have advised you to apply to him.'[30] George Howard and Fairfax Murray resolved that problem. There remained only the question of payment to Murray for his work for more than a year: 'I consider your demand extremely moderate. It was open to you to have claimed double the %age you have named. Your generous conduct takes us out of a little difficulty – we have balance in hand to pay 5%.'[31] Charles Fairfax Murray gave his services to the national collection at cost throughout his career. In April Burton wrote to Lombardi asking if he had a photograph of a suitable frame. 'Miss Lombardi said "no", adding that I had cheated her father out of his commission on the Matteo – I like that...'[32]

For much of the period of the exchanges over the Matteo di Giovanni in Siena, Fairfax Murray was engaged in a simultaneous negotiation in Florence for a Ridolfo Ghirlandaio, *The Procession to Calvary*.[33] Urgency was lent by a warning that a new circular had been sent out to all officials who issued export certificates not to grant permission without first acquainting the Ministry of Public Instruction. 'I should be glad if you would send here the Crucifixion asc. Castagno, the two Duccios, the Tiepolo and the two Panchiarottis...' Burton wrote in haste to Murray in Florence.[34]

Negotiations with the Marchese Antinori were already under way for the Ghirlandaio, with the Florentine dealer Stefano Bardini pressing his services on the Marchese on behalf of Wilhelm von Bode. The Hermitage in St Petersburg were also interested in the painting. 'If friend B[ardini] be the agent spoken of, I feel no scruple in trying to outwit him,'[35] Burton wrote. The fourth figure involved in the discussions was Giovanni Morelli, art historian and critic, and close friend of the Antinori family. 'I may mention that Sig. Morelli is executor of the late Nicolino A of whom he was the bosom friend. His good feeling towards our gallery & perhaps still more his old friendship for Sir Henry Layard make him wish that we rather than the Russians got the picture which the family are anxious to sell. It strikes me that B has the servants of many of the Florentine families in his pay and amongst the best the porter of the Casa Antinori. Now, as this man would recognise you, it would be necessary to go adroitly about the business.'

A further telegram to Fairfax Murray within days said simply: 'Act yourself to prevent B from getting commission from family + Burton London.' Despite his deep resentment of Giovanni Morelli's well-publicised animosity towards his friend Giovanni Cavalcaselle, Fairfax Murray turned to Morelli to support his offer. Frederick Burton applauded this move: 'I think you have done very well... I hope Morelli will come in time... If the family will take 30,000 I should certainly care for the reduction. But I would not risk losing the picture for the difference. I venture to feel sure that payment on the spot will not be pressed – Morelli can guarantee our good credit. But should the necessity arise of course the money will come directly from us. When we know the matter has succeeded it will be time enough to settle on the best means of getting the picture away.'[36] Giovanni Morelli and Fairfax Murray prevailed, and there was a brief moment of elation: 'Bravissimo +Burton London.'

Burton's next letter brought news that in Morelli's opinion the picture would not bear the journey to England without first being transferred to canvas, proposing that it should be sent to Bergamo to a restorer named Zanchi. 'Meanwhile we shall have some trouble about the ready money to pay the purchase price. By an Act passed some time ago, objects purchased abroad may not be paid for until they have arrived in England. We must try to get round this Act or get the money elsewhere – and I will lose no time in seeing how it is to be done. I am very sorry you should have had to make a Deposit.'[37] No sooner had Burton succeeded in arranging the purchase price within the time specified, than the problems of getting the picture out of Italy became critical. 'If on carefully examining its condition you think it safe to send it off to Venice whence it might be forwarded by ship to England, I should prefer that course to that of its going to Bergamo, since I would rather it were transferred to canvas at home than elsewhere. If it be in so shaky a state as Sig. Morelli supposes, the carting it up to Bergamo from the station after a similar trundling about in Milan (for it would have to go to Cavenaghi there first) would endanger it more than the whole journey home otherwise. [It] had best be sent to Mr Malcolm at Venice and called an old German picture – for there are some things about it that have a Tedeschi smack, such as the *marigoldo* with his back to us. But all this can be settled when you have the picture.'[38] Burton was relieved therefore to learn that Fairfax Murray had taken possession of the picture: 'I am obliged to you for taking the trouble to secure the scaling portions from falling off... I trust there will not be much difficulty about getting it passed. It would be probable Botti would be more likely to be favourable if he knew it was for the NG.'

It seems unlikely that so competent a judge as Guglielmo Botti would have been deceived into accepting an Italian master as a second-rate German painting. The deal was in danger of coming unravelled. Frederick Burton was therefore dismayed a day or two later to learn that difficulties had indeed arisen over the necessary export permit: 'Your letter received last night contains serious news ... on the chance of nothing having been done you had better write a line to Sir H [Layard] by my desire, telling him to whom the picture was consigned there.' Stefano Bardini, having complained to Burton of his not having engaged him, had, it seems, informed the authorities that it was Fairfax Murray's intention to smuggle the picture out of Italy. It was a much relieved Burton who learned that the picture had arrived in the British Consulate: 'I am happy to hear the picture is safe at Mr Malcolm's – the detectives cannot come upon it now – I think you have arranged the affair admirably ... there can be little doubt it was Bardini who gave the information.'[39] Ten days later, a grateful Burton wrote once more: 'You may send the Sodoma, I am quite content with the photograph and the price.'[40]

Close on the first success against von Bode over the Lorenzetti fresco, Fairfax Murray was contacted by his formidable adversary, beginning the business relationship that would ultimately lift him out of financial insecurity. For the time being, little would come of it, but von Bode was quick to appreciate the value of having an energetic and perceptive agent who was daily in touch with the market in Florence. He may not have known how greatly Fairfax Murray was in need of regular income. The Antinori purchase had occupied a great deal of Murray's time without a commensurate financial reward, and he was still living a hand to mouth existence. He had parted finally with Ruskin, and he had spent many profitless days away at his own expense supporting William Morris's Anti-Scrape.

Angelica was once more pregnant with their second son Eduardo, who was born on 18 October. The birth was registered by Sir Dominic Ellis Colnaghi, the British Consul in Leghorn, a career diplomat and a member of the family of London art dealers P. & D. Colnaghi. Colnaghi was himself the author of the valuable *Dictionary of Florentine Painters from the 13th to the 17th Century*. To William Spanton Murray wrote: 'I am in great disorder here and unhappy in consequence, shan't be in anything like order until the winter I fear.' His financial situation can be gauged by his being unable to travel to London to attend Dante Gabriel Rossetti's studio sale.

Among the most important works that Fairfax Murray handled in this period were six of the predella panels from Duccio's monumental *Maestà* that once dominated the high altar of Siena's Duomo. Commissioned on 9 October 1308, Duccio di Buoninsegna and his studio worked on his master-piece until 9 June 1311, when the townspeople of Siena, led by their bishops, clergy and civic dignitaries, assembled at Duccio's *bottega* to carry it in solemn rejoicing around the Piazza del Campo so that all should see it, and in to the Cathedral. Beneath the main scene of the Madonna Enthroned with the Christ Child, surrounded by Saints, Apostles and the Company of Heaven led by the patronal Saints of Siena, was a predella of 7 panels with scenes from the Life of the Virgin; on the back of the altarpiece, the clergy side, the narrative continued in 26 panels depicting incidents in the Life of Christ.

In 1505 the whole composition was taken down from the High Altar, and in 1771 the centre panel was detached from the predella. Fairfax Murray had minutely inspected the altarpiece in 1874 when he supervised its photography for Ruskin. He was on the point of moving to Florence in September 1879 when six of Duccio's predella panels were exhibited in Colle d'Alto outside Siena. Well aware of their origin, importance and position in the narrative sequence of the predella, he quietly secured them and shipped them to London, where he sold four to his client, close friend and fellow collector R H Benson. Two further panels he kept in his own collection for three years before selling them to the National Gallery.[41]

In September 1881 the appointment of Thomas Armstrong as Director for Art at the Department of Science and Art (the Science Museum was also part of the South Kensington Museum, as the Victoria & Albert Museum was then known) gave Fairfax Murray another important acquaintance in a position to purchase for the national collections in London and Dublin. The first of his sales to the South Kensington Museum was in January 1884, a sixteenth-century Lombard relief in painted and gilt wood of the *Virgin and Child between St Catherine of Alexandria and St Helena* which Frederick Burton had seen in Florence and recommended to Thomas Armstrong. Fairfax Murray had habitually dealt in paintings and drawings until now rather than museum-quality sculpture, bronzes and terracotta, but he lost little time in making good this deficit, a development which would later be of great value to him.

The acquisition of an important embroidered textile, a mitre belonging to Cardinal Andrea Matteo Palmieri, followed, and Fairfax Murray's relationship was strengthened when Thomas Armstrong began to use him as an advisor: 'I am at present much puffed up having received a long envelope with "On Her Majesty's Service" printed on it, the enclosure requesting me to inspect a work of art and report thereon!!! Her Majesty always pays double postage I find – it being necessary to use foolscap paper and envelopes of corresponding size.'[42] The same letter concluded: 'I suppose I shall flourish presently, but my inveterate dislike of a swallow-tail coat is much against me.' He later acted as negotiator in the purchase of these three important reliefs – a Benedetto da Maiano terracotta of *Pope Honorius Confirming the Establishment of the Franciscan Order*, a terracotta *Martyrdom at Ceuta* and the *Funeral of St Francis* in terracotta, bought from the heirs of the Marchesa Bianchi-Bandinelli. A *Lamentation over the Dead Christ* attributed to Giovanni della Robbia and other pieces passed through Fairfax Murray's hands to the South Kensington Museum. He gave a nineteenth-century Florentine *Virgin and Child with Two Cherub Heads* around this period and continued to act as an advisor to the Museum throughout the next 25 years.

The London art market was showing signs of resurgence after the lean years, a result stemming partly from the Settled Lands Act of 1882 which allowed trustees the resource of the breaking of entails on the estates of minors, releasing an unprecedented number of fine works of art in to the market place. The collapse of agricultural prices on which the great estates depended, the result of the invention of the combine harvester to reap the abundant wheatlands of North America for an international market, further ensured that the supply of great works (and poor studio copies) was greater than the demand. There was great scope for a connoisseur with real expertise and a keen appreciation of the new class of collectors who now succeeded the titled descendants of the Grand Tour nobility, men of financial strength and informed good taste who chose for themselves the works that they appreciated.

There was another reason for Fairfax Murray to look to London. As a dealer, he acted more often as agent than salesman, and the collectors he bought for shared his personal taste; he was not greatly interested in wealth for its own sake, and there is an indefinable element of romance in his approach to the marketplace. One of his closest and least predictable clients was the wealthy Far Eastern commodities trader, Charles Butler. Charles Butler was already past middle age when Fairfax Murray came to know him. He had entered the family firm before he reached 20 years of age, applying himself so relentlessly to the business that he was a millionaire at 40, and had suffered a complete breakdown before the age of 45. Now in his sixties, he was an eclectic but discerning collector, and Fairfax Murray's relationship with him was both close and vexing; Butler could never quite bring himself to make the major coup which he could well afford, and opportunities that Fairfax Murray recommended regularly slipped from his grasp. He did, however, support the astute but needy connoisseur whom he had learned to trust, and he financed several of Fairfax Murray's purchases in these years. Then, in 1885, this vital source of funding came to an abrupt end for a while when Charles Butler fell ill once more. 'I shall have to be careful this year, my friend Mr Butler is not at all well and in consequence indisposed to buy anything or enter in to any new business arrangements. At one time I hoped he might have backed me with such money as I want by taking the responsibility of unsold pictures. The capital required nowadays to purchase important works is considerable and makes it more difficult than it would otherwise be.'[43]

Charles Fairfax Murray was at home with his young family in Florence just three weeks in the next year. The time was fast approaching that he must take another stride and remove his business base back to London. He confided in Philip Webb: 'I expected to hear from you... I shall be delighted to find you some physiognomies to paint,'[44] he replied.

8. Return to London

Portrait of
William Morris
by Fairfax
Murray c1887,
painted from a
photograph by
Abel Lewis and
life; oils on
canvas, 85cm ×
65cm. *Private
collection*

Once more Fairfax Murray set about making a radical change to his way of life. The aspiring youth who had set out for Pisa 15 years before, still only 35, was now widely known among the connoisseurs, critics and dealers of the London art world. He numbered among his clients collectors and museums all over Europe, in Russia and the United States of America. Essentially a gregarious person despite his intense privacy, Fairfax Murray had always found in London the undemanding intimacy of people of like mind that he so greatly missed among the watchful, gossipy expatriate community of art lovers, collectors, amateur painters and dealers in Florence. He had kept in contact with the circle of patrons and collectors who had once surrounded Dante Gabriel Rossetti, Alecco Ionides, Frederick Leyland and William Graham among the most prominent. On his frequent visits to London he had nurtured his friendships with the artists of the group: William Morris, Edward Burne-Jones, George Price Boyce, Frederick Sandys, the dying Dante Rossetti and Ford Madox Brown, the mentor and supporter of the early Pre-Raphaelites. Then there were Philip Webb and Charley Faulkner, and a host of life-long friends like George Campfield, Morris's first foreman in Queen Square.

Working with John Ruskin and Burne-Jones he had come to know painters and sculptors outside of the Pre-Raphaelite descent – men like Sir W B Richmond, Alfred Gilbert and Sir Frederic Leighton. William Morris was himself at the heart of yet another circle of talents, Fairfax Murray's contemporaries, who were breathing new life in to the Arts and Crafts movement: Arthur Heygate Mackmurdo, Walter Crane, William De Morgan (whom Murray saw often in Florence) and their own followers of the next generation, Herbert Horne, Selwyn Image, Charles Ricketts and Charles Shannon. Fairfax Murray's diaries teem with meetings and engagements, dinners and social calls.

Early in 1886, on an extended visit to London, Charles Fairfax Murray called on Frederic Leighton and Sandys[1] in Holland Park Road. Frederick Sandys had been an habitué of Cheyne Walk when Fairfax Murray arrived in the Rossetti circle and he was much in evidence there until he fell out for a time with Rossetti, who had accused him of plagiarism, and went to lodge with Charles Augustus Howell. Sandys was given to the good life and frequently embarrassed for 'tin', wheedling and begging for money from Howell, who acted as his agent.[2] With his common-law wife Mary Jones he had moved to a house on Brecon Beacons to avoid the expenses and temptations of London, but by 1886 they had returned and were living in 'The Cottage' in Holland

nevertheless, one of Fairfax Murray's visitors during the first week of his return to London.

Much of Charles Fairfax Murray's contemporary importance lay in the diversity of his interests to which the decade from 1886 bears witness. Since the late eighteenth century the art world and the market for works of art had been slowly evolving the structure familiar in this century. In the span of his own lifetime, interest in art, which had long been moving steadily from the exclusive province of the noble patron to a wider market, broadened dramatically. The process that began early in the Renaissance, when artists turned to the aggrandisement of secular princes rather than painting solely religious subjects under the patronage and direction of the Church, had become the rule in the eighteenth century. Painters no longer worked as artisans under a master; patrons no longer commissioned immense works to decorate palaces and basilicas. By the nineteenth century, painters increasingly followed their own inclination in their choice of subject.

An essential catalyst in the accelerating process of change was the rise of the dealer as the mediator between the artist and the collector, finding commissions and financing the artist's work, often buying works off the easel and searching for patrons to add them to their collections, the change hastened by the development of engraving and printing methods, and the birth of photography. Dealers promoted both art and artists to a market eager to learn, and in so doing attached the symbolic values of discrimination, ownership and conspicuous taste to the price of the artists' work. Ernest Gambart saw that though few could afford original works, some could afford copies, and that many more would buy good reproductions; thus he bought not only the painting itself but the copyright, selling prints and steel engravings from the originals. Thomas Agnew pioneered the collecting of art as investment, inducing his mainly Northern manufacturing clients to buy new works not only for the prestige of owning beautiful things but also for capital growth, something the noble patron would never have considered.

Charles Fairfax Murray was the skilled *marchand amateur* personified, combining the three elements of the art world – artist, connoisseur and dealer – in one person, gifted in all three. His mastery as a connoisseur enabled him to practise as a private agent, buying and selling on behalf of a significant few discriminating collectors, public galleries and international art houses who trusted his judgement and integrity. No denizen of the elegant showroom, he detested the tag of 'dealer': 'If there is one thing I loathe more than another, it is the idea of the travelling peddler in works of art. A suggestion to bring a portfolio of drawings to any house as a boy was always sufficient to rouse me.'[10] As a collector, Fairfax Murray was first and foremost concerned with quality, provenance being to him of secondary importance. 'It does not or should not interfere with the enjoyment of a picture the fact that it is labelled by one name rather than another.'[11] As a dealer, however, he was well aware of the commercial limitations of this viewpoint, and he was a tenacious and assured defender of his attributions. He matched confidence in his judgement with boldness and decision – he once told Frits Lugt that he had found that a first bid at auction, at a slightly higher figure than his estimate of the price the opposition would be prepared to go, discouraged competitors from bidding up the price and saved him money in the long run.[12]

Although Fairfax Murray was a successful portrait painter for 20 years following his return to London (30 or more commissions can be identified), his career was now firmly based in the art market, as expert, agent, private buyer and collector. Nevertheless he found time to exhibit in London at the Grosvenor Gallery every year from 1879, when he showed *The Garland Makers* and *A Pastoral*, until 1887, with the exception only of 1886. *The Last Meeting of Helga and Gunnlaug*[13] was shown there in 1887, and following the collapse of the Grosvenor he exhibited at the New Gallery (built, in one more of the coincidences in which Fairfax Murray's career abounds, by Morton Peto). In 1890 he showed the *Concert*, which Thomas Collcutt placed in the foyer of his new Palace Theatre built for Rupert D'Oyly Carte, and he exhibited a number of portrait commissions in the intervening years, as well as making copies such as the Cavagnola he painted for All Saints, Margaret Street. Fairfax Murray was still actively painting for the market, and the number of his *genre* pictures and portraits that have a place in private collections is evidence of a measure of success. *Love's Nocturne* or *The Angel of Sleep*, an allegorical subject on the death of a young girl, commissioned by the American millionaire Collis Potter Huntington and completed in 1892, was much praised. Regrettably it perished in the San Francisco fire of 1908.[14] With uncompromising self-awareness he knew that he lacked the dedication required for greatness, but he fully understood his place in the scheme of things. Moreover, he was glad of the income he derived from painting.[15]

The imperative of keeping his business activity as a dealer and agent distanced from his rôle as artist, connoisseur and expert was that to be seen as an active trader might be held to diminish his standing as an impartial judge of quality and attribution. Few examples better illustrate the division between the artist and the merchant, or the separation of sentiment from commerce, than Fairfax Murray's successful negotiation on behalf of the South Kensington Museum to acquire a section of the mosaic decoration to the west front of Orvieto Cathedral designed by Andrea di Cione (the painter, sculptor and architect more often known by his Italian nickname, Orcagna – the Archangel in Florentine dialect.) The work was conceived when Orcagna was *capomaestro* for the enlargement and redecoration of the west front of the cathedral between 1358 and 1362 and executed by Giovanni Leonardelli. Fairfax Murray, the energetic campaigner for Anti-

Scrape, was alerted by Marie Spartali Stillman, who was then living in Rome, to the opportunity to buy one of Italy's neglected architectural fragments if the matter could be accomplished quietly. 'William took me to an antiquary today who has the mosaic from Orvieto Cathedral which is now making so much scandal – it is Orcagna's own (tho' patched up) & far more lovely in colour than the one stuck up in its place. They bought it from the Vatican works & have varnished it over to fix the patches! Pazienza!'[16]

Although much restored, the greater part of di Cione's original concept nevertheless survived. The scandal that attached to the work concerned the obscure circumstances, which later gave rise to an official enquiry, in which it passed from the Vatican *opera* into the hands of a Cardinal of the Curia, by descent to his family and thence to an Italian antiquary, where Fairfax Murray had the opportunity to secure it. Frederic Leighton, who was by now the President of the Royal Academy, made a special visit to Rome to see the piece and reported most favourably. Thomas Armstrong was already in Italy and wrote to his colleagues that it was 'somewhat restored, but an object nevertheless of great interest and importance' and recommended its purchase. John Henry Middleton, the Slade Professor at Cambridge at the time and later successively the Director of the Fitzwilliam and, from 1893, Director of Art at the South Kensington Museum under Armstrong, was much excited by the coup: 'I am delighted to hear that you are getting for the South Kensington Museum that piece of Orcagna's mosaic from Orvieto,' he wrote to Fairfax Murray. It was a very public negotiation.

Fairfax Murray enjoyed excellent official contacts in the responsible departments and, moreover, knew intimately the law governing the export of works of art. Despite the complications of establishing the disputed legal ownership of the mosaic, Fairfax Murray finally obtained the necessary license after tortuous negotiations lasting on and off for the greater part of a year. Arrangements were made in secret for the speedy removal of the mosaic as soon as the permit was granted, to forestall any change of mind. He had confidently told Thomas Armstrong that there would be no final impediment to exporting the work since the Government, if it were to refuse a licence, would be legally bound to find the money to repurchase it, and he was proven to be correct. The Finance Ministry declined to provide funds, and the mosaic arrived in London in 1891.

Twelve years later an Italian scholar saw the work in London and raised hue and cry, demanding to know how so important an art treasure was allowed to leave Italy. Professor Fumi, appointed by the Italian authorities to defend the decision to allow its export on the grounds of its extensive restoration, was the same hapless expert who had ten years earlier written a scholarly analysis of the work demonstrating that the greater part of the mosaic was by the hand of Andrea Orcagna, a marvellously fresh fragment of the Orvieto mosaics of the fourteenth century, and of inestimable value. Fairfax Murray was not readily forgiven in Rome; the official responsible for permission to export works of art was his old friend Giacomo Boni.[17]

Perhaps the most rewarding of Fairfax Murray's relationships with a private collector was with the banker Robert Benson. It was a partnership built on trust and shared enthusiasms. Robert Benson was a man of discrimination as well as wealth, and his tastes leant toward the Sienese school, the cornerstone of Fairfax Murray's early discoveries in Italy and his outstanding field of expertise. Benson was influential, too, as a leading committee member of the Burlington Fine Arts Club, and later as a founding member of the National Art Collections Fund.

Together with his wife Evelyn, he gathered together a collection of astonishing quality, sometimes advised by Fairfax Murray and often bidding at sales on his own behalf; Fairfax Murray in turn would ask Benson to bid for him if he was unable to attend an important sale. The legacy of this partnership may be found today in galleries in Washington, New York and Boston among many other American cities. Robert Benson enjoyed Fairfax Murray's company, and spoke warmly of his scholarship, his prickly self-assurance and his integrity; so close was their thinking that Robert Benson could without a qualm give Fairfax Murray substantial sums of money to invest in pictures on his behalf. A note in Benson's hand in the Burlington Fine Arts Club catalogue of the 1903 Sienese masters exhibition, against the description of four predella panels from Duccio di Buoninsegna's *Maestà* reads: 'In 1886 I gave a commission to Charles Fairfax Murray to spend £2000 in Italy. These four Duccios were part of the spoils. They came out of a farmhouse in the Val d'Elsa, near Siena.'[18] R H Benson owned also a *Pietà* of Filippino Lippi which Murray found for him, a predella panel which is now in the National Gallery of Art in Washington. Benson's handwritten note beside this in the catalogue reads simply 'Fairfax Murray bought this on Bologna Railway Station'. Murray himself remained masterfully vague as to how the picture came to be there.

A very different relationship that flourished for more than 20 years was that with Wilhelm von Bode, the able and relentlessly acquisitive art historian who was successively assistant and, from 1883, Director of the Department of Sculpture of the Berlin Museum, Director of the Berlin Gemäldegalerie – the Picture Gallery – in 1903, and two years later, Director-General of the Prussian State Museums which included the newly-opened Kaiser Wilhelm Museum. During the latter part of the nineteenth century it was almost obligatory to prefix any mention of von Bode by 'the great'; he might well have been christened 'the great Dr von Bode.' A pupil of the eminent Swiss-German art historian Professor Jakob Burckhardt, von Bode's formidable reputation was the product of authoritative scholarship combined with the lavish funding of the Berlin Museums by the standards of European galleries and museums of the time. Wilhelm von Bode was born in 1845, just four years earlier than Fairfax Murray, and they first encountered one another (though they had yet to meet) in 1877 when Edward Kaiser and Lombardi were attempting to purchase for Berlin the Pietro Lorenzetti *Group of Poor Clares* which Fairfax Murray finally secured for the National Gallery. When in 1883 the Marchese Antinori's *Procession to Calvary* by Ridolfo Ghirlandaio came to the market, and Fairfax Murray was again successful in obtaining the picture for Sir Frederick Burton against von Bode and his Florentine agent, the dealer Stefano Bardini, the two men were already well-known to one another and corresponding regularly. It did not occur to either of them to question where their loyalties lay, Fairfax Murray unhesitatingly entering the contest on behalf of the National Gallery, while von Bode took up the contention for the Berlin collection.

For the rest, it was a remarkable opportunity that presented itself to both parties, and an astonishing succession of paintings, sculpture, bronzes, drawings and artefacts passed through Fairfax Murray's hands to Berlin, both to von Bode's own Berlin Museum, the Gemäldegalerie, and to museums, galleries and private collections all over Germany which von Bode advised over the next 30 years. Once assured that the national collection was not in the market, Fairfax Murray would draw von Bode's attention to works of art at auction, or whose owners he represented. Nominally at least the deputy Director of Sculptures, von Bode was endlessly involved in the affairs of his colleagues. Dr Lippmann, the Director of the Kupferstichkabinett – the Print Room – of the Berlin Museum was a continuing buyer through Fairfax Murray over the next 15 years. The connection with von Bode quickly matured in to a closer collaboration in which Fairfax Murray negotiated purchases on his behalf, advised him of forthcoming sales and provided him with detailed appraisals and estimates of value of pictures on the market in London, Paris and Florence. By the time Fairfax Murray returned to London he was already representing Berlin, and a considerable number of German collectors, in the salerooms and in private transactions. Their dealings together were entirely one-way.

Connoisseurs of the period took a highly personal part in the continuous process of improving their collections; they were to be found in the salerooms on every major occasion, and the thrill of a hard-fought battle won or lost was part of the pleasures and despairs of collecting. In London, George Salting, for whom Fairfax Murray frequently acted, Charles Butler and Robert Benson were characteristic of these considerable collectors. In Germany, Dr Figdor, the painter Oscar Hainauer, and the wealthy silk merchant Adolf von Beckerath were their exact counterparts, the similarity extending to the time and effort collectors like Benson and von Beckerath gave to assisting their national collections. Collectors like Baron Walcher, Prince Hohenzollern, Prince Lichtenstein and Baron de Rothschild pepper the pages of Murray's correspondence with Berlin.

The collaboration with von Bode was crucial to Fairfax Murray in the development of his career as a dealer, and it was this relationship more than any other that brought him back to London. From the day he married Angelica in 1875, Murray had been faced with the problems of financing his purchases while continuing to pursue his work as a painter; and as dealing took precedence over the years, it was inevitable that as his reputation and contacts grew, so too did the difficulties of funding his acquisitions. When Fairfax Murray had been forced to appeal for help to Burne-Jones and Morris as his hopes of selling his Palma il Vecchio to the National Gallery faded, it was von Bode who was at length able to find funds for the purchase of the Palma for Berlin, and Fairfax Murray never forgot the relief this timely help had brought him: 'I am working steadily to free myself wholly from debt. The money I got for my Palma has set me on my feet but that's all, it hasn't enabled me to make any purchase of equal importance, still with your kind help I may with patience get on – I am always hoping that I may presently find a market for my own productions, this would make a vast difference...'[19] he wrote. Von Bode was, moreover, a scrupulously prompt payer, which secured him many fine purchases when immediate cash was the deciding factor between two bids.

Another early sale to von Bode was destined for the Dresden Gemälde-galerie, the Lorenzo Lotto *Madonna and Child* that was the source of a great deal of later controversy: 'I have not yet had an opportunity of thanking you for your kind offices in the matter of the Lotto – it has been of the greatest use to me and has enabled me to buy several things I have long wanted... I have sold the "Sodoma" to our National Gallery – I have bought a fine small Tiepolo and a Moretto da Brescia once offered to Pr. Lichtenstein but he let it slip being badly advised it seems to me... von Beckerath was here a few days ago.'[20]

A further bond was their shared dislike for J-P Richter, the critic and intimate of Morelli, von Bode's *bête noir*. 'The Triumvirate are here, Richter looks very much like he had never known one, Frizzoni [Morelli's pupil and follower] has just discovered that R is getting a stronger man daily as a critic... I didn't say much, but what I did wasn't favourable...'[21] Two weeks later Fairfax Murray added '...I don't think Richter worth powder and shot – I take every opportunity now of letting people know what a black-guard he is; Mr Butler took a dislike to him as soon as he saw him, but his impudence takes in a good many people...'

Fairfax Murray's account of the Graham sale at Christie's in 1886 is typical. 'I cannot tell you how much obliged I am to you for introducing me [to Dr Figdor]. He is quite one of the most pleasant people I have ever met to do business with. Mr Hainauer was rather more suspicious but he took my advice and I think he is well pleased with his purchases; I got him a fine *Madonna and Angels* attr. Fra Filippo for 630 gns and a fine north Italian portrait of a lady attr. Ghirlandaio for 230 gns. I bought a small Pordenone for 20 gns and sold it immediately to Mr Butler, a Tintoretto *Resurrection* and a fine contemporary copy of the Titian *St John the Baptist* in the Accademia at Venice.'[22] Over the years, Fairfax Murray sold paintings and drawings by Tintoretto, Teniers, van Eyck, Boccaccino, Giotto, Moretto da Brescia, Greuze, Bassano, Paris Bordone, Duccio, Correggio and a score of others to von Bode for his German galleries, museums and private clients. Leonardo da Vinci's cartoons of Christ and five of the Apostles for the *Last Supper*, now in Strasbourg, were among them.

In his autobiography *Mein Leben* von Bode refers with particular pride to a Dürer which he obtained through 'the painter and dealer Murray's agency' in 1893, the *Portrait of a Woman*. At the time there was an outcry about its going to Germany. Fairfax Murray had identified the painting as a Dürer and Sir Frederick Burton, doubting his attribution, had compounded his error by telling von Bode he should take it. On removing it from the frame, Dürer's colophon was revealed. The picture was on show with Gooden's, a firm of dealers in Bond Street where Fairfax Murray had an arrangement to hang paintings from time to time, when Sir William Gregory, MP – Austen Henry Layard's best man – went to see it after the sale to Berlin was announced in the press.

William Henry Gregory was a man of diverse interests and contradictory character, an able administrator but personally rash, a flawed classical scholar who was both intelligent and arrogant. An Irish landowner and MP at 26, the heir to considerable estates, he entered Parliament in 1842. During the Famine of 1845 he worked strenuously both in the House and on his estates to mitigate the misery of the starving, but on losing his seat in 1847, he turned his attentions to the turf and gambled away two-thirds of his inheritance in five years. Gregory returned to politics as the MP for Galway in 1857, a vociferous opponent both of Home Rule and of any extension of the franchise, but nevertheless a strong advocate of popularising the arts. He was closely involved in setting up the South Kensington Museums and was appointed a Trustee of the National Gallery in 1867 on the recommendation of Benjamin Disraeli, a position he held with some distinction until his death in 1892, though he was absent as Governor of Ceylon from 1872 until 1877.

Anglo-German rivalry in the art market in the last quarter of the century mirrored the political tensions between the two countries. War threatened as early as 1895, and von Bode, with his close relations with Kaiser Wilhelm II, was regarded by the Trustees of the National Gallery as a German imperialist. William Gregory was incensed that the Dürer should be lost to the nation, and was still less inclined to forgive when it transpired that Sir Frederick Burton had seen the portrait and declined to recommend its purchase. He raised a considerable clamour in the House of Commons, and Fairfax Murray was in the eye of the storm for a while: 'I am sorry there was any fuss, Gooden is not to blame, Sir Fredk. Burton did not believe in its being a Dürer or was at any rate doubtful and rather astonished at my view of its being indubitable, and refused to be dragged along to see it again by Ld. Carlisle who seems to have been more enthusiastic about it than usual,'[23] he wrote to von Bode. Although interest soon passed, the outcry damaged Fairfax Murray's reputation among the art establishment, where his connections to von Bode had not passed unnoticed.

As the century drew to its close, Fairfax Murray sought refuge with Lockett Agnew from the gathering storm; Germany supported Kruger with arms in the Boer War, the build-up of naval armaments continued and the Kiel Canal was opened. 'I am thinking of taking rooms near Bond Street where I can transact business... I hope there will be no war but your Emperor's message has kindled a spirit here which may go any length... the Emperor has always been regarded here as a man mad with vanity...'[24] he wrote with disarming frankness to von Bode, who was personally close to the Kaiser. A formal note crept in to the exchanges: 'Mr Lockett Agnew showed me your letter, I have no doubt that what you propose to say about the boy's portrait by Rembrandt will be satisfactory. Mr Agnew is by no means pleased at your reservation with respect to his own picture, the more so that you acknowledge that you cannot suggest another painter.'[25] The great Dr von Bode was notorious for talking down the value of any picture that he hoped he might later purchase: 'he fooled several people this way about the Hamilton Dürer.'[26]

Wilhelm von Bode had been seriously ill in 1903, and in 1905 he was appointed Director General of all the German State museums. Colin Agnew went to Berlin to open Agnew's gallery there in 1908, and direct contact between Fairfax Murray and von Bode dwindled, as Colin Agnew more and more became von Bode's representative. The last communication between them was on the brink of the Great War of 1914. 'Colin Agnew surprised me with your fine present of a bronze statuette by Jacopo Sansovino – model for the marble Neptune on the Scala dei Giganti, as I believe. The little bronze will always remember me of the good old times when we got from you and through your kindness many fine works of art for Berlin as well as for Strasbourg and private collectors here. Believe me, Yours truly, W Bode.'[27]

Fairfax Murray continued also to serve the interests of his American clients from his base in London. Charles Herbert Moore would eventually be succeeded by his young protégé, Edward Waldo Forbes, whom he sent to Fairfax Murray in 1897. Edward Forbes spent a good part of 1898 in Italy. Poor health dogged him for a while, but inspired by his maternal grandfather, Ralph Waldo Emerson, Forbes studied English Literature at Oxford. As his passion for art grew he often visited Charles Fairfax Murray at The Grange. 'For some years this was in a sense the centre of my art life in London as I later took lessons from Murray there and bought most of my pictures from him. In 1902 I bought from Murray with the help of my aunt Mrs Carey the *Madonna and Child* signed by Giovanni Bellini, and more probably executed in his workshop.'[28]

In April 1904 Edward Forbes 'decided to abandon teaching and devote myself to art rather than literature.' Richard Norton, who was Director of the American School of Classical Studies in Rome, suggested that Forbes begin to acquire Italian paintings with the thought of giving them to the Fogg. 'Norton kindly recommended Mr Murray who kindly let me come up and work in his house, under his eye. We chose a Paris Bordone *Portrait of a Man* and I made a copy of that with the underpaint and the glaze... I was still wholly incompetent, and Murray made caustic remarks about my hopeless fumbling. I think that he not infrequently took the brush out of my hand and corrected glaring mistakes, or perhaps worked over it a bit after I had gone. In any case, I had a good time and learned more or less and got an appetite for more.'[29] Forbes spent many hours with Fairfax Murray, from whom he bought pictures, including the Vivarini which Murray had first acquired in 1876 for Ruskin. This, and the Bellini, were the start of a close, second generation relationship with the Fogg.

Charles Fairfax Murray had made a passing but significant contribution to the evolution of American decorative style early in his career when he accepted a commission from the young and ambitious cabinet makers, Collinson & Lock, in 1870. As a result of the success of his series of panels for Webb's Green Dining Room at the South Kensington Museum, he was invited to paint figure panels for two pieces of domestic drawing-room furniture that were to be exhibited at international expositions. Thomas Collcutt, the designer of the larger of the two, was another of George Street's pupils who had come under Philip Webb's influence. His rosewood cabinet was shown in London in 1871, two years later in Vienna and, most successfully, at the Philadelphia Centennial Exposition in 1876. Walter Smith, the Director of the Massachusetts Schools of Design, was lavish in his praise, writing that 'the chief feature of the whole are the figures in the doors... painted by the artist Murray who stands at the head of his profession for this kind of work... the figures are executed in a free, bold manner, with strong colour-contrasts introduced, and each one is worthy of a separate and careful examination... altogether the work is an extremely satisfactory one, and an admirable example of correct taste in design and ornamentation.'[30] The second of Collinson & Lock's pieces, E W Godwin's *Lucretia* cabinet with three painted figures by Fairfax Murray,[31] was another much-admired feature of the British exhibit. The Philadelphia Exposition proved to be very influential in the next decade in American domestic decoration, and Godwin and Fairfax Murray had many imitators.

In the decade that followed his return to London the fine arts were curiously bankrupt. Only Edward Burne-Jones continued to develop the uniquely characteristic Symbolist style that so distinguished his work from that of his contemporaries, the luxuriant exoticism of Frederic Leighton and Lawrence Alma-Tadema, the immaculate, retrospective classicism of Albert Moore, and the derivative subjects of the two great painters in the late Pre-Raphaelite tradition, James Melhuish Strudwick and John William Waterhouse. These were, however, years of great ferment and lasting achievement in the sphere of decorative crafts, as the gothic revival of Pugin and Scott gave way to architecture on the domestic scale of Norman Shaw and Charles Voysey.

In the early stages of the Arts and Crafts movement the unifying conviction that embraced the paternalism of Ruskin, the socialism of Morris and the Catholicism of Augustus Pugin was that of the romantic mediaeval ideal, in which every worker – it was supposed – took his part in honest and creative toil for the good of his fellow men. It was a model in stark contrast to the sweated labour, unhealthy conditions and repetitive drudgery of work in the post-Industrial Revolutionary era, in which the common good was replaced by the profit of a few. While the movement proclaimed an idealised society in which both producers and consumers benefited from well-designed surroundings, and objects of beauty were crafted by contented labour in agreeable conditions, there was no universally accepted agreement on the neccessary steps towards achieving that goal; the choices to hand lay between the benevolent dictatorship of Ruskin's Guild of St George, the socialist Utopia of William Morris and the pragmatic approach of those like Henry Cole, who believed that the way ahead would ultimately be found in better art education for the worker within the capitalist system. None would survive the rigours of the rising demand for cheap goods.

The Guild of St George was Ruskin's essentially reactionary endeavour to assert the dignity of labour and beauty as every man's birthright, which inevitably foundered on the rock of its own well-intended contradictions. The frustrated Morris saw more clearly that the conflict between his Utopian ideal and the cost of craftsmanship was a paradox that could never be resolved. Even while he raged at Sir Isaac Lothian Bell against 'ministering to the swinish luxury of the rich' (Morris & Co were responsible for the decorative work for Philip Webb's new house for Lothian Bell), privately he acknowledged that beautiful handwork must always be more expensive than machine-made goods.

The first serious attempt by the next generation to give the crafts movement fresh impetus was made by Arthur Heygate Mackmurdo. Mackmurdo had studied under Ruskin at Oxford and had visited Italy in his company in 1874 (it is possible that Fairfax Murray met him for the first time in Rome).[32] In 1882 Mackmurdo, wealthy and well-connected and now practising as an architect, founded the Century Guild. Next year, the Century Guild opened craft workshops to design and produce quality craft manufactures for a discriminating clientele. Mackmurdo's aim was radically different from Ruskin's, in seeking to raise the perception of the lesser crafts to the level of the fine arts. Many of his circle, which included James

McNeill Whistler, Walter Pater and Oscar Wilde, saw well-designed craft work as an art form that needed no social aims to legitimise its status, and it was from the Century Guild rather than directly from William Morris that the Aesthetic movement sprung. The Century Guild was short-lived, the principals never having subordinated their own work to that of the Guild, and it was wound up in 1888. The experiment was not, however, without influence.

As Fairfax Murray was settling back in London, Walter Crane – supported by a committee that included Philip Webb, William De Morgan, Edward Burne-Jones, W A S Benson the metalworker and later a Director of Morris & Co, Thomas Wardle, who had taught Morris the craft of natural dyeing, W R Lethaby, architect and designer, Harold Rathbone, the founder of the Liverpool della Robbia pottery, and T J Cobden-Sanderson, the craftsman-bookbinder – was circulating plans for the Arts & Crafts Exhibition Society's first exhibition to take place next year, 1888. Janey Morris, Jenny her daughter, and Bessie Burden were among the exhibitors, and William Morris's *Book of Verse* with Fairfax Murray's illustrations among the items selected. The Art Workers' Guild from which the Exhibition Society emerged had set out to bring craft work of all kinds under the banner of architecture and, thereby, to raise the status of the craftworker and the quality of his output. Though not the first, the Arts & Crafts Exhibition Society was in many ways the most practical and influential approach to challenging the dominance of the machine.

The co-founder of the Century Guild, Selwyn Image, a sensitive landscape artist and the great glass painter of the English Art Nouveau, was also prominent in the Art Workers' Guild. It was Image who provided the stylistic link between the antiquarian gothic of William Morris and the spare, airy Art Nouveau of the Glasgow School. He lightened the philosophical baggage of the mediaevalists and, with Walter Crane, created a simpler style that looked forward rather than back to a mythic past. Selwyn Image was also co-editor with Herbert Percy Horne of the short-lived but influential Century Guild magazine, the *Hobby Horse,* and it was Horne who introduced Image to Fairfax Murray.

Herbert Percy Horne was born in the year that Charles Fairfax Murray joined Burne-Jones. Trained as an architect, he went to work for Mackmurdo, the leading exponent of Art Nouveau architecture in England in 1883. Image and Horne both lived at 20 Fitzroy Street in Soho, an Adam house owned by Mackmurdo and run as an *atelier*, with a ceaseless ebb and flow of artists and poets. The group included Walter Sickert, Augustus John, Charles Shannon and Charles Ricketts, a young friend and collaborator of William Morris. Herbert Horne was a man of wide-ranging taste in the arts. He had met Fairfax Murray in the early 1880s, and came to know him better through Mackmurdo in 1886. He was soon a visitor to Murray's Holland Park studio, and he tried unsuccessfully to entice Fairfax

Murray to contribute to the *Hobby Horse,* one of many failed attempts to persuade him into print. Charles Ricketts and his close friend Charles Shannon were amiable rivals to Fairfax Murray in the salerooms for Pre-Raphaelite drawings, though the dealer's longer pocket made their acquisition difficult.[33]

Fairfax Murray formed a natural link between Dante Gabriel Rossetti and William Morris and the group of younger artists and craft printers, deeply interested in woodcuts, engraving and the design and production of hand-printed books and fine bindings.[34] They met at Fairfax Murray's studio to discuss the contemporary direction of the arts; Burne-Jones was a hero to this younger generation. They saw the Symbolists, in particular Puvis de Chavanne (as they saw themselves) as the last bulwark against the rising swell of Impressionism. Charles Ricketts, with much of importance still ahead, felt threatened by the hostility of the art world and the march of modernism, very much in accord with Fairfax Murray's own view of 'that post-prandial disturbance called Impressionism.'[35] Before he died even Burne-Jones would suffer the indignity of a major work failing to sell, and he recognised that Impressionism was sounding the knell of painters whose work was rooted in the classical tradition.

On one less serious occasion Fairfax Murray led Charles Shannon, Herbert Horne, Selwyn Image and Lucien Pissarro – Camille Pissarro's eldest son and founder of the Eragny Press – on an expedition to meet Fanny Cornforth in her local hostelry, where they plied her with drink and questions about Dante Gabriel Rossetti and the days of the group at Cheyne Walk.[36] Herbert Horne also shared his interest in Thomas Gainsborough; Fairfax Murray owned a number of early Gainsboroughs which were included in Horne's *Illustrated Catalogue of Engraved Portraits painted by T. Gainsborough* in 1891. He helped Horne with his history of art in England, examining the contracts between the sculptor Torrigiano and Henry VIII, described by Milanesi in his edition of Vasari's *Lives,* in the archives in Florence.

William Morris's intense preoccupation with socialist politics in the 1880s distanced him from many of his friends who found his political views inimical to their own beliefs. Others, like Philip Webb and Charley Faulkner, stood with him. Fairfax Murray was wholly opposed to socialism in any guise, but neither Murray, whose deep conviction was that the only reliable help was self-help and who detested all forms of interference, nor William Morris, the champion of the disadvantaged, ever fell out over politics; time was always to be found for dinner at the Solferino in Leicester Square. Edward Burne-Jones on the contrary was among those who found themselves unable to reconcile their differing views, and the awkwardness between them was increased when Burne-Jones accepted a Baronetcy without mentioning it to his closest friend. William Morris read of it in the morning paper and was hurt. 'We must mind how we behave ourselves now, eh, Murray?'[37] he remarked.

The San Marco affair was forgotten and forgiven too. In March 1882, Fairfax Murray introduced Philip Webb to Giacomo Boni, the friend of Angelo Alessandri whom he had first met among John Ruskin's many contacts in Venice in the late 1870s. Boni was then a promising young architect who was deeply concerned with the deterioration of La Serenissima's unique structures and they had found themselves in sympathy on policy and practice in conservation, united in deploring the furore over San Marco. Giacomo Boni and Philip Webb became fast friends and collaborators, keeping in constant touch for many years over the concerns of Anti-Scrape. Little more than three years after their introduction Giacomo Boni was appointed, to his modest surprise, to the post of Superintendent Architect for the Ministry of Public Instruction in Rome. He visited London for an extended stay in October 1888, shortly after his appointment, and stayed with Philip Webb at his Gray's Inn Road apartment which doubled as his office, making it difficult to get any work done. Fairfax Murray had kept in touch with Boni since they first met in 1877, and he was recruited to take him on visits to the National Gallery, to see him on to the train with instructions for the journey to Kelmscott, and for working dinners with William Morris. Giacomo Boni remained in London during much of 1889, and Fairfax Murray must surely have been amused to have spirited the Orcagna mosaic from Rome while its guardian was in England, often in his company.

'As he became less of the artist and more of the dealer, he lost something perhaps of his early freshness and charm – some of his old reverence for the great men he had lived among: he never became less honourable and straightforward, less truthful, less manly, or less generous. But the atmosphere of the salesroom is not favourable to the cultivation of sentiment.'[38] Charles Fairfax Murray, the dealer notwithstanding, remained an artist, connoisseur and collector, through and through.

9. 'How happy could I be with either,
   Were t'other dear charmer away'

John Gay, *The Beggar's Opera* Act II, scene xiii, air xxxv

During 1885 and 1886 Charles Fairfax Murray could have counted his time spent at home in a matter of weeks. Philip Webb began an extended visit to Italy with John Middleton in the last days of 1884. Fairfax Murray met them at the border and travelled with them back to Florence. From here the two visitors left for Rome, where they spent much of February, with Murray joining them there at the end of the month. They returned together to Florence in March, and the three set out again a day or so later on their way to Venice. Here he introduced Webb to Giacomo Boni, and he stayed on in Venice for three weeks more to make an exquisite copy of Carpaccio's *St George and the Dragon*[1] in the Scuola di San Giorgio degli Schiavoni for Philip Webb, while Webb went to Padua. Then they all set out once more, for Ravenna and Forlì, Verona, Mantua, Brescia, Bergamo and Milan, where Fairfax Murray left them on their journey home.

He had been away from Angelica for six weeks in the company of two of his closest friends, and the contrast between their untrammelled pursuit of the great works of art that they travelled so far to see and the routine responsibilities of his own domesticity disturbed him. 'I have to go back to Venice to finish my copy of Carpaccio, or I should have left Italy at the beginning of next month... I don't think Florence suits me, I am so languid here, as soon as I get to Venice I am a different being. I wish I weren't so fast-rooted here and that my wife liked the water as much as I do – I am seriously thinking of shutting up shop here for a while anyway, I am gradually edging off from everybody and getting more and more in to my shell so that I see no-one, and that isn't right.'[2] He had been married for ten years to a girl of whom he was deeply fond for her beauty and calm, but one who, devoted and uncomplaining though she was, little understood his passions and ambitions. He probably did not attempt to explain them. To the accompaniment of a barrage of good-natured chaff from Philip Webb: 'If I did not know the extreme caution with which you mount and ride a scaffolding standing some three or four feet above the floor I shd. be somewhat anxious for your life'[3] and urging him forward 'in one hand a birch rod, proper, and the other a bag of lollipops...' Fairfax Murray returned to Venice to complete his copy.

In June he was joined in Venice by Angelica and their seven-year-old daughter Emma for a short holiday. Webb pictured them in imagination, seen 'through the glass door of Switzer's, the Signora and you (the maiden having perhaps gone to bed) and Barnaby, Boni and Alessandri all talking together. I should rather fancy the Signora may be silent but not unobservant of so much nonsense being talked...' By the end of June Fairfax Murray was back at work. 'It is with deep grief tempered with high pleasure that I condole and rejoice with you that you are once more perched on the swaying scaffolding in the beautiful chapel of the Schiavoni. Please refrain from taking snuff... you will certainly sneeze and bring yourself and my picture to the ground, and your admiring patron (what a wonderful position to hold in this wonderful world) to a premature grave.'[4] At the end of August, Fairfax Murray was back in Florence, his copy almost completed. He made a visit to Siena and prepared to set out for London by way of Venice, where he would put the finishing touches to the Carpaccio.

He expected to remain in London throughout the winter, and in the event he stayed until the following March, when he left London for Florence on 8 March and returned alone once more on 28 March. When he had arrived in London in August 1885 Charles Fairfax Murray put up as usual in Lucy's old rooms in Hugh Street, Pimlico, and he was immediately plunged deep in to a round of friends, contacts and commissions; the Carpaccio *St George* was in the hands of the shippers (though not before Fairfax Murray had exacted his revenge for Philip Webb's teasing by writing 'yr. picture's safe, anyone can finish it now', which alarmed his friend and patron mightily. A crestfallen Webb was much relieved to learn that it was a joke). Fairfax Murray's early callers on his return included Sir Frederick Burton; the irrepressibly humorous Webb pictured him 'your glib tongue newly oiled and applied to the tenderest feelings of the Director of the picture gallery of the nation on which the sun never sets...'[5] Frederick Burton's relationship with Fairfax Murray was in good order, though there had been an earlier moment when his hopes of selling his Palma to the National Gallery had been frustrated by shortage of funds and the siren calls of a rival dealer. The delay he wrote to Rossetti arose 'more likely from the peculiar temperament of its Director (between ourselves) who likes nothing that is not presented to him by a scoundrel at Milan who has already made a small fortune out of this infatuation.'[6] Their frequent contacts and later deals show that Fairfax Murray had underestimated Burton's difficulties with his Trustees.

Fairfax Murray was often to be found at the South Kensington Museum advising Thomas Armstrong, the Director, with J H Middleton, who later succeeded him as Director, and with the fearsomely acquisitive collector George Salting. Salting was an extremely wealthy Australian eccentric whose collection of porcelain and objets would greatly enrich the South Kensington Museum on his death, and his paintings and drawings the National Gallery. Wonderfully mean except in pursuit of art, Salting would invite his acquaintances to tea on Sundays. It was well-known amongst his intimates that if offered a slice of cake one must refuse because it was Salting's invariable practice to return the uncut cake to Fuller's on Monday and recoup half the price. Anyone breaking this unspoken rule of the house was not invited again. On one occasion a member of Christie's staff who was delivering a valuable Chinese vase was tipped a stale penny bun that Salting had to hand. George Salting's skill as a buyer and connoisseur of oriental porcelain was legendary. Fairfax Murray treated his idiosyncratic client with more than customary respect which Salting reciprocated in his canny way, deferring to his judgement on paintings, and trading his mistakes and second thoughts with the same ferocious determination that he devoted to his acquisitions. At times Fairfax Murray sat with him at auction, and the pair hammered out deals before they had even left their seats.

It was not until the third week in August 1886 that he arrived in Viareggio to collect Angelica, Philomena her sister, Emma and her brothers to take them back to Florence; apart from three weeks in March, he had been away for more than a year. He spent the summer in Italy, making several week-long forays away from Florence to look at pictures, and he was back in London by mid-November, this time accompanied by Angelica and the six-year-old John. They stayed in Fairfax Murray's rooms in Hugh Street, Pimlico, and remained in England until early in the following March. Christmas was spent in Bury St Edmunds with the Spantons, but the visit to London was not a success. Lengthening periods of absence punctuated by unexpected appearances had loosened the domestic ties if not the bonds of affection. Angelica was fearful of being alone in the great city with little or no English. She found the winter's rain, dark days and choking fogs as trying for her health as she had first in 1877, and she clung to him. 'Went shopping with A and John,' Murray noted, an unprecedented concession. Angelica was still as shy as when she first came to London ten years before, and it is little surprise that she failed to shine as Fairfax Murray's wife and companion.

Visits to the Burne-Joneses, Mrs Russell Barrington, Marie Stillman, the Bloods and Miss Werner (expatriate art lovers from Florence whom Angelica knew there), F S Ellis and his wife, Murray Marks and many others only served to increase her sense of isolation and feelings of despondency, and it was plain that she would never settle happily in England, far from her sister Philomena who had so long been her closest companion in Fairfax Murray's absences. 'I shall return here the same evening, my wife doesn't like being left,' Fairfax Murray told William Spanton, testily explaining why he was unable to visit Bury St Edmunds[7] overnight from a trip to Cambridge; his restless disposition was thoroughly at odds with the conventional routines of family life. Charles Fairfax Murray's almost obsessive travelling was itself an expression of his solitary nature, of his self-sufficient, compartmented personality. It was an icon for his refusal to conform, and a measure of his profound belief in the futility of laying plans for the future. In retrospect it is plain that the early years of relative domesticity in Siena after his marriage to Angelica were the real anomaly. His wandering passion for the masterpieces of art led him wherever there were paintings, drawings and books to see, to collect or deal in, and his true companions were the pictures he saw and people he met – almost all of them men – along the way. Nor was this mere self-centredness. He was generous and outgoing in his way, always deeply concerned for his children, but from his earliest years, following the illness and death of his mother, he had never enjoyed inner peace within a family. It was too late to learn.

For Fairfax Murray the highlight of Angelica's visit to London was an evening they spent together with Georgiana and Edward Burne-Jones, who had been unexpectedly elected an Associate of the Royal Academy in June 1885, and was soon involved in the affairs of that august body: 'We narrowly avoided a whole room full of portraits of her most gracious Majesty at the Academy this year – it would have been worth 6d extra as a chamber of horrors, EBJ said today...'[8] he reported. Almost from the day he arrived as Burne-Jones's assistant, Fairfax Murray had missed no opportunity to collect the work of his idol Dante Gabriel Rossetti, and of Burne-Jones and the other members of the Rossetti circle. Dining at The Grange with Angelica and Marie Stillman that evening in January, he 'took Mr Jones an illuminated choral book in exchange for a book of studies by EBJ and by this I became possessed of over 280 drawings by the master, mostly studies done between 1865 and 1870 for the *St George* series for Birket Foster, *Theophilus and the Angel*, SKM dining room windows, the Pater *Circe* and many others, also a few drawings picked from the collection.'[9] This was the world that Fairfax Murray understood.

He was also very much occupied with William Graham's sale in March 1887, for which he acted as an advisor. He took Angelica and John back home to Florence at the beginning of the month and returned on the day of the sale: 'I got back the first day, arrived at 6 in the morning after an abominable passage and called on the Stillmans and breakfasted with them before going to Christie's... Rossetti's pen and ink drawing of *Found*, the loss of which affected me so much, was going begging at Agnews ... for less than £75. I need not say that my cheque changed hands an hour later.'[10] He returned to his pictures, his studio, his work and his friends, and Florence was for a time forgotten except for a brief visit of a few days at Christmas.

His closest companions were naturally enough among the men with whom he had shared his early career. Edward Burne-Jones, Charley Faulkner, George Howard, Frederick Burton, W B Richmond, J H Middleton, the Stillmans, Walter Crane, the De Morgans (and William De Morgan's sister Mary, whose wonderful children's stories Fairfax Murray gave to his children) were frequent social companions. Only William Morris was missing for the time being as he worked tirelessly for Hyndman's Democratic Federation, almost to the exclusion of his other activities.

On 16 January 1888 'Miss Richmond came in the afternoon', and on 19

January there were more 'drawings for portrait of Miss Richmond.' On 21 January he added 'drawings for head of Miss Richmond.' So sparing are the few surviving diaries that this amount of detail is unusual and revealing, a small, inward smile, a touch of humour solely for his own amusement. With Sir W B Richmond as his neighbour in Holland Park Studios, the eminent RA was a frequent host to Fairfax Murray and as often his guest. For the first and last time, every occasion on which they met is meticulously noted, with sittings and visits from Miss Richmond intertwined. Miss Blanche Waddams Richmond was, in fact, unrelated to Fairfax Murray's neighbour, being descended from a Somerset land-owning family with their roots in and around Shepton Mallet. Her great-grandfather owned the corn mill there, and her grandfather farmed a sizeable acreage which he combined with the senior partnership in the local auctioneers' firm. Her father, the eldest son, 'travelled', probably in wool staple, and they lived comfortably in Bristol, a short walk from Queen's Square in the 'new' area of the city. His photographs show a sharply-dressed, confident young man on his way up the commercial ladder, and it must have been a severe blow when he died suddenly, from 'nervous debility and exhaustion, 10 days' in Leicester at the age of 32 while on a business trip away from home. Blanche was three years old when he died, and her mother seems to have married again, and again been widowed, by the time Blanche reached 16 in 1881. Mrs Pierce, widow, the two girls and her firstborn, Alfred, then lodged in Chelsea with a Professor of Mathematics from Bristol, where Blanche's parents had first set up home together.

Blanche's elder sister Florence Eugenie had already left the house in Chelsea when Blanche sat to Fairfax Murray, having at the age of 17 married John Bates, late of the Indian Army, known ironically in the family as the Hero of Hyderabad. John Bates, the son of the Chief Clerk of a private City bank, was the very model of a modern Major-General, arriving there as an East India Company cadet in 1841, serving in the Sind campaign and the Mutiny with gallantry and rising steadily through his commands. He was in England on retirement leave aged 56 when they met and married, two weeks after his first wife died.[11] General Bates was histrionically bemused by the bright young thing he fell for, a source of endless amusement. The two young sisters must have been a great trial to their mother.

There is no record of how Blanche came to be sitting to Fairfax Murray, and no indication of her mother's presence as chaperone at the early sittings. Fairfax Murray's diary suggests that this was a portrait commission, but it remains possible that she had modelled for him during the previous year when he worked on the *Concert Party*.[12] Blanche was a willowy blonde-haired girl of just 23 when she sat to Fairfax Murray, good-looking rather than beautiful; he was 39, on the brink of financial security. The portrait which survives – a skillful and enchanting study in pencil and black crayon with the detail of her dress and lace highlighted in white, the face lightly coloured in pastels – shows her to be strong-willed, straight-backed, and self-possessed, with a hint of the tremendous sense of fun which was one of her most endearing characteristics. By April they were lovers and Dolly, as he always called her, bore him a son, Arthur, on 2 December 1888. Since Fairfax Murray was not given to confiding in his diaries it is little surprise that there is no mention of Arthur's arrival; nor is there any reference to the birth of the third and last of his Italian sons, Roberto, who was born to Angelica in June that year. Fairfax Murray had remained in London for that event, staying until the last week in August, and he was back in London on 3 October. Blanche and Fairfax Murray set up home at 20 Rostrevor Road, a newly-built terraced house in a desirable estate development off the Fulham Road, within a short walking distance of The Grange, Burne-Jones's studio and home. It is not clear that Fairfax Murray was there a great deal, if at all, preferring to stay at his studio in Holland Park. This distinctive pattern of family life he followed not only in London but also in Florence (where his Italian family occupied an imposing villa in the hills to the south at Tavarnuzze per Montebuoni), while he had his place of business and lived alone, close to the centre. He was an unconventional family man.

In London, Fairfax Murray retained his Holland Park studio until 1892, when he moved his studio and residence to a house in Ravenscourt Park. In 1898 he moved once more to The Grange on Burne-Jones's death, and finally to an apartment over Agnew's at 4 Albemarle Street, and seems never to have spent more than the odd night with his family almost until the end. Surprisingly, despite his separate existence and long absences, Fairfax Murray kept tight control of both of his household budgets. He had found that he needed to manage the domestic expenditure of his sociable amour and the mother of his children in England, but Angelica was no less the recipient of admonition and advice.

As the English family grew larger they moved successively to a Victorian villa in Teddington, and later, first to 61 and then to 77 Barrowgate Road, Chiswick – both substantial detached houses in large gardens that stand today. The barrow-gate led into the Royal Horticultural Society's trial grounds, which occupied land owned by the Duke of Grafton, and until the RHS moved to Wisley in 1902 the area was open space, orchards and flower beds, which stretched down to Chiswick House and on towards the old village by the Thames.

The arrangement was entirely in keeping with Fairfax Murray's firmly held belief in the sanctity of discretion, and he was aided in this by the Victorian conventions surrounding family life. 'Irregularities' were not uncommon, and were judged neither hypocritically nor harshly; simply, they were strictly never to be spoken about. Amongst the Pre-Raphaelites and their friends there were many examples of relationships which were well-known and accepted but never discussed publicly. Ford Madox Brown was silent about his marriage to Emma Hill for many years, as was F G Stephens about his wife Matilda Booth. William Holman Hunt was equally discreet about Annie Miller (though they did not in the end marry, largely because Rossetti ignored the rules during Hunt's absence in the Holy Land.) J M W Turner lived two entirely separate lives, changing his attire and his way of life to conform with his identity, and on his death only Ruskin found this (and the erotic drawings of Turner's alter ego, the salty old sea-dog Admiral Booth) at all shocking. Irregular as it was, Fairfax Murray entered into a commitment the equal in every respect of that he gave to Angelica and his Italian family, and he provided Blanche and her brood with all the comforts of a wealthy middle-class home of the late-Victorian period. In the 30 years they were together they had six children, four of whom survived to adulthood; this was no passing fancy. Dolly, bright, extrovert and a little silly, was temperamentally quite the opposite to the shy, resigned Angelica, but Fairfax Murray seems to have been equally fond of both and as loyal to both in his detached manner.

There were contrasts too in the lives that the families lived. In Italy, Angelica was surrounded by her relatives – Fairfax Murray spoke of his sister-in-law as the mainstay of the family – and they lived a simple domestic family life, albeit in some style in the impressive surroundings of the farmhouse outside Florence. The family home, the Villa Murray in Tavarnuzze, was a substantial affair in splendid formal gardens with a row of tall cypress trees standing sentinel at the gate. Blanche, by contrast, together with her sister Florence Eugenie, with nine children between them and a number of cousins from General Bates's first marriage whom the Murray children detested, lived in the high style of late-Victorian suburban fashion. Ladies dressed in floating voile, *broderie anglaise* and lace with picture hats, and carried parasols to afternoon tea. The boys were got up in sailor suits and the girls in starched dresses and pinafores, with white kid gloves for visiting. Blanche shopped at Whiteley's of Queensway, which had all the cachet of the Knightsbridge of today, gave wonderful dinner parties, and would in summer embark in a string of carriages with guests, servants, cook and hampers for *fêtes champêtres* in the Deer Park at Hampton Court. Fairfax Murray's English family enjoyed a lively social life with delightful holidays in Italy and on the Riviera until Europe was engulfed in war. Muted by rationing and the loss of servants to the war effort, Dolly nevertheless maintained a good table and kept up the social round. Trips to Italy were replaced by a house in Broadstairs which was full the summer long of anonymous young men in striped blazers or subalterns' uniform making the most of their post-public school youth on their way to the trenches, in the company of a parade of young ladies in cloche hats dressed for tennis.

On Sundays from the turn of the century, the family took a carriage and drove to The Grange to visit Fairfax Murray when he was in London. The children grew up happily regarding their situation as rather exotic, the envy of their school friends, and they greatly enjoyed Sunday visits to the rambling old house in Fulham. Life for the Italian family was simpler, largely because Fairfax Murray tended to be there in the summer and, when he was with his family, to join them at the seaside. Here the invariable routine was to rent a villa for the season in Viareggio.

Holidays for Dolly's children occasionally led to exciting encounters, when their father would appear for a day or two – he was never happier than by the sea – but generally Dolly and the family travelled alone except for a maid, a nurse for the younger members and piles of luggage which included a tin bath. Sometimes they would stay *en route* in Paris, but more often they would take the train through to Genoa (where Dolly was much admired by the British Consul) or Rapallo, less often to Nice or Monte Carlo. On one such expedition, Dolly had decided that it would be good for the children's colloquial French if they were to stay in a small Left Bank hotel-pension instead of their usual English-speaking *belle-epoque* hotel. Their French vocabulary was improving remarkably, if not in *delicatesse*, when Fairfax Murray – issuing from his apartment on the Boulevard des Malherbes close to the Madeleine – was compelled to spend a morning looking for them. By noon they were established in their regular hotel off the rue de Rivoli, and Fairfax Murray had gone on his way.

He was generous and tolerant so long as he was not called upon to be present, and his comings and goings were as entirely unpredictable as his visits to his family in Italy. His daughter recalled his arriving from Paris unannounced in Chiswick late one evening when she was ten or eleven years old; sending the parlourmaid to fetch her discreetly, he waited in the shadow of the porch. 'Is your Mother giving one of her parties?' he whispered; and learning that there was indeed a dinner party in progress, he produced a *baguette* from the folds of the enveloping black travelling mantle he always wore, kissed her on both cheeks and silently returned to the waiting cab. He was very fond of his children.

Almost everyone in the circle of painters, sculptors and their clients knew of Angelica, and many, though not all, had met her. John Ruskin, Edward and Georgiana Burne-Jones, George Howard, William Michael Rossetti and the Madox Browns knew her. Marie Stillman and Spencer Stanhope knew her particularly well as neighbours in Florence, and Janey Morris met her there. The De Morgans, and Marie and Lisa Stillman, knew both Blanche and her children as well as Angelica and the four children in Florence. Angelica was in London in 1876 and again for five months in the winter of 1886–87. Fairfax Murray's neighbours in Holland Park, who included the Prinseps, Frederic Leighton, W B Richmond, G F Watts and Frederick Sandys – and who knew between them the entire Victorian art world – all knew Angelica. She had stayed in Bury St Edmunds with William and Madge Spanton.

The question of whether Blanche was known in the same milieu was carefully obscured. Since discreet 'irregularities' were perfectly acceptable in Victoria's reign, it is easy to conclude that Dolly led a hidden life. In fact, she was far from the deepest of secrets over the years. They were often to be seen together at the opera. The English family were close to the Morrises – when Fairfax Murray was not at home at The Grange, Dolly's three younger children would walk on summer Sundays to Matins in the church where Hogarth is buried in the old Chiswick village, and thence after the service along the Mall to visit the widowed Janey Morris and May for home-made elderflower wine and cake before returning home. Richard Norton was a frequent guest in Chiswick, and Lockett Agnew was godfather to Murray's daughter Elizabeth Florence (named for her aunt and not for the city). All knew that Angelica was living.

Sydney Cockerell knew all about Dolly from William Morris almost from his first day with the Kelmscott Press, and the English family can only be described as an open secret, if secret it was at all; Cockerell made frequent, studiously oblique, references to the complications of Fairfax Murray's domestic affairs without any hint of surprise or disapprobation.

In the wider context of the international dealers and their patrons, John Pierpont Morgan's librarian, Belle da Costa Greene who once alleged, vividly though inaccurately, that Fairfax Murray had a household in every capital in Europe, was certainly aware of his two families. She was in touch with all the major dealers in Europe and the United States, and routinely heard the gossip of the art market. Her true name was Belle Marion Greener, the daughter of the first black man to graduate from Harvard and a mother of mixed race[13]. Both parents were light-skinned, and the fiction of her part-Portuguese descent explained her attractively exotic appearance; few knew she was coloured and she 'passed' in conventional upper-class New York society. She was a confident and flamboyant young woman, widely (though probably wrongly) believed to be Morgan's mistress. Her dramatic taste in dress and jewellery, the signature green handkerchief at her wrist, her endless round of parties, concealed a degree of scholarship and ruthlessness which fully equipped her for her task of building up the banker's library. Belle da Costa Greene's tangled relationship with Bernhard Berenson, who fell passionately though unhappily in love with her when they met in New York in December 1908, ensured that the circle that frequented the Villa I Tatti also knew of Fairfax Murray's situation, and thus by full circle the matter was privately known to the art world and ex-patriates of Florence.

It is not surprising that Fairfax Murray had once turned to Dolly for companionship. She was young, vivacious, good fun and attractive, and she had a warmth and charm that instantly appealed even in later life (she survived him for 34 years). She was bright and well-educated, though undeniably frivolous in her youth. Fairfax Murray at 39 was leading a bachelor existence for nine months of the year and would, so far as society was concerned, continue to do so for another 20 years. He now knew that his wife would never live in London where his livelihood lay. He felt the need of feminine company in his mannish world and Dolly for her part recognised the qualities of the man he had become, perhaps with greater understanding than did Angelica. There was trust and affection between them, and she always spoke well of him in later life. Whatever regrets she may have felt went with her to her grave.

There is little doubt that Fairfax Murray fully intended to bid farewell to England as the war clouds gathered over central Europe. There is no mistaking the sense that Fairfax Murray was clearing away the past and preparing himself for a fresh, final chapter of his life surrounded by his books and pictures, at peace with Angelica and their children while he awaited the grandchildren he so much wanted. He was by nature ideally cast in the rôle of grandfather which he did not live to play, though he would have filled it with great distinction. The last of Dolly's children, Edmund, was born in March 1905. In planning to take his honourable leave of England, the English family were not to be abandoned or forgotten. As early as 1909 Fairfax Murray had settled the Barrowgate Road property on Blanche when she became, officially, the resident and ratepayer. His name was removed from the electoral roll at the Chiswick address in 1910, although he continued to pay all the household accounts. He told Marie Stillman that he estimated that the contents of the house would, if realised, give her a comfortable income for life; to Mrs Stillman it seemed there must be more to it than a matter of money, and she felt sorry for Dolly and the children.[14] She had long known both Blanche and Angelica and was intimately aware of the pull of opposites that Fairfax Murray felt. Nevertheless, time and again he postponed the break with England until Europe was at the very brink of war.

He said goodbye to Georgiana Burne-Jones in October 1913, sending her a postcard of the Villa Murray with news of his three sons by Angelica (and a grandchild on the way), and her reply shows that his departure had been long discussed: 'I should very much like to see you before you leave England (though I am sure you will many a time return to it for visits).'[15] Ever the energetic organiser of other people's lives, 'that dragoman of friends, the interpreter of all needs,'[16] Sydney Cockerell went, early in 1913, to see Fairfax Murray, who was 'packing all his books for Italy, and will be giving up his Albemarle Street rooms in March (unless he changes his mind as he is very apt to do)',[17] and a week later 'called on Fairfax Murray . . . very cordial but will soon be moving to Paris the pictures he has on loan to the Museum.'[18]

At Charles Fairfax Murray's death, the Italian family claimed to have known nothing of Blanche and the English family, although Dolly later insisted to Marie Stillman that John knew of the English children. He represented his father in his absences from Florence, and dealt in pictures from his home in Florence. It seems unavoidable that he would have learned of Dolly from his contacts in the trade if not from his father. Eduardo, the most 'English' of the Italian sons, knew or was made aware of the family when he came to see his father in February 1918. They may have hoped to spare Angelica, though it is hard to believe that his wife of 44 years could have remained completely unaware of another attachment. At Fairfax Murray's death public announcements in the Italian papers asserted that the Italian family had no legal claim to any of his Estate in Italy and that nothing must be sold by them or bought from them. This move, so directly contrary to Fairfax Murray's Will that it could under no circumstances have been sustained in an English court, can only have been intended as a legal manoeuvre to gain time to examine his business and private affairs. One result was that the greater part of his library was returned to London and sold at Sotheby's in a series of badly organised sales that failed to raise the true value of the collection in 1920. It was hardly the tactful concealment he would have wished. While friends and colleagues in England could discuss the revelations discreetly and sympathetically, the dismay of Angelica and his Italian family was blazoned on the pages of the *Corriere della Sera*, and they considered an attempt to challenge the Will in the English courts. The truth, however, was that much the greater part of his Estate was in Italy and specifically left to Angelica, and the matter was quietly settled.

It was doubly sad because Charles Fairfax Murray was a proud man who cared deeply for both of his families and both of his women. He was acutely aware of the position he had placed them in. Angelica had been his companion in the early years of his struggle to achieve a measure of success and stability, and she had patiently, dutifully stood beside him through difficult times, often alone. She was beautiful but not intelligent, content to look up to him from her place in the home and to keep his house and bring up their children in accordance with his surprisingly detailed and informed instructions. She possessed the ultimate charm of always being there to welcome him whenever he appeared and by her acquiescence of allowing him to live the life he wanted to lead, seemingly without complaint or questioning his ever-longer absences. Perhaps she was glad to be relieved of the almost continuous pregnancies of their early years of marriage. It is apparent that by 1886, when he moved with his work to London, Fairfax Murray had become weary of the domestic constraints of matrimony and the not infrequent additions to his children; but he always thought of her fondly. He needed her at hand, he needed the warmth of the Tuscan sun and to be surrounded by beautiful things. Florence represented to him every possible contrast with the darkened world of the salesrooms in London, the gaslights and the cold, foggy English winters that caused him such difficulties with his health. His home, his pictures, his books and his early love were in Florence, and long before the First World War engulfed

Europe he had fully intended to retire from the commerce of the auction rooms to read, to study and perhaps to write – time for which he had never allowed himself.

How happy might he have been with either. . .

10. The Critics

Photograph of
Charles Fairfax
Murray by A.
Braun, Paris
1902 European art historical scholarship in the nineteenth century was
marked by remarkable leaps in knowledge and methodology
among a growing number of critics whose careers shaped, or at
any rate served, the development of taste and knowledge among
the new middle classes and the interest in works of art created by
access to great paintings in museums and in reproduction. Until
late in the eighteenth century, the method and perspective of the
art historian had altered very little from the pioneering biographical approach of Giorgio Vasari, whose *Lives of the Artists*, an
important source in spite of its inaccuracies and bias in favour of
the Florentine school, was first published in 1550.[1] He was
followed by Ascanio Condivi, whose *Life of Michelangelo*, published
three years later, provides an early example of differing opinions
between critics.

The mood changed in the late eighteenth century. From the
tranquil contemplation of the works of the supreme masters of
painting and sculpture within the enclosed world of private collections in the great houses, the field of art scholarship developed
quite suddenly under the influence of social and cultural change,
the increasing accessibility of the arts in public collections and the
rise of the *marchand amateur*. By the beginning of the nineteenth
century, elegant disputation between erudite amateur commenta-
tors had evolved into strident confrontation between influential
critics, set against a background of conflicting academic theories.
Personal rivalries of extraordinary ferocity became the common
coin of art criticism.

In the chronology of art historical scholarship, Charles Fairfax
Murray's reputation as connoisseur and critic was built between
1870 and 1885, between John Murray's publication in London of
Crowe and Cavalcaselle's third volume of *A New History of Painting
in Italy* in 1866 and the furious acceleration of the pace of the art
market that followed the arrival in Europe of a new generation of
American art lovers and connoisseurs in the 1890s. These were the
early years of the great American collections of John Pierpont
Morgan and Henry Huntington, Henry Clay Frick and P A B
Widener, to be followed by others, such as Samuel Kress. Earlier
American connoisseurs were often expatriate collectors, of whom
James Jackson Jarves (1818–88) was perhaps the most important.
With skill and discernment he had built a collection, mainly of
Italian *trecento* and *quattrocento* paintings, from his home in
Florence which he intended should ultimately be permanently
exhibited in the United States; but public galleries in his native
America displayed great reluctance to take it, and he had consider-
able difficulty in arousing any interest in 'such a startling novelty

as a large collection of Italian paintings'.[2] It was only through the powerful advocacy of John Ruskin's close friend Charles Eliot Norton that a home was at last found for a major part of the collection at Yale in 1869. James Jackson Jarves was a prophet without honour in his own country. Twenty years would pass before the tide of American demand for European painting washed over the art market.

Fairfax Murray was established as a connoisseur and *marchand amateur* by the time he was 30 in 1879. Thus his expertise was already recognised by critics, museums and collectors as much as 20 years before the full flowering of nineteenth-century academic scholarship, before the social historians, art theorists and psychoanalysts entered the field of art criticism, and before the appearance of any scientific aid in the service of attribution and criticism. There were no x-rays to reveal overpainting and *pentimenti*, no chromatography for the analysis of pigments, no infra-red reflectography to examine *sinopia*, the artist's underdrawing, and no dendrochronology to establish the age of wood on which panels were painted.

Disdainful of the academics of his day, Fairfax Murray's practice was to record in sketchbooks and notebooks, in an ever-expanding collection of photographs and in an apparently boundless memory, every detail and nuance of the paintings he studied hour upon hour, day upon day in his incessant travels. His rapid judgement derived from an all-embracing familiarity with all of the major European schools and periods – he was considered a leading authority on the German and Flemish painters as well as on the early Italian Renaissance.

Nothing was as valuable to him as the close contemplation of a canvas. His 'natural instinct for detecting artistic quality … it's a gift, and you can't do much in the way of collecting without it…'[3] in his own self-deprecating words, was in truth painstakingly honed over years, and refreshed daily. 'I can never describe the despair I am in when I cannot rub my nose against a picture, I think my eyesight is as good as that of most people but the loss of pleasure in the workmanship of a good picture appears to me so great when it is hung so that you cannot see the sweep of the brush – pictures look too much alike at a distance & I defy anyone to judge accurately of the quality of a picture hung over the door even of an ordinary room, nor is one helped by a glass however powerful, nothing is satisfactory except the panel or canvas a few inches off one's nose…'[4] he insisted. He was accustomed to sit for hours at a stretch studying intently a single canvas or even a figure in a landscape background within a composition, and he made hundreds if not thousands of sketches and notes of the paintings he studied for later reference.[5]

Fairfax Murray chose early in life to rely only on his own, confident judgement. His dislike of theorists was grounded in a conviction that the only dependable foundation of the critical faculty was the discipline of practising as an artist, and that writers approaching the subject from an academic standpoint were unable to bring a complete understanding to their task. His career spanned the transition from the artist-connoisseur to the academic historian as authority and arbiter. He had a painter's eye for artistic merit, and since his earliest days as an art lover he had nourished a particular interest in the relationship between sketches and drawings and the masterworks they related to, developing an acute understanding for the process of composition and the finer points of technique. Fairfax Murray was among the last of a long line of artist-connoisseurs – Peter Lely, supreme portraitist and one of the greatest of all collectors, Joshua Reynolds, the first President of the Royal Academy, Thomas Lawrence and Charles Eastlake, the first Director of the National Gallery for example – who combined the practice of painting with distinguished connoisseurship. Fairfax Murray was perhaps unique in combining the pursuit of the fine arts with an equally perceptive and appreciative understanding of the crafts of ceramics, textiles, printing and the decorative arts; the distinction between arts and crafts would not have been understood in the Italian Renaissance, and it was one which he deplored.

Fairfax Murray regarded the rise of the new class of academic art historian with all the suspicion that a skilled practitioner of an older generation reserves for innovation. He was, nevertheless, acutely aware of the gaps in his own and others' knowledge: 'we are still almost at the beginning of knowledge with regard to the painters of the 14th and 15th centuries,' he wrote.[6] Exceptionally equipped in his time for the practice of his profession, for more than 40 years – from the late 1870s, when he was still living in Siena, until the First World War – Charles Fairfax Murray was considered by many to be the leading authority of the London art market. Arthur Benson, Cambridge don and the author of a sympathetic memoir, thought of him as an appraiser – 'he could illustrate, he could not analyse'[7] – the intellectual's approach to an expertise that Fairfax Murray saw as essentially a question of skill and experience. He would not have hailed the distinction, which was entirely foreign to him. Lockett Agnew described him simply as 'the finest judge of art in the world.'[8]

Among the earliest and most valuable of the scholarly German critics of the nineteenth century was the now almost-forgotten Karl Freidrich Felix von Rumöhr, the author of *Italienische Forschungen,* who died in 1843. He brought together an historical approach to art and patronage with the critical examination of signed, authenticated examples of an artist's work from which he extended his careful attributions, going only so far as a rigorous interpretation of the evidence allowed. Inevitably, he rejected many popular attributions. Until Rumöhr the methodical analysis of style and attribution had been regarded as something of a black art. The art world had tended to rely on written, often imaginative, provenance and hearsay, and the colourful accounts of Giorgio Vasari.

Rumöhr's academic rigour provided the stimulus for the thorough,

comprehensive studies of Italian art undertaken by Giovanni Battista Cavalcaselle and the English diplomat Sir Joseph Archer Crowe. Neither was an academic. Cavalcaselle was trained as an artist. Crowe, the writer in their collaboration since Cavalcaselle had little English, came from an artistic family background. The two first met in 1847, and their partnership was forged when Cavalcaselle was exiled to London for his revolutionary political views. They began their influential work with the study of *Early Flemish Painters*, which was published in 1857, but thereafter they focused their researches on the art of the Italian masters of the early Renaissance. The historically significant (and much republished) survey, *A New History of Painting in Italy*, was published in three volumes between 1864 and 1868, the third volume coming out just a matter of months after Fairfax Murray joined Edward Burne-Jones. Crowe and Cavalcaselle's 'new history' documented the work of the major Italian artists and the members of their schools over five centuries, identifying unattributed works on stylistic grounds of technique, colour, chiaroscuro and movement, making closely reasoned attributions of each artist's work and school, correcting errors and bringing up to date Vasari's historical and biographical approach to art criticism by the intensive examination of the works themselves.

Almost concurrently, Jakob Burckhardt was taking a fundamentally different scholarly approach to the study of Italian art. His authoritative examination of *The Civilisation of the Renaissance in Italy* of 1860 – a study of social structures, political and religious institutions, and the growth of learning – led him to discuss the history of art in terms of the environment in which art was created.[9] In his uncompleted work on the circumstances and constraints within which the artist worked he identified 'the task' as the triangular relationship between the artist's skills, the demands of the patron and the liturgical and iconographic requirements for the finished piece. Burckhardt's subsequent discussion of technique and media, the special demands of commissioned religious works and the propagandist purposes of secular paintings, set the history of Italian art in the context of the Renaissance as a whole.

Cavalcaselle was already the author of *The Early Flemish Painters,* his first collaboration with Crowe, when Morelli began to concentrate his critical attention on the construction of a theoretical approach to the processes of attribution, publishing his first major work in German under the anagrammatic pseudonym of Ivan Lermolieff in 1873. Giovanni Morelli is generally credited with the evolution of the 'scientific method' of art-historical criticism. Morelli's prescriptive approach was based on the concept of observable correlations between regional physiognomy with regional schools of painting, rather than through the study of individual artists. He set out to show that, historically, local schools of painting in Italy had developed to a considerable degree independently of each other, progressing to their highest levels of achievement by a kind of Darwinian process of evolution, and thus at different times. Morelli also believed that the Italian schools could only be studied *in situ*, a stipulation of some importance since it provided frequent opportunities for his pungent assertions that Germans in particular were incapable of understanding Italian painting (a view he shared with his friend Sir Austen Henry Layard, who expressed his contempt for the 'meaningless profundities' of German critics).

Morelli emphasised the essential importance of form over aesthetics, citing such details as background landscape, colour harmony, the shape and execution of the hands and ears, facial expression and pose in identifying the painter. It was Morelli's extraordinarily competitive, dogmatic and dismissive approach to other connoisseurs and writers that elevated these fundamentally unexceptionable observations to the level of major controversy. He relished contention. Burkhardt's social historical approach to art history was so opposed to Giovanni Morelli's evolutionary theories of regional schools as to ensure it a barrage of mocking criticism.

Trained in Germany and later in Paris as a physician, although he never practised, Giovanni Morelli was appointed in 1861 at the age of 45 to the Presidency of a Government Commission charged with listing all important works of art in public institutions. In the post of Secretary to the Commission, the Government appointed Giovanni Battista Cavalcaselle. It was a lively irony that threw Cavalcaselle together with the art critic who was to be his implacable rival. Both Morelli and Cavalcaselle were staunch patriots, but of dramatically differing hues at a time of extreme volatility in Italian politics. Morelli was a political moderate who favoured the monarchist Cavour; Cavalcaselle was a revolutionary republican who supported Mazzini. Morelli's was a provocative, didactic personality, Cavalcaselle was of a thoughtful and melancholy disposition; neither was easy to get along with, and it is unlikely that they could ever have enjoyed one another's companionship.

Professionally they differed as much in their approach to connoisseurship – the artist and the anatomist – as in their politics. They differed over the question of policy on the export of works of Italian art, and they differed too on such vital technical concerns to their work as the preservation and restoration of fresco, Morelli favouring cleaning, which Cavalcaselle considered likely to cause further damage, preferring instead their stabilisation by protective varnishing. Their relationship was antagonistic from the beginning, and the difficulties of their working together cannot have been eased by their being compelled to travel the length and breadth of Italy by diligence in one another's company.

Morelli was a man of 55 years and widely respected in the Italian art world when Fairfax Murray first arrived in Italy in 1871. His influence was considerable, since he held an official position of great importance in regulating the sale abroad of Italian works of art. Alongside the Antinori he enjoyed close relations with many other titled families with important collections of Renaissance pictures, and with as many of the leading figures of the art establishment in England. He was equally the familiar of experts such as Cavenaghi the restorer, Baslini the Milanese dealer, and Otto Mündler, Sir Charles Eastlake's official agent in Italy. Unofficially, he was also an advisor to the National Gallery and regularly consulted by successive Directors – Eastlake, Boxall and Burton. Sir Austen Henry Layard was a friend whom he advised on his personal collection.

Crowe and Cavalcaselle's strategy of painstaking comparison with authenticated works could scarcely have been further from Morelli's attempt to determine the correct attribution of a work by means of a hypothetical template, even though in practice he was often obliged to dispense with theory. Both by conviction and experience Charles Fairfax Murray was in Cavalcaselle's camp. He was distanced by his regard for Cavalcaselle from the group of art historians, critics and collectors surrounding Giovanni Morelli (though he was careful to maintain at least a formal contact with Austen Henry Layard, who was a leading Council member of the Arundel Society, and thus, with John Ruskin, his employer as a copyist).

There was constant sniping between the two sides within the narrow confines of the art world in Italy, England and Germany. Wilhelm von Bode was a prominent figure in the tangled relationships that marked the struggles of the last quarter of the century among collectors, museum curators and dealers for the prime pictures, encounters often masked by personal attacks and strident claims of superior connoisseurship; it was, when all was said and done, a hunt for prestige and profit from a steadily diminishing supply of pictures of the top rank. As early as 1875 von Bode had crossed swords with Morelli, who had used his official connections as a legitimate matter of patriotic concern for Italy's art heritage, to prevent the export of Giorgione's *Tempest*, which von Bode had acquired for the Berlin Museum. As a result of his intervention the painting remains in Italy, an outstanding work among the masterpieces of the Accademia in Venice. Wilhelm von Bode and Giovanni Morelli became enemies that day, and remained enemies, Morelli adding coals to the fire whenever the occasion presented by his contentious opinions on German connoisseurship.

Fairfax Murray's friendship with Giovanni Cavalcaselle was based on mutual respect and shared interest. Between 1878 and 1884, their correspondence[10] discloses a carefully considered dialogue concerning the complex iconography of *trecento* panels and frescoes with their myriad saints, bishops and benefactors, and details of inscriptions and dating, particularly those of the Sienese school, the importance of which Fairfax Murray had recognised at a time when scholarship was still concentrated on the Florentine and Venetian schools. Cavalcaselle invited his help in research for the *Storia della Pittura in Italia,* his sequel to the *New History*, and Fairfax Murray's reply, painting by painting, skirted deferentially around the issues on which they disagreed, although he was at pains to list them. The lengthy catalogue of works by Pietro and Ambrogio Lorenzetti which Fairfax Murray prepared for Cavalcaselle in the summer of 1879 included a number of works that had passed through his hands, among them the fragment of Ambrogio's fresco of *A Group of Poor Clares*.[11] There were additions and new attributions among the nearly 50 works he listed and described. The *Pala della Beata Umiltà* altarpiece, which is today in the Accademia in Florence, is one such instance. It was attributed by Boccaccio to the shadowy figure of Buffalmacco, and ascribed by Crowe and Cavalcaselle to the 'Sienese School'. Fairfax Murray demonstrated that it was the work of Pietro Lorenzetti by identifying a panel in the Berlin collection as a missing tile from the altarpiece (misattributed there to his younger brother Ambrogio). There is no clear evidence of the date that Fairfax Murray was invited to Berlin by von Bode to examine their early Italian pictures, though his assistance was credited in the catalogue.[12]

The exchanges between Cavalcaselle and Fairfax Murray embraced questions of best practice in the restoration of damaged frescoes, and they debated the aesthetic considerations of how far work that had been destroyed or obscured by inept over-painting should be returned to its supposed original state.[13] Until business took Fairfax Murray almost continually to London after 1885, he acted regularly as a sounding-board for Cavalcaselle's thoughts on these controversial issues for which he had responsibility in his position as the Inspector General. Ten years after they first met in Rome, Marie Stillman wrote to Fairfax Murray: 'William saw Mr Cavalcaselle today in the street who spoke of you with enthusiasm, saying you knew far more than he about Old Masters, far more than anyone – greater praise could no man speak.'[14]

Giovanni Morelli maintained a war of words with his former colleague until his death in 1891, five years before Cavalcaselle's, and his many friends continued to promote his theories. Lady Eastlake's article, 'The Patriot and the Critic' in the *Quarterly Review* of July of that year, in which she praised Morelli the man and the connoisseur, was but one such panegyric that drove Fairfax Murray to sketch out the three known drafts of a fierce polemic against Morelli, his 'scientific method' and his attacks on Giovanni Cavalcaselle. One indictment, furiously dashed off, crossed out, and amended begins: 'This gentleman imposed on his generation by pretending that ancient works of art could be easily reduced to a formula ... a [person] of somewhat imposing presence, an able linguist and easy writer, his first pseudonymous book caught the fancy of the ignorant public .... his abuse of Cavalcaselle from whom he learned what little he knew ... holding up to ridicule a man who whatever his shortcomings did more to clear the ground for future writers on art than any man of his time...' Words tumbled on to the page with scant regard for punctuation, sentences incomplete. 'The first duty of a writer is to know whether a work of art is good or bad, a masterpiece or a common production of little value.

Morelli's judgement will not stand this simple test'[15] he added. Of Morelli's method Fairfax Murray commented 'there is little or nothing new in the Morellian "system" so called except a pretence of being founded on a scientific basis. Every art-critic before Morelli was born knew that "except the face, no part of the human body was more characteristic than the hand"[16] and without making such a fuss about it took in to account the manner of drawing the draperies, the peculiarities of landscape, method of painting colour...' On the question of his attributions, which he dismantled in detail and at length, he concluded: 'I know of no one else to compare with Morelli for the magnificence of his blunders ... a greater number than have ever been committed by any empiric since the days of the great Dr Waagen.'[17]

Wilhelm von Bode too carried on the furious debate. On the occasion of Morelli's death he declined the usual civilities, writing instead that: 'As a surgeon he had his attention directed to the form of the human body, and especially its extremities, and when thus engaged he thought he discovered that every great artist, even in painting portraits, made use of his own extremities as models for the subject in hand. Later he issued a catalogue of the ears, noses and fingers, the former property of Sandro, Mantegna, Raphael, Titian & Co and with this schedule in hand every lover of art is to patrol the picture galleries, when he will be able unerringly to single out the different masters, in spite of all the wretched mistakes of the directors.'[18]

Fairfax Murray's article remained incomplete and unpublished. Nevertheless there is little doubt that it was intended as a serious response to Morelli's dicta, which were influential in the burgeoning interest in European art scholarship in the last quarter of the nineteenth century. There were other publishing ventures that failed to reach the printed page, or where Fairfax Murray is not credited as part author or editor. In November 1885, J H Middleton,[19] William Morris's friend and the Slade Professor at Cambridge at the time, proposed a collaborative project to publish a series of papers on the subject of false attributions and forgeries. The first of these articles was to be concerned with Mantegna's drawings, misattributions of Mantegna's work to others, forgeries, and a drawing by Francia in the Louvre attributed to him. Fairfax Murray supplied Middleton with notes, but no attributable piece has been found. 'Costa is the author of several false Mantegna's'; and of *Judith* in the Uffizi: 'no design of Mantegna's seems to have given rise to so much employment to his contemporaries – there are three designs and pictures in England in private collections – I saw them at Leeds. I was too young then to say much about them but I don't think that either of them was an original'[20] he added.

They intended also to examine the two versions of Leonardo's *Lady of the Rocks*. A critic following Morelli 'with the discrimination that marks the rest of the article' had compared the National Gallery version unfavourably – 'a sham Leonardo' – to that in the Louvre: 'most writers hitherto have been content to either accept [the present attribution] and as if it were necessary in doing so, to prefer it to the Louvre picture, or to reject it summarily as a copy with variations from the original. I am not aware of anything that has been advanced that is convincing either way' Fairfax Murray commented. There is no doubt that, setting aside for the moment his resentment of Morelli's animus towards Cavalcaselle, he harboured the gravest doubts as to his competence.

One of Fairfax Murray's few published contributions was to Jakob Burckhardt's *Cicerone*, a much-reprinted popular guide to Italian art that went to several editions in German and English translation. Intended for the discerning traveller, it was not primarily a scholarly work, but its quality attracted both Joseph Archer Crowe and later von Bode as editors after Burckhardt's first edition in 1855. Fairfax Murray collaborated with von Bode in the 1884 edition, as a collector of the Sienese school and an authority on Pietro Lorenzetti.

Charles Fairfax Murray was no writer. 'I am not a literary cove'[21] he remarked cheerfully, alas accurately. Dante Gabriel Rossetti had observed this weakness in Fairfax Murray's armoury long before. He was inhibited by the act of writing formally, although his vivid personal letters flow without hesitation. The drafts of his article on Morelli present a graphic picture of a gifted and perceptive man with a rich fund of knowledge and carefully-formulated views, tormented by the problem of setting down his thoughts as they outstrip the pen, until there is more crossing out and transposition than text and the thread is lost, and biting scorn replaces reasoned argument with each successive paragraph.

There was another, considered justification for his reluctance to publish. Fairfax Murray was deeply aware of the pitfalls of attribution and the problems of writing critical commentaries that might survive even a few years' exposure to continuing scholarship. He was scathing about the pretensions of those critics who postured as infallible, and defended the older critics 'who were under great disadvantages in comparison to their modern brethren ... travelling was costly and difficult and they were under the necessity of trusting almost exclusively to memory for impressions of what they had seen...' To William Spanton he confided '...I have a good deal to say on the subject – mostly criticism of ancient pictures as to authenticity, but it is a difficult subject. I don't know any work which is not full of errors – one is obliged to modify one's opinions from day to day. The critical faculty requires so many qualities almost impossible to find in the same individual. First you require some knowledge of art – technical and historical – sufficient imagination to discern quality in another and not to mistake chalk and cheese, and yet not so much as to carry your judgement along with it under special circumstances. You require to be enthusiastic and yet cool-headed – there's the difficulty.'[22] Fairfax Murray was neither falsely modest nor beset by doubts about his judgement or discernment. His failing was that, once the pen was in his hand, cool-headed he ceased to be. The combative side of his nature soon took command. 'I hope when you come to write your book that you will deal tenderly with Morelli & not antagonise his many friends'[23] his ally and client, the English banker R H Benson, wrote; Fairfax Murray's foibles were well-known, and his close supporters were alert to this danger to his acceptance among the cognoscenti, many of whom numbered Morelli among their personal friends and acquaintances.

Charles Fairfax Murray's distaste for Morelli prefaced a far greater challenge to his unassuming authority. Bernhard Berenson, 16 years Fairfax Murray's junior, arrived in Florence in 1889. He was in a class of his own as a rival in expertise, as impeccably prepared for his expert role as Fairfax Murray but in a very different school. With two years of intensive study of Italian painting funded by the irrepressible Mrs Isabella Stewart Gardner of Boston, with the intellectual armoury of a Harvard student of Hebrew and mediaeval German literature and art, and a working knowledge of Arabic (as well as his native Lithuanian, with which he might pass as Russian), Berenson was overweeningly confident that the path of connoisseurship and aestheticism lay at his feet. There was a vast divide in their method. Fairfax Murray, the self-taught connoisseur, versus Berenson, the university-educated intellectual and advocate of the Morellian 'scientific' method; Murray, the accomplished and practising painter, against Berenson, the aesthete who had never held a brush. They differed as widely in their personalities. The observant, candid Murray, with his disdain for the pretentious, could never have brought himself to be 'on terms' with the egotistical Berenson with his court of intellectuals – the '*unsereiners*', our kind.

Moreover, Fairfax Murray was already long-established while Berenson had yet to make a name. In his search for controversy by which he might establish his expertise and authority, Berenson clashed soon after his arrival in Europe with Murray's close friend William Stillman. Berenson briskly dismissed an article that Stillman had contributed to the art magazine *The Century*, concerning a painting known as the *Apparition of St Mark* in Venice by Tintoretto. He endeavoured amongst other criticisms to show that Jacopo Tintoretto's picture was in Milan and not Venice, and by implication that Stillman had not troubled to examine the painting he was writing about. It was an ill-judged and personal attack; Stillman was writing of a *St Mark* by Domenico Tintoretto, the son, that Berenson seemed not to know. It was an early instance of Bernhard Berenson's methodical personal vendettas.

Berenson's successful emergence as a formidable expert and self-publicist came with a loan exhibition of Venetian Old Master paintings at the New Gallery in February 1895. He wrote a closely argued and lengthy appraisal of the major works in the exhibition. He stated flatly than none of the Veroneses was by the hand either of Paolo or Bonifacio Veronese, that only three of nineteen Bellinis were by that family of masters, that 32 supposed Titians were misattributed, and that only a small number of the 'Giorgiones' were genuine. The furious reaction of angry owners and the dismay of dealers and experts alike testified to the impact of this new star in the art firmament, and it is noteworthy that a majority of the re-attributions of his early years as critic are accepted today, while many of his later attributions have been revised. There were good business reasons for seeking an opportunity to take the conceited young man down a peg, and Berenson never felt entirely secure or welcomed in the London market after this spectacular but tactless intervention.

Bernhard Berenson's aggressive and egotistical manner of establishing himself in the European art world, and the publication of Morelli's *Kritische Studien über Italienische Malerei* in an English edition in 1892–3 led Fairfax Murray to draft a second attack on Giovanni Morelli. 'I have been reading lately the *sproponti* of the defunct Morelli & I really think it will rouse me to add to the literature on the subject...' he wrote to Wilhelm von Bode.[24] Direct criticism of Bernhard Berenson might well have missed its target since many, collectors and critics, were uneasily aware that Berenson was generally correct in his judgements at this time, before he allowed commercial considerations to influence his attributions. When Berenson had first arrived in Italy he had been greatly impressed by Morelli's attempt to postulate a 'scientific' approach to the attribution and authentication of works of art by the study solely of the internal evidence of technique and style. The concept appealed to Berenson, who attached no value to provenance and who had a leaning towards theory (his theory of 'tactile values' is an example). He refined Morelli's approach, systematising his general principles in to a series of rules for attribution. Since the Morellian 'system' earned Fairfax Murray's withering scorn as combining the obvious with the ridiculous, Berenson, Morelli's pupil and disciple since their first meeting in Milan in January of 1890, was readily identified with his method. 'For many years I have been irritated by the reverent attention paid to a band of critics whose continually growing influence is a real danger in more ways than one ... *nil nisi bonum* has no weight with me when the influence is living'[25] Fairfax Murray started one piece soon after Morelli's death. (See Appendix.)

Berenson was also becoming known in the circles in which Fairfax Murray moved in Rome, Siena and Florence, a shifting world of expatriates, critics and art dealers who included, in addition to his close friends the Stillmans, the novelist and writer on aesthetics Violet Paget (better known as the novelist Vernon Lee), Herbert Horne, Enrico Costa, Robert Langton Douglas, the Anglican priest turned critic and dealer, and Frederick Mason Perkins, an American critic. Berenson, a personality of seething jealousies, would later clash with his first patron, Charles Loeser, with Vernon Lee whom he thought had plagiarised his work, with Langton Douglas over the question of which of them had first found a Sassetta and Horne, who knew too much about Berenson's business dealings. Fairfax Murray saw early on that Berenson was beginning to find his way in the art market from his vantage point of supposedly disinterested critic, looking out for paintings for the American collector E P Warren, who advised the Museum of Fine Art in Boston, and for the American millionaire Theodore Davis. Their rivalry would crystallise in to enmity when Berenson began to act in a covert commercial capacity while he continued to masquerade as an impartial connoisseur. Charles Fairfax Murray was by the 1890s openly if informally linked to the London dealers Agnew's and was generally regarded as their agent in Italy. Berenson was closely but surreptitiously linked to their Bond Street rivals, P. & D. Colnaghi. He acted both as intermediary and advisor to his American clients and as agent for Colnaghi's, regularly taking fees from both sides, though he was careful to stay at one remove.

For all his acknowledged expertise, there was unease about this confident and egregious young man. J P Morgan, who had succeeded Frederick Rhinelander, a Berenson supporter, as President of the Board of Trustees of the Metropolitan Museum of Art, put the resources of his banking intelligence network in Europe at the disposal of the respected New York dealer Henry Duveen to look into Berenson's role in the art market. There was already some suspicion that his financial involvement might be at odds with his ostensibly unbiased opinions, a view stoutly reinforced by Isabella Gardner's husband Jack, who suspected him of taking secret commissions from Colnaghi's on his wife's purchase of three Rembrandts from the Hope collection, and went on to prove it. It seems improbable that Mrs Gardner was unaware of Berenson's activities in the market place; he was supremely successful at buying the pictures she wanted for Fenway Court, and that was enough.

These well-founded doubts were, however, ultimately to cost Bernhard Berenson any prospect of the Directorship of the Metropolitan. Berenson, as always intensely suspicious of anyone outside of his circle, attributed this setback to the hostility of Agnew's, 'whose game he had spoiled more than once,' and to Richard Norton, whose father, the Harvard Professor, had concluded that Berenson's ambition outstripped his ability when he studied under him there and had once refused him a bursary to study in Italy. Most of all, he blamed Charles Fairfax Murray.

Bernhard Berenson, moreover, was fallible, an occupational hazard among critics as Fairfax Murray was always ready to point out, but a question which Berenson elevated to a matter of life or death. Giovanni Morelli had owned a profile portrait of a girl said to be by Leonardo da Vinci, the so-called *Donna Laura Minghetti* Leonardo from the name of its owner after Morelli's death in 1891. Berenson listed it as an early example of da Vinci's work in his first important book, *Florentine Painters of the*

Renaissance, in 1896. Two years later the portrait, which Morelli had always refused to exhibit, was sold to Berenson's client Theodore Davis. It quickly proved to be a fake, and the London art market fell on it with a degree of satisfaction bordering on glee. Charles Fairfax Murray, who had the opportunity to examine the picture in London on its way to the United States, wrote that it was 'a forgery of simple character such as only the most inexperienced should have been deceived by it'. The Florentine restorer Luigi Cavenaghi claimed to know the man who painted it, which was not unlikely. Richard Norton, delighted, informed Isabella Gardner that it was Berenson who had recommended the picture to Davis. (Herbert Horne was equally emphatic that it was J-P Richter, another critic in the Berenson circle, who had advised him.) He was unabashed when Theodore Davis, who continued to regard his purchase as a genuine Leonardo (or refused to admit his mistake) refuted his allegations, and doubts about Berenson's probity – though not his expertise – lingered.

Three years after the *Donna Laura* episode, Fairfax Murray had a taste of the secretive partnership between Berenson and Colnaghi's. It arose from Prince Chigi's sale to Mrs Gardner of Botticelli's *Madonna of the Eucharist*, one of a handful of Sandro's work with unassailable provenance in private hands. Richard Norton first drew the painting's availability to her attention, to Berenson's furious dismay; he could admit no trespass on his personal preserve. Norton on the other hand was it seems concerned only to enrich the artistic heritage of his native Boston, and he took no commissions from any party in the transactions that he initiated. He was, however, particularly close to Agnew's through his father's connection and his personal friendship with Fairfax Murray. Agnew's tried and failed to secure the *Madonna* with two successive bids; a number of rival bidders were said to be interested, including von Bode. Colnaghi's, represented by Edmond Duprez, finally secured the picture and moved it discreetly to Luigi Cavenaghi's studio in Milan. Berenson, who had not been involved in the bidding but was kept closely informed, was then invited by Colnaghi's in his capacity as Mrs Gardner's agent to whisper to her the likely price of owning the Botticelli in Boston. He negotiated a price that paid him a handsome secret commission from the dealers in addition to the retainer he held from Mrs Gardner. The question of getting the painting out of Italy now arose.

When he first came to Italy as Mrs Gardner's protégé to research Italian art, Berenson had seen a version of the Chigi *Madonna* in the Panciatichi collection, a genuine work of Botticelli's *bottega*, although in poor condition. This he now acquired through Haskard's in Florence where it was 'touched' by Isabella Gardner's 'gnome', the Boston artist Zozo Smith.[26] He had been sent to Italy to make a copy of the original *Madonna* for Prince Chigi, a normal condition of sale in order to make good an obvious gap in a collection, but which was also intended to help circumvent Italian export regulations by delaying exposure of a sale. Haskard's offered the restored

Panciatichi picture to Fairfax Murray, and in May 1900 Agnew's bought it. The Chigi version remained meanwhile in the studio of the restorer and dealer Luigi Cavenaghi while Zozo Smith made his copy for the Prince. (It is said that so pleased was he with his work that he made another head-and-shoulders version which Berenson sold to Herbert Horne, who passed it in turn to the Marquise de Turenne as a genuine 'school' picture.)[27]

When the Panciatichi picture appeared on the market in London at Agnew's, the Italian Government prosecuted Prince Chigi for breaking the law on the export of works of art, but his fine for evading the law was reduced to a nugatory sum when it became clear that Agnew's Botticelli was not the Chigi *Madonna*. Under cover of the turmoil, Cavenaghi smuggled the Chigi picture to Colnaghi's. The greater of the two Botticellis was exhibited in Bond Street on its way to Boston, to the discomfiture of Agnew's, and shortly after it arrived to great acclaim in Boston. The laurels in this skirmish unquestionably went to Berenson, whose name did not feature, although he had profited handsomely. Charles Fairfax Murray never forgot a slight, and it may well be that Berenson's later suspicion that Fairfax Murray had set J P Morgan against him was not without some foundation.

Behind the grave air of connoisseurship the unseen rivalries of the art world and the struggle for advantage and reputation continued unabated. In February 1898, Berenson published an unsigned piece in the *Saturday Review* in which he castigated Sir Edward Poynter's stewardship at the National Gallery, and which included a remarkable personal attack on Charles Fairfax Murray. 'No 1416 *The Virgin & Child with Two Saints* by Filippo Mazzola, purchased from Mr Charles Fairfax Murray for £120. The interest in this picture begins and ends with the fact that it was painted by the father of Parmigiano. Feeble in conception and execution, this wretched painting has nothing to convey to us except the sorry truth that even in the Golden Age of Italian art there were accredited painters no less incompetent as any now living ... however, the cheery thought remains that its acquisition greatly redounds to the genius of Mr Fairfax Murray as a dealer, though scarcely, perhaps, as much as his famous 'Lotto' at Dresden.'[28] (The Lorenzo Lotto in question was the *Madonna and Child*, which had earlier been dismissed by Morelli as a counterfeit of the 'Bridgewater' *Madonna* 'coarsely executed by some Flemish painter', later amended to a seventeenth-century Bolognese painter. Berenson had himself described it as a school picture. Frizzoni said it was Bergamasque in origin. Loeser later found a signature which he considered genuine, and that Fairfax Murray's attribution was correct.) Berenson had an unpleasant way of attempting to belittle any other authority or reputation, particularly if he believed his carefully concealed business interests to be threatened in any way.

Mary Berenson wrote that 'Bernard has the reputation of being a man who cannot bear other men as he is furiously jealous of their reputation.'

Fairfax Murray merely said that he was used to being slandered by Berenson. After they had visited P. A. B. Widener's collection, Mary Berenson claimed that Agnew 'had dumped off all his unsaleable rubbish on this ignorant millionaire', and accused Agnew's of 'prettying up' a picture that Berenson had declined to buy and selling it to Widener as a 'priceless Filippino'. Fairfax Murray carried on the battle to the end of his days: 'It is singular the unlimited confidence this gentleman of Jewish extraction enjoys in America in spite of his unblushing impudence and obvious "interest" in all the deals that go through with his connivance however worthless the work is (if not which he backs.) He is in regular pay for this useful quality.'[29] The immemorial, mindless anti-Semitism of the nineteenth century did not intrude elsewhere either in Fairfax Murray's personal or business relationships; it was nevertheless a convenient stick with which to beat Berenson who was deeply and uneasily aware of the *stetl* he had left so far behind and his rejection of his Jewish patrimony. 'The same individual "crabbed" my Botticelli and induced the owner to return it to Agnew's' Fairfax Murray wrote to Edward Forbes. This was far from the only occasion of Berenson's financial interest influencing his attributions. He had down-graded three paintings in the collection of Fairfax Murray's client R H Benson to the Venetian Marco Basaiti, an artist much influenced by Bellini; when the Benson collection was sold on his death to Joseph Duveen, Berenson rapidly re-assigned them to Giovanni Bellini, the younger son and most accomplished of Jacopo Bellini's workshop. Berenson provided expert opinion for Duveen under a lucrative secret contract that gave him 25% of net profits arising from his attributions.

On the first occasion that Bernhard Berenson saw the Mantegna *Sacra Conversazione* that Richard Norton had bought for Mrs Gardner he promptly denounced it as a 'palpable forgery', withdrawing stealthily by stages. Three years later it was, he conceded, a 'school' picture, and 15 more years passed before he acknowledged it as a genuine Mantegna. Richard Norton was by then in his grave, the victim of a German shell in France, where he was driving a civilian ambulance near the front in 1916. Fairfax Murray too was dead. It was Bernhard Berenson's way of doing business.

At the turn of the century Fairfax Murray was already at the start of the long process of dispersing his collections. He was, however, still as active as ever in the art market. He was now Agnew's partner and agent in Italy, and he continued to travel ceaselessly. If he could be said to have a routine it was that he might generally be expected in Florence or by the sea with his Italian family from mid-July to September, but in the event he was seldom in any one place for more than a week or two. Much of his time in Italy was spent in Siena, where he had made some of his most valuable discoveries. When there he might often be found of an evening in the company of Robert Langton Douglas, the clergyman son of a clergyman who had come to Italy as Church of England chaplain in Leghorn in 1895 at the age of 31. He served in Siena for a year in 1899, and in 1900 he relinquished Holy Orders to devote himself to Italian history and the history of art. They would sit of an evening in the Piazza del Campo outside the 'Toscana' with Edward Hutton, another of the English connoisseurs and *marchand amateurs* who peopled the Italian art world at the turn of the century, and Frederick Mason Perkins. Edward Hutton fondly recalled Fairfax Murray for his habit of rapping his heavy stick on the café table and calling out 'Bring out your Madonnas, two hundred lire,' a tactic which surprisingly resulted in some successes.

Robert Langton Douglas was a congenial and gregarious man of great charm and considerable learning, whose success with women was matched only by his failure to stay out of trouble with them. He had for a time been part of the Berenson circle and he numbered Gustavo Frizzoni, the art historian and Morelli's disciple, among his mentors in the arts. In London, he counted George Howard, D S McColl, the Director of the Tate Gallery, Walter Pater until his death in 1894, Oscar Wilde, the playwright George Meredith and Henry Wallis, the painter of *The Death of Chatterton*, among his circle. Langton Douglas edited a new edition of Crowe and Cavalcaselle with Stanford Arthur Strong, the Librarian of the House of Lords, after Cavalcaselle's death in 1897, and he was for two years Dean of the Faculty of Arts of Adelaide University (until another domestic entanglement forced his resignation); he ended his career as the Director of the National Gallery of Ireland.

Prior to this last appointment Langton Douglas was for a time a successful dealer in Bond Street. He shared with Henry Wallis and Fairfax Murray a personal interest in majolica. Murray, who had anticipated the collectors' vogue for majolica by some 20 years, was authoritative on its history and had sold nearly 50 choice examples to the South Kensington Museum in 1889. He supplied Langton Douglas with other museum-quality examples and helped him with historical background and the identity of coats of arms portrayed. Langton Douglas's scholarship on the *trecento* did not, however, pass muster with Fairfax Murray, who gave him a good deal of assistance but did not spare the rod, tracing pictures, and lending him examples of *bicherne* – the sumptuously-bound accounts books of the Sienese administration in the fourteenth and fifteenth centuries for an exhibition in 1904.

The offer of acknowledgement in the catalogue provoked an example of Fairfax Murray's robust approach to connoisseurship: 'I think you hardly appreciate the reason of the objections I have to some points in your notes on Crowe & Cavalcaselle and in the Burlington Fine Arts Club catalogue. I certainly thought you exaggerated the importance and claimed too much credit for what I regarded as very small and obvious discoveries, known to me many years previous; but to me the mistakes and your obstinate adherence to them was far more important.'[30] A placatory reply, in which Langton Douglas pleaded that 'I regard you as one of the three or four connoisseurs whose opinion really matters', was met with 'What I complain of most is that, not content with several more than hazardous attributions at the last BFA Club exhibition, you should have gone out of your way to attribute to a Sienese master a picture which was certainly intended by the artist (not long dead probably) for a Piero della Francesca. There could be no possible resemblance between this forgery and the artist you attribute it to. If you had recognised it as modern as you should have done, you could not possibly have made this mistake.'[31] They remained on surprisingly good terms for years, Langton Douglas continuing to seek Fairfax Murray's advice ('I haven't asked anyone else because I want this to be all my own work')[32] and borrowing rare books.

It was a generation of rich discovery and the rapid development of scholarship in the art world, hastened by the commercial imperatives of the sudden leap of interest and profit arising from the founding of the great American collections. It was an era also of disputatious and egocentric connoisseurs and academics who sought by every available means to publicise their expertise and confound their opponents. Charles Fairfax Murray contrived to keep his opinions out of this arena, adding daily to his personal connoisseurship; dealing mostly for personal clients, he remained scrupulously honest though undeniably shrewd. There was method as well as modesty in his reluctance to enter the public debate in print, but his failure to publish is regrettable. Art historians of the next generation were deprived thereby of his carefully developed store of knowledge and insights that bridged the careful researches of Crowe and Cavalcaselle and their contemporaries and the post-scientific age of archival and technical resources in the service of the arts. At the same time, perhaps deliberately, he allowed his reputation as a critic and the awareness of his contributions to the nation's collections to fade gradually as those who relied on his judgement left the scene.

Epistola de Contemptu Mundi di frate Hieronymo da Ferrara dellordine de frati predicatori la quale manda ad Elena Buonaccorsi sua madre, per consolarla della morte del fratello, suo Zio.

11. High Water, 1885–1900

Title page of
the 1894
Kelmscott Press
limited edition
of Savonarola's
letter to his
Mother, *Epistola
de Contemptu
Mundi*. The
autograph was
from Fairfax
Murray's
collection, and
the woodblock,
designed by
him, was cut by
William
Harcourt
Hooper

The 15 years that lay ahead as the century drew to a close were years of public recognition in the art world of Fairfax Murray's self-taught expertise, and in private the fulfilment of his youthful ambitions formed in the days at Cheyne Walk. Between the ages of 35 and 50 Charles Fairfax Murray built three astonishing personal collections – one of paintings, one of Old Master drawings and another of books, incunabula, autograph letters and illuminated manuscripts. He fathered and educated his two families, enjoyed a successful career as a painter and portraitist and built a formidable reputation as a critic. As a dealer he numbered among his private clients four of the most important collectors in the London market – Charles Butler, Robert Benson, George Salting and von Bode – whom he advised, buying and selling on their behalf. He was employed as an agent by the South Kensington Museum and consulted by them regularly for expert opinions and from time to time by a host of others from Boston to St Petersburg.

A thread that runs throughout Fairfax Murray's life is a passionate interest in learning. It was natural that he should be drawn to Cambridge, and to a friendship that was to carry him to the heart of the University. John Henry Middleton was an archaeologist, an Orientalist and unconventional scholar, a flamboyant personality (and chloral addict). Like Fairfax Murray, Middleton drew people to him or put them against him in equal measure. He had met William Morris on his second visit to Iceland in 1873. Fairfax Murray had later met him in Florence with the Stillmans, and their friendship had grown. John Middleton was appointed Slade Professor of Fine Arts at Cambridge in 1886, the year that he married Bella Stillman. Within weeks of signing the lease for the Holland Park studio, Fairfax Murray was back in Cambridge in his company. He had visited John Middleton the previous summer, and there had met A G Dew-Smith, one year older than he, a wealthy Old Harrovian who had stayed on in Cambridge after getting a rather poor Third in Natural Science from Trinity. Dew-Smith's two great interests were collecting – books, manuscripts and jewellery – and photography, and they quickly found a great deal in common. Fairfax Murray was soon invited to stay at Chesterton Hall. Angelica was in London with young John, and at Christmas there was a note from John Middleton to say 'the Darwins want a portrait of Mrs Darwin; Dew-Smith wants to meet your wife'[1], followed a three weeks later by a note from Dew-Smith: 'come down and bring Madame with you... Mr Trotter wants a portrait.'[2]

Albert Dew-Smith had recently formed a partnership in the

Cambridge Scientific Instrument Company with Horace Darwin, a son of the great evolutionist and author of the *On the Origin of Species by Means of Natural Selection,* Charles Darwin. Fairfax Murray was quickly on terms both with Horace and his brother George, and their fellowship led to a series of Darwin portrait commissions, commencing with the widowed Mrs Charles Darwin and including both George and 'one of the daughters'. There were others within the University, and he became the court painter for a while. More importantly, Murray's acquaintance with Middleton and Dew-Smith ensured him a comfortable welcome to the University he had so long admired from a distance, and introductions to a number of the dons. Dew-Smith had been accorded the privileges of a Fellow of Trinity in recognition of his generosity to the Physics Schools, and he and Fairfax Murray together with John Middleton took their dinners at the High Tables of Trinity, Trinity Hall and King's ('not nearly so fine as Trinity') and spent relaxed hours in the Master's garden by the Cam. Cambridge provided a congenial, masculine atmosphere in which Fairfax Murray could pursue his consuming delight in rare books among scholars of like mind, and it remained the place in England in which he was most at ease until the final few weeks of his life.

Fairfax Murray's study of mediaeval manuscripts and early books began under the tutelage of William Morris in the earliest days of his involvement with Burne-Jones and the Firm. William Morris had devoted hours to the intensive study of the manuscripts in the Bodleian Library during his time as an undergraduate at Oxford, and he was an expert judge of the field. Over and above his keen appreciation of the artistic nuances of mediaeval script and design, he was extremely well-informed on the materials and technicalities of calligraphy and book production in the Middle Ages; the quills, vellums, papers, pigments, inks and bindings. Fairfax Murray, always the student, quietly absorbed William Morris's reverence and discrimination. From the day he returned to London in to the 1890s, as William Morris's health declined and Fairfax Murray's business activities prospered, he was once again an intimate of the Morris household and a frequent visitor to Kelmscott House. He bought early books for Morris. They traded four pages of the superbly illuminated Aldenham Psalter of 1270, which William Morris longed to own, for five pages of early fifteenth-century Italian drawings that Fairfax Murray greatly desired; (happily, in his last year Morris was able to acquire the rest of this Psalter and restore the missing pages to their proper place). It was in this atmosphere of companionship, scholarship and aesthetic pleasure that Fairfax Murray made the character-istic decision to build a personal collection of books and manuscripts to rival his Old Master paintings and drawings in interest and importance. The resolution made, he set out to implement it with energy and resolve. Tammaro de Marinis, himself a notable collector and dealer in rare books who knew Fairfax Murray, his senior by some 30 years, and who eventually acquired a substantial portion of his French books, said of him 'an expert in pictures, he devoted all his profits to the purchase of ancient books'. His prime suppliers were Ildebrando Rossi in Rome, Dotti & Franchi in Florence, and later, Tammaro de Marinis, Edouard Rahir in Paris, J & J Leighton, Bernard Quaritch, Leo Olschki and Jacques Rosenthal.

In the early years in Italy, his purchases were confined mainly to ancient Italian books, particularly of the fifteenth and sixteenth centuries, many of them ornamented with wood engravings; but in 1897 Fairfax Murray bought the 15th-century French manuscript in three volumes of *Lancelot du Lac in the Quest for the San Graal* at the Ashburnham sale. In 1899 he bought *en bloc* the library of the Marchese Girolamo d'Adda, for which he had printed a catalogue in a limited edition of 62 copies.[3] The Adda catalogue had been preceded by another, also compiled by Guiseppe Cavalieri, containing descriptions of 2,276 books in Fairfax Murray's collection, in the main great works of Italian literature. When the Sneyd collection was sold at Sotheby's in 1903 Tom Hodge, the auctioneer, announced publicly that Fairfax Murray was assembling a major collection (a revelation which may have given some private amusement to the secretive collector who was already possessed of a remarkable library). He made a number of purchases from the Patrizi sale in Rome, but his attempt to acquire the Pirovani collection a year or more earlier ended in a rare failure. A catalogue for the sale had already appeared, put out by Dario Rossi. The sale, however, did not take place, and the catalogue is now itself a collector's item. Fairfax Murray was, nevertheless, an eager buyer under his habitual pseudonym of 'Mr Archer' when part of the collection came up for auction later in London.

He was more successful when he asked de Marinis to negotiate the purchase from the bibliophile Cavalieri de Ferrare of the unique example of a Florentine fifteenth-century edition, a pamphlet entitled *La Compagnia del Mantellacio per Bernardo Zuchetta* decorated with a superb woodcut. By 1905 the struggle to get hold of Italian imprints became so intense between Fairfax Murray and Prince Essling that prices rose higher and higher. De Marinis went to Ferrare and obtained the precious incunabula without much difficulty, having accepted without discussion the asking price of 3,000 lire, an enormous sum for the time. Fairfax Murray, delighted, pressed him to accept 10,000 lire, a small fortune. On learning of the purchase Prince Essling flew into a great rage, pacing up and down his library and crying out 'Ah the brigands, the brigands...' The brigands, it transpired, were Leo Olschki and Jacques Rosenthal who, having been given the same instructions, had failed. In 1907, Fairfax Murray put out a list of the ancient books he possessed with short descriptions, to serve for the time being; they numbered 4,144.

It is a fascinating commentary on the parallel worlds of the collector of art and the collector of books that so little is known of Fairfax Murray's activities in the bibliographic field. William Spanton, his close friend for 50 years, does not so much as touch on his remarkable library in his memoir. Fairfax Murray was a voracious though discriminating collector. His interests were very wide, ranging from illuminated manuscripts through blockbooks printed from single engraved wooden blocks to incunabula, the earliest printed books from movable type, to autograph manuscripts; of the latter, Fairfax Murray built up spectacular collections of letters of historical interest from kings, queens, dukes, generals and prelates, of writers, composers and artists and their noble patrons. Among the correspondents were Machiavelli, Cosimo di Medici and Cesare Borgia, Giorgio Vasari, Marsilio Ficino and Raphael, Nicholas Fouquet, Marquise de Maintenon and Cardinal Mazarin, Henry VIII, Mary Queen of Scots, Charles I and Charles II; there were many of equal importance. In one month alone he acquired the manuscript of Swinburne's *Poems and Ballads* and the Hayley correspondence 'full of information concerning Romney and Gibbon ... over 2000 letters to go through ... and 100 letters of Southey's.'[4]

Already rich in Italian books, Fairfax Murray turned to the purchase of illustrated French books. Helped by Edouard Rahir in Paris, he was able to put together a superb collection of 700 volumes in a short time, the cataloguing of which he entrusted to Hugh William Davies of J & J Leighton, the antiquarian booksellers who provided so many of Fairfax Murray's acquisitions; this work, itself a masterpiece of learning and precision, remains a precious bibliographical tool on account of the great number of reproductions of woodcuts and printed pages. Among the superb rare books and fine bindings of Fairfax Murray's French collection were volumes from the libraries of Colbert, the chief political advisor to the Sun King Louis XIV, Madame de Pompadour, the Duc de la Vallières and Diane de Poitiers. The dedication of the catalogue, a splendid example of hand presswork and fine binding, reads 'This catalogue ... which I had hoped to have the honour of dedicating to that unique poet Charles Algernon Swinburne is now inscribed to his memory.'[5] Fairfax Murray never forgot the good friends of his days among the circle of Dante Gabriel Rossetti's friends at Cheyne Walk.

German printed books did not escape Murray's attention, and he collected 477 works, some printed in Germany, some in Holland, Belgium and Switzerland,[6] for which he confided the cataloguing to Hugh Davies once more. Among them, appropriately, were a number of books once owned by Thomas Howard, 2nd Earl of Arundel and Surrey, the doyen of the great aristocratic collectors who lent his name to the Arundel Society. There were others from the libraries of George I, Jean Grolier, Chancellor of France until 1565 – perhaps the most famous bibliophile and collector of all time – and William Morris, to whom the catalogue was dedicated: 'To the memory of William Morris, to whose intimate knowledge of early books I owe my first inspiration as a collector.'

One of the most interesting parts of the collection was a complete set of the various editions of *Bernhard von Breydenbach and his Journey to the Holy Land, 1483–4*, first published in 1486. This is a fascinating work, a travel and adventure story to rank alongside the voyages of Marco Polo, describing in the first person the adventures of the German monk Bernhard and a number of companions along the way from his monastery in Bavaria to the monastery of St Catherine in the Sinai desert. It was a great popular success and much sought-after from the day of its publication, and *Bernhard von Breydenbach* came to be translated and reprinted in French, German and Spanish. The bibliography of 24 editions of this memorable work was based entirely on copies in Fairfax Murray's library.[7]

When in 1906 the Hodson Library, the property of the Wolverhampton brewer and collector was sold, Fairfax Murray was at last able to possess the greater part of the original manuscripts of William Morris's works. It was a further step towards achieving his private goal of accumulating the manuscripts, drawings and personal papers of the three colossi of his early years, Morris, Burne-Jones and Rossetti. At the time of Fairfax Murray's return to London, William Morris was dedicating his enormous energies to the short-lived breakaway Socialist League, but in 1888 he still found time to write the *House of the Wolfings*, paying his customary attention to every detail of the typeset page at the Chiswick Press before its publication. The task focused his attention once again on the aesthetics of producing the perfect book, and he pondered the design of a face to express the feeling of his text. The Kelmscott Press which grew from this seed was to become the last great focus of his flagging energies; at only 54, he was in failing health. The first Kelmscott sheet was pulled in January 1891.

Arthur Mackmurdo liked to claim that he had shown William Morris a copy of the Century Guild magazine, the *Hobby Horse*, and 'discussed the difficulties one had to overcome in getting a page of printed text that was a pleasure to look at … he there and then resolved to master the situation by setting up a press of his own.' Without doubt the *Hobby Horse* set a new standard in the production of periodicals, both by its beautifully proportioned typography and by the handsome woodblock cuts that Horne, Image and Mackmurdo employed to illustrate the text; while the literary emphasis of the Century Guild and its frankly elitist approach to craft had a certain resonance for William Morris, despite his socialist principles. But the inspiration for the Kelmscott Press was deep in Morris's soul, and among those with whom he shared his consuming interest was Fairfax Murray.

If Fairfax Murray did not contribute directly to the Kelmscott Press as greatly as William Morris wished, it was because he was out of the country or engaged in expert appraisals and catalogues too often to fit into the regular pattern of work required for producing illustrations for wood-engraving to conform to the printer's timetable. The early Kelmscott prospectus for William Morris's *The Well at the World's End* in 1892 stated that it would contain 'four wood-cuts designed by Charles Fairfax Murray', but in the event first Arthur Gaskin, and ultimately Edward Burne-Jones, undertook the illustrations. Fairfax Murray found time at least to assist Burne-Jones. 'I have handed over the *Garden of Eden* design to Mr Morris to get photographed. Leave out anything you like and simplify to make it go with Heaven – the leafage everywhere may be too complicated ... and of course the shadowing on the figures of Adam & Eve is nonsense. I only put it there to help myself with the outline...'[8] He also painted a fine portrait of Morris 'with the quality of an Old Master' from the Abel Lewis photograph, with his subject close at hand.

It was very like the early days. Fairfax Murray was to have transferred Burne-Jones's designs for the last and greatest of the Kelmscott books, the *Chaucer*, to wood blocks, but he took three months over the first and the task was given over to Robert Catterson-Smith. Fairfax Murray did, however, work on the title-page of *The Golden Legend* which William Morris designed. He helped too when Morris was editing his *Poems by the Way* for the Press. William Morris was greatly surprised to receive from Fairfax Murray the manuscript of an early poem of his: '*Catherine* puzzles me – I have not the slightest recollection of any stanza of it. Did I write it? ... the two stanzas are certainly mine, though these also I have utterly forgotten.'[9]

Fairfax Murray also designed and illustrated, with a woodcut by William Harcourt Hooper, the privately-printed edition of the ascetic monk Girolamo Savonarola's letter to his mother Elena Buonaccorsi on the death of her brother Zito, the *Epistola De Contemptu Mundi*. Savonarola's high-minded religious ideals and his spiritual delusion that he received his instructions directly from God, together with his unrelenting sermons against the corruption of the Church in the face of a ban on his preaching in public, resulted in his being condemned to death by the Pope in 1498. He was burned at the stake in the Piazza della Signoria in Florence in front of an invited audience, and his ashes were tipped into the Arno to prevent any cult growing up around his remains. His pious exhortation to his mother to reject the world was a treasured recent addition to Fairfax Murray's autographs, and the rare Kelmscott Press edition, which was circulated privately, of which only 150 copies were pulled, 6 on vellum, is more than a nod towards the historical importance of its author. It was said that Fairfax Murray was the only person whom William Morris allowed to publish a work under the Kelmscott imprint that was not personally designed and edited by him.

The Savonarola was printed two years before William Morris died, in the year in which Sydney Cockerell joined the Press as Morris's business manager. Fairfax Murray knew him as Ruskin's sometime companion in the later years of his decline, and they quickly became allied. After William Morris's death F S Ellis and Cockerell, his executors, agreed to sell him Morris's library as a whole for £20,000, though Fairfax Murray later withdrew in the face of legal problems over an agreement to pay over three years, which the executors were unable to reconcile with their obligations to the estate. Instead he took his choice of the library for £2,000, and the rest was sold to the Mancunian collector William Bennett for £18,000 (the bulk of which passed to the Morgan Library in 1902).

Almost from the moment Fairfax Murray was settled back in London his services as connoisseur and disinterested agent were called for, though it was also evident that there were those in positions of influence who regarded him with a measure of personal animus which stemmed from his rôle as a dealer, and embraced his lack of concern for the social niceties. A startled American visitor found that he kept important paintings in the bath. He was scornful of poses, of dressing the part, uncomfortable with the pleasantries of social occasions and lacking the least facility for small talk. He 'never gushed, never exaggerated, never was influenced by title or wealth ... he was friendly and sympathetic, but no flatterer...'[10]

An early occasion on which social prejudice openly declared itself came when George Howard, his long-time friend from the early days with Burne-Jones and his close companion in several battles for possession on behalf of the National Gallery, proposed Fairfax Murray as a member of the Council of the Arundel Society in 1889. John Ruskin had been forced by ill health to retire, and no-one knew better the works that merited their publication than Fairfax Murray, who had worked for Ruskin and the Society for 15 years. It is not clear that George Howard consulted him first, but neither might have been surprised at the lofty, class-conscious response of Sir William Gregory, the former colonial Governor of Ceylon: '...why not sound out Lord Savile if he would join us?... I quite concede in your view as to Murray's merits, but I fear the apples of discord being sown among us and it is inconvenient that a professional artist should sit in judgement and decide on his brethren ... of course, very big men like Leighton or [Watts?] would be different, but Murray is more on a level with our copyists and is a dealer besides ... all this between ourselves.'[11] Fairfax Murray was in trade. Merit must be sacrificed to breeding.

This did not inhibit the Trustees of the National Gallery, of whom William Gregory was a dedicated and effective member, from turning to him only days later when it became known that Lord Darnley was discreetly offering his great Veronese *Allegories of Love*[12] for sale. Fairfax Murray had in truth been acting on behalf of Lord Darnley since June of the previous year, and had first offered them to the National Gallery. Frederick Burton was unenthusiastic and neglected to inform the Trustees that they were available to a suitable purchaser. Fairfax Murray had therefore felt able to offer them to von Bode, who was seriously looking for funds to purchase them: 'Fairfax Murray was with me this afternoon and he told me that the four beautiful Veronese pictures from Chobham exhibited at the Royal Academy some years ago are for sale...' Thomas Armstrong wrote to George Howard. 'I remember these pictures very well for they seemed to be the freshest works of the period I have ever seen, admirable specimens of painting and most interesting and instructive. I am afraid Burton is inclined to poo-hoo them. Do try and get them for the Gallery... they would be a famous acquisition for any Gallery and I hope Berlin or some French jew will not lay hands on them....'[13] George Howard, who had not long succeeded as the 9th Earl of Carlisle, wrote by return to Fairfax Murray asking him for 'a note which I could *show* about them'.[14] Fairfax Murray's reply enabled George Howard to raise the matter formally with his fellow Trustees over Burton's head. It was an instructive instance of the Director's prerogative in the matter of acquisitions which was to become an issue five years later.

It seems that the long pause in the discussions that followed had its origins in Frederick Burton's indifference and a shortage of funds. It was not until May of 1890 that Darnley's nephew, Lionel Cust (later Director of the National Portrait Gallery) wrote once more to George Howard, to say that the pictures were now in the hands of Agnew's, where Fairfax Murray acted as adviser. The first was sold to the National Gallery later in the year and two of the remaining three in 1891 (with a Tintoretto thrown in), Lord Darnley giving the fourth to the nation. The sale was negotiated by William Agnew, and the purchase price of £5,000 was astonishingly lower than the £12,000 which Fairfax Murray had recommended to Lord Darnley two years earlier, when he had hopes of passing them to von Bode in the absence of interest from the National Gallery. Lord Darnley was far from happy with the outcome: 'I have persuaded myself by your strong advice to accept a price I never believed I should descend to' he wrote to William Agnew.[15] The repercussions of this incident were felt in 1894, when Lord Darnley offered Titian's *Europa* to the art market at large for £15,000. He declined to consider it his patriotic duty to sell at a lower price to the National Gallery, and possession quickly became a contest between Berlin and Berenson acting for Mrs Isabella Gardner. This magnificent painting is a jewel in her remarkable, eclectic collection at Fenway Court, the gallery she built to house it in Boston.

Fairfax Murray was much in demand for expert opinion in the last decade of the century. George Agnew, on the advice of his father Sir William Agnew, recommended Murray to the Hon. Evelyn Ashley 'as being conversant with old drawings'[16] to give an opinion on a collection formerly in the possession of Lord Palmerston. The Duke of Portland required a catalogue of his collection in 1891 and consulted R H Benson, who unhesitatingly recommended Fairfax Murray. Portland was a little apprehensive, but the introduction proved a success: 'I have just seen Mr Murray and have taken a great fancy to him. He says he can come to Welbeck with you next Friday'[17] he wrote to Benson. Charles Fairfax Murray's polite lack of deference intrigued hereditary aristocrats. 'I have more or less agreed his demand for £100 and I do not think it too much to give him. I should like to pay him well and then he will go into the work *con amore* – however, I am sure he will anyway.'[18] It was to prove a labour of love at the price. He found that of the numerous portraits attributed to van Dyck, three only were by his hand. Four years had passed when, in January 1895, the Duke wrote to Fairfax Murray that 'a copy of the picture catalogue has just arrived, and I must write to say how delighted I am – it far exceeds my expectations. I am so much obliged to you for the care and trouble you took in compiling it. The Duke of Sutherland wrote to me the other day to ask for your address... when will you commence the catalogue of minia-tures?'[19] (The Sutherland assignment came to nothing, although Fairfax Murray visited Trentham to see his pictures, leaving the coachman aghast at his having insisted on being driven up to the front entrance.) The Duke of Bedford consulted him for a second opinion on a catalogue of pictures at Woburn compiled by George Scharf, the Director of the National Portrait Gallery. Lord Balcarres sought his help in finding a copyist for a Perugino triptych and received a reply suggesting instead an original picture from Certosa that Fairfax Murray thought might fill the bill more usefully; his advice was accepted. Lord Beauchamp was another possessor of a family collection which, like so many dating from the days of the Grand Tour, was in some need of re-attribution and cataloguing: 'Mr Benson told me that I could have no better opinion than yours & I shall be glad to have it – without regard to my feelings!'[20] One feels that he could have had no better agent than Robert Benson.

Galleries and exhibitors consulted him. He valued the important Roscoe collection on its transfer to the Liverpool Royal Institute, the nucleus of the Walker Art Gallery. Fairfax Murray advised and edited the catalogue for the acclaimed 1893 Signorelli exhibition at the Burlington Fine Arts Club, which drew exhibits from several European galleries. Though his connois-seurship was sought he was not, however, eligible for membership on the grounds of his livelihood in dealing. Sensibly, this did not bar him from using the Club's excellent library where he was welcome, but the social imperatives were nevertheless observed. The New Gallery were not governed by similar rules, and Fairfax Murray was a member of the Committee for the 'Italian Masters 1300–1550' Exhibition the following year. He was able to remedy a lack of sculpture of the period in English collections by loans from Berlin through his relationship with Wilhelm von Bode, and in a notable departure from his usual practice, he also wrote a critical column on the exhibition for the *St James's Gazette*.[21] Several of the books he commended came from his own collection.

In the autumn of 1893, Sir Frederick Burton announced his resignation from the post of Director of the National Gallery which he had held for 20 years, touching off a rush into contention of a number of candidates who were regarded, or who regarded themselves, as suitable candidates. He left his post at a juncture when there was fast increasing competition for museum-quality works of art, and for Italian painting in particular, both from Germany and from the emerging millionaire collectors of the United States. The vacancy provided the occasion to air a number of fundamental issues concerning the conduct of the Directorship, and in particular the incumbent's relationship with the Trustees. While the issues were ostensibly those of organisation and responsibility, there was also a personal edge to some of the questions raised. Among the more establishment-minded of the Trustees, particularly Gregory and Layard, there was the widely touted view that Frederick Burton had proved something of a dead hand on the development of the collection, and in truth his later judgement was somewhat erratic. They elected to ignore his continued strengthening of the early Italian schools. They pointed instead to his reluctance to go after the Darnley Veroneses, and his failure to negotiate for the Dürers that had gone to Berlin, while choosing to forget the storm of criticism they had raised over his purchase of a Piero della Francesca *Nativity* early in his Directorship. The real issue was whether the Director or the Trustees should decide future additions to the collection.

Among the more liberal of the Trustees, who included George Howard, the 9th Earl of Carlisle, John Postle Heseltine and Lord Savile, there was support for Frederick Burton's record, a greater respect for his judgement as a painter himself, and recognition that lack of funds had made his task difficult. The convergence of these factions was a patched-up agreement to recommend that future Directors should sit with the Trustees and share with them the responsibility for purchasing policy and the decision-making process, rather than exercise absolute executive control (Carlisle pointing out that this was exactly how Burton had in practice worked). The point that continued to divide them was between those Trustees who believed that the post must go to a painter by profession and those who favoured an emphasis on scholarship and administrative experience, thus increasing the influence of the Trustees in making acquisitions.

The candidates who entered the lists were Sidney Colvin, Keeper of Prints and Drawings at the British Museum and before that at the Fitzwilliam, Edward Poynter RA, painter and Thomas Armstrong's predecessor as Director of Art at the South Kensington Museum, Walter Armstrong, the Director of the National Gallery of Ireland, Charles Lock Eastlake, who had held the post of Keeper of the Gallery for the last 15 years and whose uncle Sir Charles Eastlake had been the second Director, and Charles Fairfax Murray, painter, connoisseur, collector and dealer. There was a sprinkling of other names put forward, including that of Lord Carlisle, who was nominated by the critic Stopford Brookes. They were soon discounted or withdrawn. Walter Armstrong was quickly eliminated for, despite his obvious credentials and persistent campaigning, he was suspected of taking commissions on purchases for the Dublin Gallery. Another early entrant, Humphrey Ward, collector and dealer, was tarred with the same brush, and his energetic later submissions on behalf of his friend Walter Armstrong did him more harm than good. Charles Eastlake suffered the fate of many loyal seconds-in-command and he was again overlooked, the Treasury going so far as to recommend the abolition of his post when he persisted.

At first blush it is surprising that Charles Fairfax Murray, the artist-dealer who lacked the least interest in becoming the ornament of any drawing-room and was wholly unknown to the Establishment, was ever nominated. In fact, behind the scenes as always, he played an important non-speaking part in the politics of the decision. The selection of the new Director commenced under William Gladstone's administration in which Carlisle had a powerful voice and, had Gladstone remained in office, Fairfax Murray might likely have emerged as the middle way as the contest polarised between the merits of Sidney Colvin and Edward Poynter.

He was under no illusions about his place in the tactical struggle, as he told von Bode: 'I have withdrawn from all business matters for some months as I am one of the candidates for the National Gallery Directorship – I am only running as a second to Poynter more than anything else to oppose Colvin who seems to me to be the least capable of all who are running for it.'[22] It was an act of self-denial in support of George Howard and the artist-Director Trustees who needed a credible reserve candidate; yet the prize might have been his.

Fairfax Murray was proposed both by Lord Carlisle and by Sir Edward Burne-Jones as their second choice. Both recommended Edward Poynter as artist-Director (in Burne-Jones's case because Poynter was also his brother-in-law), and he was supported by Holman Hunt. Early in the contest, Poynter was confident enough to let it be known privately that he had been as good as offered the position, which caused Burne-Jones some embarrass-ment and led to further support for Fairfax Murray. 'Where (in Praeterita is it?) is a note of Ruskin's about you? Tell me. The question of the Nat. Gallery is NOT settled, I know – nor likely to be at present, the Prime Minister told me so on Saturday.' Fairfax Murray discussed the position with Thomas Armstrong at the South Kensington Museum, the latter duly reporting the conversation to Lord Carlisle: 'Fairfax Murray wants very much to see you about the NG... moreover, FM says that Mr G declares that he has not made any appointment and he intends to look closely into the matter before it comes to a decision.'[23]

William Morris typically took the direct path and urged his appointment in unequivocal terms: 'I am quite sure that he has a remarkable and altogether unusual instinct for *style* in art, and that he has cultivated that gift assiduously until he has, to my mind, gained an unrivalled knowledge of the history and qualities of pictures. I believe his appointment would be a great gain to the public.'[24] William Morris stressed Fairfax Murray's superior art historical scholarship, and his view that he spanned both sides of the argument.

Sidney Colvin, without publicly announcing his own candidacy, was well-placed as a senior civil servant to press the case for a scholar-Director with good administrative experience, and this he did in letter after letter to a host of supporters in Government and among senior civil servants long before Burton had formally resigned. He pointed out that an artist-Director would not be a full-time Director, a telling point against Edward Poynter, who was in the running for a future Presidency of the Royal Academy.[25] William Gladstone was himself not in favour of the two most prestigious (and highly paid) posts in the national arts firmament going to one man, and Colvin's star was in the ascendant for a time. The critics D S MacColl and Marion Spielmann wrote on his behalf. Dr Bredius of the Hague, a widely respected scholar-Director, strongly supported Colvin, pointing out that there was no great gallery in Europe under the direction of a painter; the art historians had won long since. Less predictably, G F Watts, Frederic Lord Leighton PRA and W B Richmond preferred him, perhaps because they were set against Poynter.

In March 1894 the 84-year-old Gladstone made way for his Foreign Minister, and the decision on the Directorship was taken in June under the premiership of Lord Rosebery.[26] To the very end of the contest the artist-Director faction were fearful that Gladstone's objection in principle to the two most prestigious posts in the arts being held by one man might prevail under the new administration. Edward Burne-Jones wrote once more, now to Lord Rosebery, supporting Fairfax Murray's claims in case Edward Poynter should be ruled ineligible: 'Mr Fairfax Murray is both an artist and an expert ... about thirty years ago he was introduced to me by Mr Ruskin who was struck by the boy's energy and gifts, and I have known him ever since. As he gained experience in his art, he also developed an outstanding power of judgement and discrimination of schools of painting both ancient and modern ... his practical knowledge of the art is invaluable and his reputation as a judge of art is so good that some years since he received an invitation through Dr Bode of Berlin to go there and examine and pronounce on the early pictures in the Gallery... the Italian Govt. has also commissioned him to make purchases on their behalf...'[27]

In June the proposed changes to the relationship between Director and Trustees were confirmed, diluting the authority of the Director, and Edward Poynter was appointed to the post. The decisive factor against Sidney Colvin was that he was widely regarded as having neither the eye for a painting (his considerable experience being with prints and drawings) nor any real knowledge of painters. It was something of a Pyrrhic victory for the artist-Director faction. Edward Poynter was generally considered by his contemporaries to have been the weakest holder of the office in the history of the National Gallery. He retired in 1904 and was succeeded by Charles Holroyd, the first Keeper of the Tate Gallery, in 1906.

Fairfax Murray 'bears his disappointment well' Lockett Agnew wrote:

'... personally I must own to some regret that he did not get the post. He has what many artists have not, a broad and comprehensive mind.'[28] He had felt it his duty to stand, and once in the fray fought well, although it would certainly have reduced his income had he been appointed. He was confident that his qualifications as a connoisseur and artist outweighed his lack of administrative experience, particularly since he could rely on the support of Keeper Eastlake, with whom he enjoyed good relations. He would have been pleased and willing had he been offered the post to put his energies and knowledge into raising the status and quality of the national collection. He was, however, also aware of his perceived lack of social connections, the blemish of his bowed legs and unfashionable appearance, and the suspicion that attached to his being 'in trade'. The prejudice and snobbery enraged and saddened him.

He was commissioned by the Gallery to act for them at Lady Eastlake's sale shortly after Poynter's appointment; it was not a precedent. 'With regard to the National Gallery ... I have absolutely no connection with it – whether the commission to buy for them at the Eastlake sale was given purposely "as a sop in the pan" immediately after Mr Poynter's appointment I know not; one thing is for certain, they have not consulted me again.'[29] The months of waiting in the wings cost him dear. 'That Jordaens I offered you for £300 which you said was dear was afterwards sold to the Brussels gallery for £1000 ... my loss of it was part of the price I paid for my transient ambition to become Director of which I have been well cured. I wouldn't take it now if they offered me double the salary!'[30]

In July 1902, Fairfax Murray was incensed when Poynter moved a *Family Group* by Vermeer, which he had donated to the Gallery two years earlier, to a markedly inferior position on a window wall, and reattributed it: 'I did not present what I considered, and still consider, the most valuable picture I owned to the Gallery to be extinguished in this manner ... you saw fit after accepting the picture without reservation as by Vermeer to change the inscription to "attributed to". Of this I took no notice, the merit of the picture remained ... the present position given to the picture amounts to a challenge to myself that I will not submit to in silence.' He added: 'It is unnecessary, at least at present to go into other matters that have led up to this present situation, the springs of which are possibly as well known to you as they are to me.'[31] Fairfax Murray had a long memory.

There was an unexpected end to the chapter which would have meant far more to Fairfax Murray than any public office. Frederick Burton died in March 1900; three months had passed when a letter arrived from Dublin. 'My uncle, the late Sir Frederick Burton, desired me (as his Executor) verbally to be sure to give you a very interesting book, viz. Blake's *Songs of Innocence and Experience*, painted by himself. I understand that it is intrinsically of great value... Sir Frederick spoke most highly of you as his friend & appeared most anxious that you should have the book as a memento...'[32]

followed a week later by a package and a second letter: 'I now have great pleasure in sending the book of Blake's *Songs of Innocence* ... my uncle spoke very highly of the valuable services you rendered to him during your residence in Italy.' It was a wonderful gesture of friendship and respect. Fairfax Murray was to enjoy possession of this unique volume for five years before giving it, with a number of priceless William Morris, Christina Rossetti and Dante Gabriel Rossetti manuscripts, to the Fitzwilliam, where their preservation and retention in Britain was assured. It was an early example of his gifts to collections that were open to the public rather than hidden away in the rich man's castle.

There were many other services, small and large, freely given to old friends over the years. For William Morris, Fairfax Murray's last, sad service was to make three gently rendered, simple pencil drawings of his friend and mentor in death, at peace in his bed in the garden room at Kelmscott House on the morning of 3 October 1896. Burne-Jones was in frequent need of assistance: 'If you have 5 minutes to spare could you run across this morning and help me with advice about a portrait – the sooner the better for me but I mustn't waste your time, come when you can'[33] was typical; or '...SKM haven't got in the Library an Albert Dürer triumphal car ... if you have one will you lend it for a few days, I will take mighty care of it.'[34] He relied once more on Fairfax Murray's discretion when Charles Augustus Howell's estate came to auction. Nobody cared to think of the past relationships, alliances and reproaches that might be exposed by private letters written 25 years earlier, and it was generally believed that 'the Owl' had collected tales from the gossipy Rossetti circle for future use, by whatever means came to hand; in particular, he was thought to have letters relating to Burne-Jones's passionate affair with Maria Zambaco. 'Today a chap told me that there had been or was to be a sale of letters written by friends to Rossetti, that man quaked for fear that some of his should be for sale... I also felt troubled ... what a bore it is to have to even think of this. How are you? Don't sell this letter, there's a dear boy'[35] he wrote. Fairfax Murray attended the sale on his behalf, but on that occasion at least Burne-Jones need not have worried.

After William Morris's death came another request which might have caused Fairfax Murray great embarrassment, since it would have involved his arbitrating between two close friends. 'I am much in need of your help,' Burne-Jones wrote. 'There appeared a week ago in one of the newspapers some reproductions from designs by Richmond for the new mosaics in St Paul's. One of them ... an outstretched figure of Christ on a tree where branches filled the lunette was so very like the one I made for St Paul's American Ch. in Rome that the similarity was noticed by many and reported to me.'[36] Fairfax Murray was narrowly spared the dilemma. Next day Burne-Jones had learned, he said, from W B Richmond that 'the authority is no longer a manuscript – now it's anything in S Clemente – it may be changed to S Agnese in Rome & to sculpture in Rheims – so don't bother at all – I can't pursue the matter all over Europe...'[37] He was very angry. In the end it was simply to rekindle the memory of the days in Kensington Square that he called on his first studio assistant: 'Oh Little Muvy, Ain't you never coming to see me...'[38]

Fairfax Murray was no less accustomed to the technical queries that reached him from The Grange. One such was a request from Georgiana for advice that Burne-Jones was probably embarrassed to ask himself; if he were to overpaint a picture varnished in copal, would the overpainting be removed in subsequent cleaning? Fairfax Murray was a regular visitor in the Spring of 1898. He bought a number of chalk drawings from Burne-Jones to add to his collection: 'Are you going to write a biographical sketch of me that you wanted those 2 particular heads yesterday? Deal gently. Yours aff. EBJ[39]. Almost five years earlier, in August 1893, Murray had received an altogether deeper cry of pain and desperation: 'My picture of *Love among the Ruins* has been utterly destroyed, it was lent to Goupils and there they varnished it with white of egg – the whole thing has gone as though it had never been done...'[40] The picture carried poignant memories of Maria Zambaco, and Burne-Jones could not steel himself to attempt its restoration. The years passed and at length he wrote once more to Fairfax Murray: 'Do you remember the watercolour *Love among the Ruins* that they poured white of egg over, in Paris 5 years ago? I have promised the owner to try and work upon it ... but how should I remove the horrible stuff before I begin...?' Fairfax Murray went to The Grange next day and the two painters worked side by side once more, Murray experimenting with ox-gall to remove the clouded coating of albumen. They succeeded in cleaning away the film that covered the head of Polia, the likeness of Maria Zambaco: Burne-Jones lovingly repainted the damaged features while 'Mr Fairfax Murray ... treated in the same way the portion of the background that still remained filmed over. It seemed something like a miracle when at last the whole picture shone out again.'[41] Six weeks later, Edward Burne-Jones was dead.

There were other calls on his expertise. The irreverent Philip Webb – 'I hear tell of you now and then but never see you – the big-wig reputation you've earned is I suppose the cause...'[42] – called on Fairfax Murray for help with the affairs of their old friend, George Price Boyce. 'The good Boyce's affairs are being knit together on account of his incapacity for managing them, and the lawyers want inventories of the contents of West House ... for the pictures it wants a specialist – and who so specious – beg pardon, special as you. Could you without too great inconvenience make this inventory?'[43] He could, of course. Philip Webb was among the first to receive a copy of the Kelmscott *Epistola*: 'And so you thought that *I* should have a copy ... one more of so many precious gifts of books will not make me blush after so much practice at hiding shame ... my stars, Mr Murray, what a kindly New Year's gift for an old man … it stirred up my dormant memories of St Marco di Firenze … and of 1884–5 when you took in the belated traveller and did for him…'[44] By February the inventory was completed and Philip Webb could write that 'Mrs B tells me that it pleased poor old Boyce to have you in the house busy over his much loved pictures.'[45] These were three companions who understood one another perfectly over the years. 'I'm glad you are busy for I'm fond of good temper,' Webb added.

William Stillman was another who benefited from Fairfax Murray's humanity. During his last illness, Murray sent him Turner's gouache and watercolour of *Devonport and Dockyard*, to hang at the foot of the bed and cheer him. The painting is one of the series of *Picturesque Views in England and Wales* that Turner painted in 1830, which he had acquired from Ruskin's estate in 1900. When Stillman died the following year, Fairfax Murray donated the picture to the Fogg in his memory.

In September 1899, as Charles Fairfax Murray reached the age of 50 and the height of his influence in the art world, that world as he knew it was already passing away. His three great mentors were gone. Dante Gabriel Rossetti had died in 1882. William Morris had died, the fire burned out, in October 1896, and Edward Burne-Jones, who had never quite recovered from the loss, had followed him in June 1898. John Ruskin was less than a year from his grave in Coniston, silenced by his madness since 1889. Of the artists of Cheyne Walk circle of 30 years ago, Ford Madox Brown had died in 1893, George Price Boyce in January 1897. Murray's great friend W J Stillman was already an invalid and would die in 1901. Fairfax Murray would be their pall-bearer.

He was now recognised as the absolute authority on the Pre-Raphaelites. Dante Gabriel Rossetti's reputation was already in decline, and the prices of his works falling. As the Impressionists succeeded Symbolists, only Edward Burne-Jones's work commanded any attention on the Continent, and Fairfax Murray, as his one-time pupil and assistant, was much consulted by the French; Léprieure, editor of the *Gazette des Beaux Arts*, consulted him at length on Burne-Jones's technique and the English Symbolists, publicly acknowledging his debt. In England, his lasting contribution to the Pre-Raphaelites still lay ahead.

He could, however, preach the Pre-Raphaelite gospel in the United States, and the opening came his way in 1892. Lockett Agnew introduced him to a feisty American cotton mill owner, Samuel Bancroft Jnr. Self-educated in the arts and nine years older than Fairfax Murray, Bancroft was of recent English descent, related by marriage to Walter Crane. His cousin was an architect in Manchester, and he already owned Rossetti's *Water Willow*. He was as splendidly pugnacious and outspoken as Fairfax Murray; they formed a natural partnership. He was Bancroft's mentor and forthright advisor as well as dealer until the latter's death in 1915. Fairfax

Murray introduced Bancroft to Edward Burne-Jones, Fanny Cornforth, George Price Boyce and Janey Morris, and between them they built the greatest public collection of Pre-Raphaelite works outside the United Kingdom, including numbers of Rossetti sketches and drawings, his paintings *Lady Lilith*, *Found*, and *Veronica Veronese* among others as well-known, Millais's *A Waterfall in Glenfinlas*, Sandys's *Mary Magdalene* and Edward Burne-Jones's *Council Chamber* from the *Briar Rose* series, as well as Charles Fairfax Murray's own *Last Meeting of Helga and Gunnlaug*.[46]

At the turn of the century Fairfax Murray had reached the high-water mark of his career. There was one more debt to repay to his Pre-Raphaelite mentors; to Edward Burne-Jones, who had passed on his own hard-won knowledge of painting technique and provided him practical experience, much as he had himself learned the craft of painting from Dante Gabriel Rossetti, to William Morris, who gave him his love of books, the opportunity to study early manuscript illumination and to share in the process of making new works as beautiful as their exemplars, and to Dante Gabriel Rossetti himself, to whom he owed the spur to forge his talent and refine his skill as a discerning connoisseur. He would be the guardian of their flame, and he set out to secure recognition of the significance of their work and their memory from generations yet to come.

12. Nunc Dimittis

In October 1898 Fairfax Murray moved into The Grange, just three months after Burne-Jones died. He left no comment on his feelings as he took over the rambling house that held so many memories of his earliest days, but Dolly would later speak of his quiet satisfaction. It was notice to the art world, if any were needed, of his considerable achievement. To Georgiana Burne-Jones it was a token of continuity: 'It is a real comfort to me to think that you will go and live in it.'[1] The Grange became his principal place of business, his lodging – where he lived in spartan simplicity, guarded by a housekeeper – and the home of his London collections. In addition he kept a substantial house, a mile or so away in Barrowgate Road, Chiswick, for his English family, an apartment in Paris in the Blvd Malherbes where he kept a store of pictures and rare books, a town house for his most valuable pictures and the library of early Italian books in the centre of Florence, and the Villa Murray at Tavarnuzze for the Italian family. His two families included six sons in universities and private schools. Although he gave up painting professionally around 1903 as his hand became increasingly rheumatic, he was now enjoying the fruits of his knowledge and experience.

War, which had long been threatening, was now a gathering storm as German naval rearmament increased in momentum. The art market was becoming destabilised and values were set to fall. Fairfax Murray, who was increasingly turning to early books, began to liquidate some of his collection of paintings, a long process which would demand all of his experience and skill. He consulted both Sotheby's Tom Hodge – the undisputed master of the book auctions – and Frank Sabin, the leading picture dealer. Sabin made an offer of £130,000[2] for the entire collection, but Fairfax Murray knew that he could better it in separate lots if the need arose, and he did not proceed immediately. He was anxious, as he had always been, that pictures of museum quality should find their way in to public collections such as those in which he had found his vocation, and he had on many occasions passed on works at prices below their market value or refused commissions, regarding himself as their steward and not as the owner. He was deeply conscious of his responsibility to future generations: 'I don't want to leave a great collection behind me, or a great fortune. I want to provide adequately for my family on simple lines, but I have got more than my share of beautiful things, and I intend to distribute many of them before I die.'[3] The house in Barrowgate Road and its contents, including many valuable pictures, was made over to Dolly.

Charles Fairfax Murray's close personal friendships with the later Pre-Raphaelites within the circle of Rossetti's acquaintances, his extensive collection of their sketches, drawings, paintings and manuscript poetry, and his deep sympathy with their work (which he correctly recognised as an important English school, although at the time it was at its lowest popular estimate) combined to make him the most eligible of all their associates to write a definitive life of Rossetti. In contrast to his reluctance to write on other aspects of connoisseurship, Fairfax Murray commenced a *catalogue raisonné* and critical examination of Rossetti's drawings in 1892. His original intention to write it himself soon gave way to a collaboration in which he was to write the catalogue and criticism, while his partner – most probably William Stillman, who was preparing to leave Italy to retire to Surrey – would write the biographical sections. They had co-operated before.[4] Fairfax Murray made considerable inroads into the preparation of a catalogue of Rossetti's own work and studio replicas; but by July 1893 the biographical material had not progressed and Fairfax Murray was ruefully coming to accept that he would have to undertake that task in addition if his catalogue was to see the light of day.

In August 1893, Samuel Bancroft wrote from Wilmington to tell him that he had received a letter from one Frederick Holland Day, whom he did not know, a fellow Rossetti enthusiast who hoped to publish a slim volume on the painter. Holland Day, it soon transpired, was no mere tyro but the editor of a magazine called the *Knight Errant*, conceived along lines similar to Horne's *Hobby Horse,* and a partner in the Boston publishers Copeland & Day. 'Forewarned is forearmed,'[5] Bancroft added. Day was in London for the Ford Madox Brown sale that summer and, meeting Fairfax Murray there, suggested that Copeland & Day should publish his Rossetti drawings and critical notes. The terms he later proposed were firmly rejected. Neither Holland Day nor Fairfax Murray published their work on Rossetti.

Nevertheless, his debt to his early mentors, his admiration of Dante Gabriel Rossetti, his friendship with Edward Burne-Jones and his brotherhood with William Morris remained a discrete theme of Fairfax Murray's compartmented life. Cheyne Walk and Queen Square were Charles Fairfax Murray's university,[6] and it was his lifelong aim to give back something of that which he had taken out. Dante Gabriel Rossetti's inspiration was returned in unqualified admiration, unhesitating loyalty and awe. 'All the man is in his eye,'[7] Fairfax Murray once said to Spanton. 'It is no good asking me to criticise him,' he told Arthur Benson. 'He was such a great man – a man who gave the impression of greatness, of genius ... and of such irresistible generosity and kindness.'[8] He was now the undisputed authenticator of their work and the guardian of their reputations. Only the rigorous and solitary William Holman Hunt was denied his approval. Hunt's claim to have been the only true Pre-Raphaelite, and his criticisms of Rossetti, were more than Fairfax Murray could condone. When Hunt's book *Pre-Raphaelitism and the Pre-Raphaelite Brotherhood* appeared in 1905

Fairfax Murray wrote to F G Stephens, who had reviewed it for the *Athenaeum:* 'I have your very temperate and kindly reply to that abominable book of Hunt's. You couldn't say less and would have been justified in saying much more, but the book destroys itself & I hear but one opinion of it. As to Hunt's relative merits in comparison to his contemporaries, time will settle that effectively however loud he wails... I have what I believe to be Hunt's first letter from the East to Rossetti, it is quite sufficient to dispose of Hunt's pretensions to pose as the head of the confraternity, and shows the same evil spirit of deprecation of Seddon who he was evidently jealous of.'

Henry Marillier, the managing director of Morris & Co after Morris's death, turned to Fairfax Murray for a *catalogue raisonné* of Rossetti's drawings, for the loan of more than a dozen major works and Rossetti manuscripts, for letters and guidance on matters of fact when he published his *Dante Gabriel Rossetti, an Illustrated Memorial* in 1899. As the price of his co-operation, Fairfax Murray insisted on removing from the text anything that might be pejorative concerning Dante Gabriel Rossetti's relationship with Janey Morris, having in mind that Janey and May were still living. He rigorously excluded any mention of his personal connection. 'Your method of administering advice and information with a pick-axe is rather alarming...' Marillier wrote. 'I cannot promise to take out all reference to yr. name ... you are more identified with Rossetti's name than anyone else, and everyone accepts you as the leading authority.'[9] But he wrote again a few days later: 'about Mrs M I have been as discreet as possible.' Fairfax Murray's legendary pugnacity was accepted by all whom he allowed to know him well as a carapace to keep out intruders. A C Benson regarded his 'unabated ferocity' after an illness as a welcome sign of recovery.

Georgiana Burne-Jones was in frequent correspondence with him as she wrote her *Memorials of Edward-Burne-Jones.* 'I will tell you now in confidence,' she wrote 'that my heart is set on making that early part live again ... those wonderful, seething days.'[10] To Cockerell he remarked only that the *Memorials* were 'nothing but a collection of facts that may be useful to a future biographer, but they give an uncomplete picture of him from much being omitted, purposely of course.'[11] For the same reason he refused Edmund Gosse, who was writing his biography of Algernon Charles Swinburne, access to the many letters he possessed: 'Personally, I consider Swinburne a remarkably fine character at bottom and a most loveable personality – but, alas, just think if his letters were published in any considerable numbers, what the effect would be! ... I am against giving intentionally false impressions of people, simply by leaving out what is considered detrimental,' he wrote to Cockerell. Moreover, Swinburne's sister Isobel was still living, and Fairfax Murray considered it impossible to give a rounded picture of the poet, the brilliant and the tawdry, while his close relatives were still alive. Half-truth was less acceptable than silence, he would not condone posthumous gloss. His memories were sacred to him, and he was outstandingly loyal in a disloyal milieu, as silent as the confessional throughout his life. When J W Mackail, Edward Burne-Jones's son-in-law, was researching the 'official' biography of William Morris four years after his death, he turned to Fairfax Murray for original letters, manuscripts and information. The price was always the same; his anonymity.

In January 1903, Charles Fairfax Murray completed the sale of some 260 Rossetti drawings and 226 by Edward Burne-Jones to the Birmingham Museum and Art Gallery at a sum well below their market value. J R Holliday, the Birmingham solicitor, book-lover and friend of William Morris, raised a subscription among the public figures of Burne-Jones's native city to ensure their permanence as a collection. Next year, Fairfax Murray gave the Museum 35 cartoons for stained glass by Burne-Jones. Three years later, Holliday again found the funds for the purchase of more than 300 drawings by Madox Brown, Frederick Sandys and John Everett Millais from his collection, creating almost at a stroke the basis for the world's pre-eminent holdings of Pre-Raphaelite drawings, and assuring their legacy. It was part payment of his debt. Fairfax Murray's familiar stipulation was that his name must nowhere appear. 'What *shall* I tell the press, they are bound to ask?' wrote Whitworth Wallis.

Fairfax Murray felt something of the same affection and debt to Cambridge which he scarcely knew before the age of 30. Two of his sons, John from his Italian family and Arthur from Dolly's, were Cambridge-educated, John at Pembroke and Arthur at Christ's. Two years separated them, and M R James must have been among those who knew his 'secret'. 'Monty' James, a specialist in early manuscripts and incunabula, succeeded John Henry Middleton as Director of the Fitzwilliam in 1893. His close friend Arthur Benson, an Etonian contemporary, introduced him to Fairfax Murray in 1904. 'I went by appointment to see one Fairfax Murray who possesses many mss., he doesn't know how many, but between 200 and 500. He gave me one to take away ... and expresses his intention of giving them all eventually to the Fitzwilliam. This is all extremely pleasant. Fairfax Murray is only anxious that no public notice should be given of his gifts,'[12] James wrote in astonishment to his father. He received 30 more manuscripts in 1904–05. 'Murray,' he wrote, 'has none of the affectations of the art critic.'

Arthur Benson recorded their meeting in his diary: 'He was showing him the most sumptuous mss; he showed him about 15 of these ... suddenly he said "I'll send you all of these if you like, and I want to give you all of my autographs of Italian painters and all of the original mss of Morris and Rossetti. I have a very great objection to death duties, and there are certain things in my hands I don't want to get sold... I want no sort of recognition – I hope it won't get in the press..."

'The rest of the afternoon was spent just wandering about among his wonderful things and looking. He carried a great branch candlestick ... to wander about those great, warm darkening rooms, with these splendid and beautiful things everywhere, did one good. He is a very delightful and simple man, and I have a great affection for him. I can't quite make out his mind... I think he has the mind of a collector through and through ... his big head, frank eyes, and the simplicity, kindliness and child-like honesty of his talk make him an attractive fellow.'[13]

Fairfax Murray remained active in the art market, buying as often as selling, his enthusiasm frequently overcoming his prudent intention to reduce his collections. He savoured a modest triumph at Poynter's expense when the newly formed National Art Collections Fund approached him to join their failing efforts to save the Velasquez *Venus at her Toilet*, the 'Rokeby Venus', for the nation. Edward Poynter was cool to the picture, and certain of the Trustees thought that so provocative a nude had no place in the National Gallery. He had already given 'generously' but the Fund was far short of its target when he was invited to a meeting to decide what might be done. He immediately pledged a further £5,000, an enormous sum, from his future income with Agnew's if others could be persuaded to find the rest. His gesture reached the ears of George, Prince of Wales and he was commanded to lunch at Kensington Palace on 2 January 1905; one wonders how he dressed for the occasion. Impressed, the Prince made his interest known and the money was not long in coming. Fairfax Murray was relieved of his obligation, and Agnew's sold the painting for a good deal less than they could have realised in Berlin, having already given £5,000 to the Fund. Poynter had resigned the Directorship in October 1904, and the Velasquez cast a 'comfortable glow' on the incoming Director, Charles Holroyd. Fairfax Murray resumed the re-arrangement of his collections.

An excited Arthur Benson wrote a hasty note to M R James in September 1907: 'Dear Monty, I was at Fairfax Murray's house yesterday – he is full of schemes for *giving* away the greater part of his collections. He told me that he had for years been collecting specimens of portraits of foreign artists who had worked in England, as well as typical examples of English portrait painters. He said "would there be any place in Cambridge that such things could be hung?" On the Directorship of the Fitzwilliam he said that he had little doubt that it ought to be Waldstein, but if not he thought that Cockerell would be a very suitable and thoughtful Director.'[14] To Sydney Cockerell, Fairfax Murray simply wrote 'my advice to you is to go in and win.' He gave gifts of Blake, Rossetti and Morris manuscripts to Trinity Hall to form the nucleus of a collection of autographs, and a fine Hogarth portrait of Matthew Prior, without his wig, to Trinity in 1908.

James and Benson scoured Cambridge for a suitable site for no less than 46 portraits, which included a van Dyck, two Hogarths, a Lely, a Gainsborough and others of great importance, but in the end it was Dulwich that took the prize. Henry Yates-Thompson, the bibliophile owner of the *Pall*

Mall Gazette and a pre-eminent collector of manuscripts who was said to have the finest collection in England after Sir Thomas Phillips, was Chairman of the Trustees of the Dulwich Picture Gallery. He was also widely held to be the rudest man anybody knew, but the bibliophile Fairfax Murray got on with him remarkably well. Yates Thompson's offer to build a separate wing to the Gallery to house the collection as a whole was finally instrumental in this remarkable benefaction going to Dulwich rather than Cambridge, as Fairfax Murray had originally intended.

He had long been closely associated with Agnew's, and the chronicle of their joint ventures, which included pictures in which he had a half-interest and later purchased outright, is a catalogue of Italian primitives and European Old Masters of the quality of Matteo di Giovanni, Botticelli, Filippino Lippi, Raphael, Titian, Dosso Dossi, Tintoretto, Rubens, Van Dyck, Hogarth, Hoppner, Gainsborough and Angelica Kauffmann. Fairfax Murray was personally close to Lockett Agnew, who assumed the running of the business with his cousin Moreland when William Agnew retired at the close of 1895.[15] They were as different as two close relations can be, Moreland Agnew the courteous, retiring, skilful judge of pictures, Lockett ever the ebullient salesman, possessed of a keen appreciation of pretty girls and the good life. They were a strong team as partners, but their personal relationship was less happy, leading eventually to Moreland's early retirement.[16]

Lockett Agnew and Fairfax Murray were equally a strong team, Murray providing the seemingly inexhaustible flow of fine pictures for Lockett to sell to his roll-call of distinguished clients and friends in the trade, while the closeness between them[17] permitted him to use the firm as his capital base. Moreland Agnew perhaps disapproved of this lax arrangement, and around 1900 a formal agreement was concluded, bringing Haskard's Bank in Florence, Charles Fairfax Murray and Agnew's into equal partnership to deal in Italian Old Master pictures. Agnew's provided the shop window and clients, and Haskard's the working capital, while Fairfax Murray continued to bring in the stock in trade: 'that strange and gifted character Charles Fairfax Murray ... had a dwarf-like body, a noble head and a marvellous eye for pictures and drawings of all schools, especially the Italian and early Flemish ... [and] was a most valued business associate. One of our greatest joint coups was the purchase in 1902 of a group of pictures from the de Somzée collection. These included the Maitre de Moulins now in the Louvre, the Maitre de Flémalle which passed through Salting to the National Gallery and the Gerard David altarpiece [now in the National Gallery of Art in Washington] and two predellas [Toledo and Edinburgh].'[18] There were Memlings, a Lucas van Leyden and a Coninxloo. These and many more great masters passed through the joint account: Palma il Vecchio, Andrea del Sarto, Greuze, Hals, Canale called Canaletto, and a Jacopo de' Barbari that figured prominently in later recollections pepper the ledger pages.

When the next generation joined the family firm in 1906, Lockett was no man to stand aside, and it was inevitable that Fairfax Murray, not of his choice, should be identified with a faction. While their close friendship was broken only by Fairfax Murray's ill health and Lockett's sudden death almost one year to the day before his own, the business relationship seems to have declined after the curious affair of the Jacopo de' Barbari. In 1907, whisper went the rounds of the art world that Charles Fairfax Murray was in financial difficulties. Frits Lugt, the dealer and historian of the art market who was 22 at the time, spoke of his recollections at the end of a long life. 'There was a rumour that Fairfax Murray needed money and was thinking of selling his collection. The matter was in the hands of Mr Hodge, a senior member of Sotheby's... Murray made a mistake in the acquisition of a major painting, and Agnew's made him personally responsible for the loss.'[19] Murray, he added, 'must have had something in mind', as a catalogue of his Old Master drawings had been prepared in 1905. Agnew's ledgers tell a less colourful tale. Fairfax Murray having secured the picture, the Italian government denied it an export permit, and in 1904 Agnew's were repaid exactly the purchase price. The picture remained in Naples, where it can be seen today. Curiously, Colin Agnew repeated the tale years later: 'a Jacopo de' Barbari painting in Naples which was not right ... may have precipitated a crisis.'[20] In the end it was all hearsay and innuendo, the common coin of the art market.

Agnew's seem, however, prudently to have insisted that Fairfax Murray balance his book as the art market slowed once more as war in Europe became daily less avoidable. Thomas Hodge, the senior partner in Sotheby's, made a substantial private sale from his mediaeval manuscripts collection to Dyson Perrins, one of the great collectors, 'at the request of Agnew's.'[21]

Fairfax Murray was seriously ill with pleurisy in 1909 and slow to recover. It affected his heart, and at 60 he knew that this was a serious setback. He hastened the completion of his master plan that had perhaps given rise to rumours two years earlier, without in any way curtailing his punishing travelling. In September 1909, Fairfax Murray sold 1,400 Old Master drawings to the American railroad and banking magnate John Pierpont Morgan, including works by Andrea del Sarto, Francia, Rubens, Poussin, van Dyck, Tiepolo, Claude Lorraine, Adrien van Ostade, Jan van Huysum, Fragonard and Watteau.[22] Morgan through Belle da Costa Greene, had turned down the offer at a figure of £45,000, made through the antiquarian booksellers Henry Sotheran two years previously; now, encouraged by Sir Charles Hercules Read, the Keeper of British and Mediaeval Antiquities at the British Museum, and possibly even by Berenson whom Belle also consulted, Morgan acquired the collection for £50,000; 'the *whole* of his collection is certainly worth having. He is about the best judge of such things here' Read had replied. Wagging tongues in the art market spoke of

Fairfax Murray scurrying around the London dealers buying up further works to supplement the collection but the whispering may be ascribed to envy; £50,000, some £3,000,000 in today's money, was an immense sum for a collection of drawings which were only then becoming seen as important. Ten years earlier, the collector J P Heseltine was accustomed to pay perhaps £200 to £300 for a Rembrandt drawing. In October 1910 Fairfax Murray gave up The Grange to Richard Norton. He had met his father in the same house in 1867 at the age of 18, 43 years earlier. His London address was now at 4 Albemarle Street, the building at the rear of Agnew's Bond Street premises which, rumour had it, Lockett had bought so that he could escape unwelcome visitors by the back door.

With Sydney Cockerell's appointment to the Fitzwilliam in 1908, Fairfax Murray entered into an even closer relationship with Cambridge. Cockerell's acquisitive nature matched his own; Murray started letters 'Dear Cormorant'. Over the next ten years, Charles Fairfax Murray gave the Fitzwilliam an astonishing array of fine art which included more than a dozen Constables and as many Wilkie watercolours, five early Gainsborough portraits, a hoard of Pre-Raphaelite paintings, drawings, sketches and printed books, a Corot and most spectacular of all, the superb Titian *Tarquin and Lucretia*. Dolly greatly resented 'greedy Mr Cockerell', but in truth Fairfax Murray had long considered his intention to place many of his pictures in permanent collections open to the public for the benefit of a wider audience.

A man unused to honours or public recognition which he sedulously avoided, he was startled to receive a letter from Sydney Cockerell in October 1911 informing him that the Syndics of Cambridge University 'unanimously appointed him to the office of Honorary Keeper of Paintings at the Fitzwilliam Museum' in recognition of his outstanding benefactions and critical contribution to the arts in Cambridge. Cockerell foresaw difficulties: 'If you do not decline this appointment you will be the first to hold that exalted office. In any case, it is intended as a compliment; so do not say "no" hurriedly … there are no duties attached unless you wish it.'[23] The letter reached Fairfax Murray in Montebuoni: 'I have been wandering again … I am afraid I cannot accept the honour which yr. Committee has been kind enough to propose. I do not see the use of an office or position that has not *some* duties attached to it and I am unlikely to have much opportunity if any in the near future of attending any meeting … respecting the care of the pictures which I should feel it my duty to look after…'[24] Early in the New Year Cockerell tried again; Fairfax Murray's reply had a note of finality: 'I have quite made up my mind that it wd. be an absurdity for *me* to accept the honour…' Throughout his life he had been unable to compromise; the honour, however well-intended, seemed to him humbug. He stuck to his principles to his last day, but there were times in his life when he could have made his path smoother. Nevertheless, he spent many weeks of the following year with Cockerell, unrecognised, appraising the Marlay Bequest to the Fitzwilliam.

In 1912, Fairfax Murray was more involved with the National Gallery than he had been since Burton's directorship. He gave Jan Lievens's *Portrait of a Man* and he was called to give evidence to the Parliamentary Committee chaired by Lord Curzon of Kedleston, set up to examine ways in which pictures of international importance could be kept in Britain in the face of prices offered abroad, notably by American collectors. His uncompromising argument in favour of market forces and Estate Duty relief on bequests was probably not regarded as a politically acceptable contribution to solving the problem, but he spoke with authority and the final Report did not contradict him. His friend of 46 years, George Howard, 9th Earl of Carlisle, died, and his widow Rosalind sought Fairfax Murray's help in deciding the future of the Castle Howard collection.

He was involved also in discussions with the Trustees about the repatriation of the Layard Bequest from Italy. The Italian Government had embargoed the export of Layard's collection on his widow's death, despite their earlier firm agreement that the pictures would remain in Venice only during the lifetimes of Sir Austen and Lady Layard. Fairfax Murray offered to get the bequest out Italy, legally and at negligible cost, an offer tardily accepted by the Gallery's Trustees. So slow were they to accept that the Foreign Office was able to intervene, insisting that negotiations must be conducted through diplomatic channels, and the Gallery were forced to withdraw their instructions to Fairfax Murray. The Layard Bequest languished in Venice throughout the First World War, and by the time the issue was again live, Charles Fairfax Murray was dead and Sir Charles Holroyd, the Director, retired.

Fairfax Murray had once again made up his mind to leave England in March 1913. He was out of tune with the times, and the world order that he knew for 65 years was about to collapse into war. His last three and a half years were dogged by the illnesses that slowly, inexorably took away his life, not without a characteristic struggle that he was determined to win, almost to the last hour. He was constantly on the move between Italy, Paris and London from May to October 1913. He spent the five winter months in Albemarle Street preparing for a major sale that would, he hoped, settle all but his personal collections, but he was again unwell in January. He was able to return to Florence for two or three days only in the first week of April 1914 before setting off once again for Paris to undertake the final stages of putting his collection of Old Master paintings on the market at the George Petit Galleries. He was exhausted and in unusually low spirits, but from Paris he pressed on to London to meet Sir Charles Hercules Read with whom he was to travel to New York. They sailed together in mid-April. John Pierpont Morgan snr. had died in Rome in March 1913; they were to start work on appraising the collection and advising the young J P Morgan.

Fairfax Murray was compelled by his trip to New York to miss the English Arts and Crafts Exhibition in Paris to which May Morris loaned enough of her father's treasures to fill a Morris Room. He wrote to her in Paris before he left England: 'My future plans are hazy enough, only I am removing my books and pictures such as I keep to Florence where I have built myself a library & may I hope that even if Kelmscott sees me no more that I may one day see you in Florence. I hope so; it is a very nice house that I have bought with a garden and one huge room that I have converted in to a library, and the other half in to a picture gallery. Always yr. aff. Charles Fairfax Murray.'[25] In the midst of the chaos of unpacking and displaying her Morris examples she replied immediately: 'I am so sorry you have been bad ... the Morris Room is quite splendid,' adding a few days later: 'I hope the rest on the sea will do you good in spite of 700 at dinner ... receiving the King and Queen pretty tiring and dull...' By the second week in June, Fairfax Murray was back in Paris, having crossed the Atlantic twice in less than six weeks, a little recovered from the rheumatic illness that continued to plague him: '...as you can see I am safe and sound and until a few days back in much better trim. But the damp has undone for the moment the good effects of the heat I enjoyed in New York.'[26]

Charles Fairfax Murray's most important attempt to disperse the larger part of his remaining pictures was held the following week at George Petit. The sale received a mixed response in a market unsettled by the imminence of war, and the best that might be said was that under the circumstances the results were satisfactory. The quality and breadth of taste reflected in the pictures offered are some indication of the collection he had amassed; he had by that time already given collections that might have stood on their own both to the Fitzwilliam and to Dulwich, and the walls of his two houses in Florence, and in the English family house in Chiswick, remained covered from floor to ceiling with valuable and beautiful things. The Paris sale included Rembrandt's *Portrait of his Brother*, Reynolds's *Death of Dido*, Bellini's *Toilet of Venus* (a school picture), a Gainsborough self-portrait, Botticelli's *Infant Jesus with the Virgin and St John*, a Boucher, another Rembrandt, a French fifteenth-century diptych of *La Vierge aux Donateurs*, and Anthony van Dyck's superb portrait of *Lucas Vosterman*. (Bought in after failing to reach its reserve, this was among the pictures sold at Christie's later in the year that Murray died. The war had by then ended and confidence was beginning to seep back in to the art market; the van Dyck fetched a passable premium over its Paris sale reserve.) Other pictures were moved to Florence. Shortly after the sale Fairfax Murray went to London to attend to his business there and then left for Italy. He was in Italy less than a month, travelling much of the time and leaving from Venice to London in the first week of July.

He was in Paris when war, which he had so long dreaded, was declared on 4 August 1914. For a short time travel was comparatively easy, but with each successive week the difficulties of moving among his collections, his houses and his families increased. After a short holiday in Italy during August, he returned to Paris en route for a return to New York. The trip commenced inauspiciously when the journey to Paris, which had once taken less than a day, became so extended by delays and travel restrictions that he missed his sailing from Le Havre. Nevertheless, he arrived in New York by the middle of September and settled down to work on cataloguing the Morgan pictures. He met up once again with Francis Lathrop, the American painter he used to go with to the opera after a day at Kensington Square, now 'living on fruit dipped in alcohol, for fear of microbes[27]' to his great amusement.

New York delighted and restored Fairfax Murray to something like his usual self: 'This is an extraordinary place, I am nearly used to it, as used as I can get to any place where I haven't a place of my own, but I managed through a friend to get very comfortable rooms, so am spared the hotel life which I loathe. Here people are much divided about the war, as there are so many Germans and people who have married Germans. I take no notice and never discuss the war, my coolness rather irritates the wobblers as I always assure them that there is no doubt of the issue, that it is only a matter of time. Here they are still in the condition of William the Weed himself, when he began it and didn't reckon England and Belgium at all, and look upon Germany as having a good chance of winning... They are very good natured here, I was promptly presented to one of the best clubs for a month, last time I was here I had 3 to choose from but this is better than those with one exception and that was too magnificent, the Dining Room being like the Ducal Palace at Venice for size and height – the company where I go is the happy medium, frequented by artists of all kinds – musicians, architects and painters etc... The artists have a very Boheme resort called the Salmagundi. I dined there one night with one of Tiffany's men. The shops leave us nowhere for luxury of architecture on 5th Avenue...'[28] As ever, he was ready to talk of pictures, but there was now a significant emphasis on art, not as a calling as in the old times, but as a commodity. Fairfax Murray too was conscious of this change: 'There are great collections here but I haven't bothered much about them, the fact is that I am rather blasé as to seeing things. If they were for sale and I could buy them it would be another matter.' Fairfax Murray was tiring even of the great works that had been his Grail throughout his life. The clear fall days of New York suited him, and his thoughts were turned once more to the sun of Italy, and to almost 50 years of friendship with William Spanton. 'I am leaving here I hope in the 2nd week in November but I do not expect to stay in England, in fact if practicable I shall land in Italy direct or in the south of France. It is quite warm and pleasant here and I dread the change of climate. Personally I am not pleased to be so nearly 70! You are a little nearer than I am, but a better life, and you are now I think my oldest friend, Hughes was the last near you coming as he did a few months or weeks later than you – I met him at Heatherley's.' This was his last long letter to Spanton. 'Always yours affectionately, C F Murray' he concluded. Edward Hughes had died the previous year.

Fairfax Murray made the dangerous return sea crossing late in November 1914, already planning a further visit to New York the following October. The Kaiser had told his armies leaving for the front in August that they would 'be home before the leaves fall', but the opposing armies were by now bogged down in the mud of Flanders after the inconclusive Battle of the Marne. At sea, however, the sinking of the *Lusitania* with the loss of 1,100 lives testified to the dangers from U-boats and armed merchantmen. Arriving unscathed in England instead of in France as he had intended, Fairfax Murray was forced for a time by the fighting along the Western Front to postpone his plans to go to Italy, and he remained in London until May 1915, where he experienced the first Zeppelin bombing raid on London from his apartment in Albemarle Street. He was probably safer there than in Chiswick with Dolly and the family. The anti-aircraft battery on Barnes Common broke most of the windows in Barrowgate Road but failed to impede the progress of the Zeppelin overhead.

He wrote to Samuel Bancroft in April to tell him that he had hopes of travelling to the States for a third time that fall, but also that he had been ill with a severe attack of bronchitis. This, too, was the completion of unfinished business, the closing chapter of their productive, sparring relationship; there had been a long pause in their correspondence since June 1911, when Bancroft had unwisely broadcast his opinion that William Michael Rossetti had attempted to pass off spurious copies of the *Sybilla Palmifera* and the portrait of *Mrs Morris in a Blue Dress* as his brother's. They were, as William Michael had attested, Dante Gabriel Rossetti's unfinished work which had been worked on after his death by Ford Madox Brown. Fairfax Murray's arctic rejection of the charge effectively marked the end of their collaboration. Bancroft broke the ice only in January 1914, and Murray too thawed sufficiently to reply in a carefully polite letter. They corresponded in a desultory fashion once or twice over the year, the spell broken, but Samuel Bancroft was not to read this warmer, last letter. He had died four days before.

Fairfax Murray contrived to get to Paris during May 1915 and put up, as he had so often in the past, at the Hotel Brébant et Beausejour. Here he passed two months in the company of his friend, dealer and fellow bibliophile Edouard Rahir, in the ornate, gilded Empire arcade of shops dealing in books and antiquities, the Passage des Panorames. By the end of July, he was able to obtain the necessary permissions to make his way to Italy, and he arrived in Florence in the first few days of August. He had been away from Angelica and his family in Florence for 15 months, much of the time without any contact because of war; his business affairs in Italy had been left in the hands of his eldest son, John. Fairfax Murray paid his respects to Angelica and stayed a few days in the villa at Tavarnuzze before returning to his house in the city.

He was destined not to enjoy the pleasure he had so long looked forward to, of sitting in his newly fitted library overlooking the shaded garden, surrounded by his personal collection of paintings and books, in his private residence in the via Marcilio Ficino. In August 1915 he suffered a stroke from which he took three months to recover his strength sufficiently to travel alone to Monte Carlo. There he stayed a month in the Hotel de Paris to convalesce before returning to Florence for Christmas. He wrote to Sydney Cockerell in the following January to say that he had once again spent a week in bed – a lifetime to the restless Fairfax Murray – but that he was fairly well again though not over-strong. He divided his time between his house in the via Marcilio Ficino and the family villa throughout the spring and early summer, making some progress in regaining his strength but complaining frequently that his memory had suffered from his illness of the previous August. Two letters written in June are in a clear, firm hand and he seemed to be slowly on the mend. One, to his daughter Elizabeth in London, bears the return address of Haskard's Bank in the Palazzo Antinori; Fairfax Murray continued to keep his two families carefully segregated.

He had been in Italy for ten uneven months when he suffered a second, far more serious stroke in June 1916. John and his Belgian wife, Flora, coped with the angry, helpless Fairfax Murray as he lay paralysed. In a letter to Edward Forbes, John told him of the situation: '... my father has been dangerously ill since June, and though now he is making steady progress towards recovery it will be a long time before he is well again. He had completely lost the use of his right side and he was for several weeks unable to speak... I am glad to say that he is now able to speak quite clearly which is a comfort to him as his intelligence remains as bright as ever.'[29] With extraordinary courage and an iron will, Fairfax Murray now set himself the task of regaining his independence and the use of his bent and paralysed legs. By September he was able to walk once again, although his right arm and hand remained of little use. Slowly he taught himself to manage on his own, and as he progressed a plan evolved in his mind to resolve the conflicts over his estate and possessions that he knew must inevitably arise between his Italian and English families if he did not act while he had enough strength and his faculties left to him. An Englishman at heart, he had little liking and no confidence in Italian lawyers, and he knew that he must have his affairs settled, and his Will proved, under English law.

Towards the end of September he announced to his astonished family that he would go to London. It is some indication of his unquestioned authority over Angelica and his children that no-one, dismayed as they were by his weakness, was able to dissuade him. They parted in great apprehension, and Fairfax Murray set out alone on his journey across Europe at war; feeble, driven and brave. He arrived unassisted in the centre of Paris at Edouard Rahir's door, shaken and with his right hand still useless, almost two weeks after he had set out from Florence. Rahir, although he had been warned of Fairfax Murray's intentions, was deeply shocked by his appearance and the state of health when they met, and insisted that he rest and sleep; but on 26 October Rahir wrote to John Murray to tell him that his father had insisted on struggling on to London and that nothing would deter him: 'he was so anxious to go to London that, having already reached Paris his morale was better ... he was happy to have made a great part of his journey. I accompanied him to his train, and I have had news of his arrival from one of his friends who knows Mr Agnew...'

Fairfax Murray arrived, utterly exhausted, dishevelled and completely unexpectedly, late one evening in the last week of October in Chiswick, where he had to be helped from the cab and was put straight to bed. His startling and unforeseen homecoming and his desperately low state cast a grim shadow over the household, the servants now reduced to Dolly's faithful parlourmaid Mary. They managed between them to nurse him back to some semblance of health and strength in the weeks that followed and to contain the disruption that surrounded the caged and defiant Fairfax Murray, who had seldom spent more than the odd night under his English domestic roof. The winter bombing raids were a particular trial. Brightly, Dolly would lead the family down to the cellar when the alarm was raised, the reluctant Fairfax Murray refusing to follow until the aircraft were almost directly overhead. When the night raids increased in intensity and frequency he reversed the process, retiring each evening to pass the night in the wine-cellar which he had had furnished with a fine Turkey carpet, the most comfortable chair in the house, a supply of books, candles in case of failure of the electric supply, a little table and the other comforts of a fine library. When there was a raid in progress he suffered the intrusion of the household into his new domain. Sydney Cockerell, who had seen him when he first arrived, visited him again in late November and found him still far from strong: 'It is sad to see him so broken. He is a little less nervous than he was three weeks ago, but it is obvious that he can never again be his outspoken, vigorous self',[30] adding as an afterthought, 'He gave me Gainsborough's watch.' With the New Year, Fairfax Murray removed himself to his apartment in Albemarle Street. He was not a submissive patient.

Sydney Cockerell visited him from Cambridge several times in January 1917, writing letters to his dictation and helping him put his affairs in order. Fairfax Murray resumed his flow of gifts to the Fitzwilliam, this time a Flaxman sketchbook: 'that he should foresee the rehabilitation of Flaxman does not surprise me in so steady and admirable judge of Art; that the sketch book should be a gift does not surprise me either. Murray has often shown a generosity which might be studied by richer men,' Charles Ricketts wrote.[31] Marie Stillman, now in her seventy-third year, expressed her concern that her old friend of nearly 50 years remained so prevented: 'I wish one could help him somehow but he is so unwilling to allow one to do anything.'[32] At the end of February, Cockerell noted in his diary 'called on Fairfax Murray who was unwell, just leaving for Chiswick,' where he stayed only a few days; he was soon back in Albemarle Street, and Sydney Cockerell recorded in the minuscule hand in which he wrote his diaries: 'Murray told me about his 2nd family which I have known about for 20 years.'[33]

In May, Fairfax Murray gave the Fitzwilliam six mediaeval ivories; later in the month Cockerell called once more and Murray lent the Museum his exquisite Donatello bronze of *David*. Fairfax Murray, he thought, was giving up his rooms next week, but nothing came of this idea. There was an important discussion in August between Lockett Agnew, who was Murray's executor, Sydney Cockerell and Fairfax Murray when they met to consider the best way in which to handle the division of his estate between the two families and how best to approach the scandalous issues that must, sooner or later, inevitably arise. The next day, Sydney Cockerell called and took him up to Cambridge by the 4.50 p.m. train, dined with him at his lodgings at Rider's in Trumpington Street opposite the Fitzwilliam, and saw him safely to bed. Fairfax Murray was five days in Cambridge, spending a day wandering about the Fitzwilliam, attending Evensong at King's, lunching with Monty James, the Provost, next day, and taking tea with the Master of Christ's another. Five days later, Sydney Cockerell brought him back to London: 'his visit has been a decided success.'[34]

Fairfax Murray spent occasional nights in Chiswick during September when the air-raids reached their peak; 22 airships bombed London, of which 13 were lost. On the night of 19 October the raiders lost a further five out of the eleven Zeppelins that reached London to Royal Flying Corps fighters, the remainder scattered by storms over the North Sea, and the campaign came to a halt. For the most part, however, Fairfax Murray was in his rooms in Albemarle street; Sydney Cockerell visited him on six occasions between November (when Murray gave him a parcel of Mrs Browning's letters for the Fitzwilliam) and the New Year, to write letters. Then, in January he was absent and it was not until the beginning of February that Cockerell noted 'to Albemarle St where at last I found Murray – he had been ill and looked very run down.'[35] He was at a low point again and Cockerell suggested he should 'hold back a Titian that is being packed for us but he would not hear of it.' Later in the week he 'spent some time with FM, discussed his affairs with Lockett Agnew. Called at Dickson's to arrange[36] removal of some pictures Murray has given us.' Meetings to discuss Fairfax Murray's capacity and the estate were now almost a weekly event. A letter from Sydney Cockerell, or perhaps dictated to Cockerell, alarmed the family in Italy; Eduardo, who served in the British Army throughout the war (his refusal to renounce his British joint citizenship was to cost him a long spell of imprisonment in Italy during the Second World War) arrived at Albemarle Street in the middle of February to see for himself his father's true state of health. It was evident that he was in no condition to return to Italy for the time being. To J R Holliday, Cockerell wrote: 'FM is as you know in a delicate state of health & it doesn't do to contradict him ... his memory is getting very erratic ... the strange thing is his memory is, on the whole, so good.'[37]

It had not appeared so good to him two weeks previously. In the middle of February, Sydney Cockerell brought the Donatello *David* back to Albemarle Street. Fairfax Murray's intention to send it to Florence is clearly set out in a letter to his son John in Florence, but Cockerell appeared to think that having been lent it he now had some prescriptive right to acquire it for the Fitzwilliam. This was almost an exact reprise of the overbearing tactic that had cost the Fitzwilliam the bequest of Henry Yates Thompson's manuscripts collection the previous year. Cockerell persuaded Sir Otto Beit to give £6,000 for the *David* and to bequeath it to the museum, and he was extremely put out to find, two days later, that Fairfax Murray denied that he had offered it to the museum for that sum or had any such design, which Sydney Cockerell affected to attribute to his memory having gone to pieces. In an operatic gesture he rushed to Lockett Agnew's office only to find that he had died there that morning, suddenly, from a heart attack, putting an end for the moment to all thoughts of further dispute over the Donatello. (Even so, Fairfax Murray's solicitors had to demand its return, eight months after he too was dead.)

In one bitter moment, Fairfax Murray lost one of his most intimate personal friends and his trusted Executor. Lockett Agnew was no stranger to marital entanglements and would doubtless have dealt with everything with tact and efficiency. His death was an unexpected blow not only to Fairfax Murray, but all those who wished him well and foresaw the problems that must arise. J R Holliday and Sydney Cockerell, who felt obliged to decline to succeed Lockett Agnew in the task of handling Fairfax Murray's affairs, discussed the likelihood of difficulties in letters almost as a matter of course, and no doubt the question arose in many other minds.

In the event Fairfax Murray, casting around in increasing desperation for a friend to replace him, appointed the 78-year-old T E Collcutt – his friend and colleague from the 1870s when they worked together for Collinson & Lock. Thomas Collcutt was bemused to find on Murray's death that Arthur, the eldest son and sole Trustee of the Estate, knew nothing of the family's complexities. Fairfax Murray had deceived only himself. The unfortunate result was that he clung to the belief that it would be possible for his English children to remain unaware of their illegitimacy. Neither Fairfax

Murray nor, after his death, Dolly could bring themselves to tell the children, and it was left to Marie Stillman, the closest and staunchest of Fairfax Murray's women friends, to explain the family's situation. For, despite his ingrained Victorian chauvinism – the product of the age – and for all of his detestation of humbug and conformity, he was deeply aware of the stigma of illegitimacy. He had once been genuinely concerned for the nine children of Frederick and Mary Sandys, who were unmarried, his wife being alive: 'I suppose I know more about him than any outsider, but it's a difficult subject to handle, the more so as he has several children'[38] he told Samuel Bancroft. It was a subject very close to home.

For a moment Fairfax Murray faltered. On 4 April Sydney Cockerell went to Albemarle Street as was now his habit and found that he had departed, along with his remaining pictures and books, without a word to him. He had gone to Chiswick and from there to the coast, putting up at the Officers' House on the shingle at Pevensey with Dolly to look after him. He loved the sea and the salt air and the freedom to travel that all of it stood for in his mind, and the memories of the Portsmouth Dockyard and trips to the Isle of Wight with his father. He was there for much of April and all of May, and the rest did him good. Once settled, he addressed himself to a matter of considerable irritation, Dolly writing to Henry Yates-Thompson at his dictation: 'I am told by a friend of mine who has been to Dulwich within the last few days that my picture by Andrea del Sarto is labelled as "presented in 1917." I never gave you this picture. If you look at your notes of our meeting you will not find any mention of the picture. I cannot understand how this mistake was made.'[39] His friend was the faithful Spanton. The matter was resolved within a week and Fairfax Murray, mollified, offered Dulwich Picture Gallery a Gainsborough sketch. Refreshed, he went with Dolly back to Chiswick and almost immediately announced his resolve to return to Cambridge.

In the middle of June, Fairfax Murray arrived unaided in Cambridge with the intention of staying in lodgings for an indefinite period, and put up at 4 Little St Mary's Terrace. There are five days of visits to the Fitzwilliam noted in Cockerell's Diary; J R Holliday was there and they dined together at the University Arms. 'Murray was at his ease and the talk was very interesting.'[40] Then he left suddenly 'for London by the 12.59' and was away for a week. The abrupt decision caused consternation; Sydney Cockerell was by no means certain that he was up to the journey alone, but he underestimated both Fairfax Murray's dogged perseverance and the wanderlust at the depths of his very being. He was away once again for a fortnight in August, which he spent with Dolly and the children at the house in Broadstairs that she had rented because of the war. Billy, who was now in barracks at Driffield, learning to fly before being posted to France, was the only absentee.

Then, as unexpectedly as he had left, Fairfax Murray was back in

Cambridge once more. He met Henry Yates Thompson and Sydney Cockerell took them to lunch at Trinity, where the portrait of Matthew Prior which he had given them years before hangs in the Combination Room. He spent days in the Fitzwilliam poring over the William Morris manuscripts he had given and sitting in front of his Titian. His own books and his paintings were an impossible journey away and he knew he would never see them again, but there was plenty here to give him pleasure and satisfaction.

As autumn gave way to winter which he loathed, Fairfax Murray returned to Chiswick, and on 26 October the blow fell from which he did not recover. Billy, 20 years of age and recently promoted from cadet to 2nd-Lieutenant, was killed in a flying accident with 2 RAF Fighting School, Marske by Sea, piloting a Sopwith Camel behind the lines in France. Armistice was signed two weeks later; it was one more tragic, terrible waste of a fine young man. Charles Fairfax Murray revised his Will on 11 December 1918 at 4 Albemarle Street, in the presence of his executors, Thomas Edward Collcutt and Arthur Maurice Collcutt, and his solicitor, John Downey. On 23 January Sydney Cockerell 'heard that Fairfax Murray had a stroke on Monday and was on the point of death'. Two days later he 'went to London by 4.23 to see Mrs Stillman about Fairfax Murray. I learnt that he had died at 77 Barrowgate Road at midday – Mrs Stillman was in the house at the time. Had a long talk with her and then went to see Ricketts & Shannon.' Next day he took over some of the necessary arrangements: 'wrote letters to various people about Fairfax Murray's death.'[41]

He wanted his ashes to be scattered in some quiet place without a stone or, better he said, at sea. Instead, Charles Fairfax Murray was buried beside his daughter Evelyn in Isleworth on the last day of January. The ubiquitous Sydney Cockerell wrote a neatly turned précis of the day in his diary. 'Picked up Mrs Stillman and went with her to the house at Chiswick, whence we drove to Isleworth in bitter weather. No-one except the three children of the English family,[42] Mr Collcutt the executor, ourselves and a Mr Taylor who had been a neighbour at Teddington. A dreary cemetery and a gabbled service. Went back as far as Gloucester Road with Mrs Stillman and Dover Street with Mr Collcutt, who is 78 but very alert and full of interesting talk. Both he and Mrs Stillman had known Murray for more than 40 years.'[43]

Few of the circle of friends in his later life touched the old days. There were to be sure, May Morris, William Spanton, Sydney Cockerell, Graily Hewitt, Georgiana Burne-Jones and, especially, Marie Spartali Stillman. Charles Fairfax Murray was guarded in his friendships. Few of those who knew him knew him well. Only days after he died, Georgiana Burne-Jones wrote perceptively to Sydney Cockerell: '... I have often wished I really knew him, but I did not – though I would have trusted him as a friend, and hoped that he felt the same with regard to me. But nothing ever brought us really together. I have always felt a strong sympathy with him but as I said never came very near him. He was fortunate in the friendship of that good and beautiful woman Mrs Stillman and I am glad she was near him at the last.'[44]

May Morris knew him better and loved him from her childhood: '...an intimate friend of my family ... a great expert and well-known collector of works of art of all kinds. His knowledge of all such matters was inexhaustible, his taste unerring and severe as he cared for nothing but "the very best", and did not collect mere curiosities.'[45] William Spanton wrote his professional epitaph: 'Early in life he cultivated his critical – to the neglect of his creative – faculty. The critical faculty, indispensable to the collector and dealer, is fatal to the art-student unless it is subordinated to the creative faculty.'[46] He was a consummate portrait painter and a skilful draughtsman who chose instead to make his way as *marchand amateur;* connoisseur, collector, dealer and intimate of the great names of the art world, he had few rivals in his time. His legacy is to be found in galleries and museums from St Petersburg to Melbourne.

His death passed almost unremarked by all but the tiny handful of connoisseurs, patrons and beneficiaries of his astonishing donations, and his reputation endured only in the same discerning circle until they, too, went. Charles Fairfax Murray had in death secured the anonymity he so ardently sought. It was the final achievement of the unknown Pre-Raphaelite.

Appendix
Charles Fairfax Murray and three
unpublished drafts of articles on
Giovanni Morelli

sion. 'L'Amico di Sandro' was Bernhard Berenson's confection which he later disowned, an invented artistic persona whose work did not fit easily into the accepted vision of Sandro Botticelli's style nor the work of Filippino Lippi, but of a standard above that of the obvious school picture. The mention alone of 'L'Amico' suggests that the real target of this late posthumous attack was no longer Morelli but Bernhard Berenson, a dedicated follower of Morelli's method in the early 1890s, and long after an implacable rival of Fairfax Murray. The timing may be significant; in 1907 Berenson had concluded an arrangement with Duveen that gave him 25% of the net profit on any works which he was called in to authenticate.

It seems likely that the length and detail (in the likely second of his drafts) of Fairfax Murray's notes on the National Gallery's version of the 'Virgin of the Rocks',[6] and the depth in which he compares it with the Louvre version, results from his earlier intention to write an article on this subject in collaboration with John Henry Middleton,[7] the Slade Professor at Cambridge. It is also an example of his enthusiasms overtaking his intention (which was to criticise Morelli's method and expose his 'number of blunders of the grossest description'). Morelli's notorious dismissal of the London picture as a 'sham Leonardo' provoked instead some 1650 words on this single picture, a piece of pure art criticism.

'As the previous writer upon whose book the whole of this article is founded has devoted a few words to this picture[8], I may also say something in defence of the present attribution (*to Leonardo*). Writers have been content hitherto as far as I know to either accept it & even, as if it were necessary to its acceptance, to prefer it to the Louvre picture, or to reject it summarily as a copy with variations from the original. I am not aware that anything has been advanced that is convincing either way, one critic limiting himself to the statement *expressing the opinion* that Leonardo never repeated a picture as if he had been his bosom friend & knew all about his sentiments on this subject.'

Fairfax Murray described the NG picture in minute detail, making comparisons with the Louvre version, and ended '*Putting aside for the moment the question of the preservation of the picture* A careful consideration of the differences in the two pictures forces one to the conclusion that the National Gallery picture was used by the painter as a draft of his subject & that he abandoned it when he found the alterations required in the design became too numerous & important to be made without difficulty on the dark ground. No doubt the National Gallery picture was left in a very unfinished state.' The analysis of Leonardo's technique which follows this passage demonstrates his painter's understanding of the painter's method.

'To sum up, my observations point to the conclusion that the NG panel cannot be, as has been hastily asserted, a copy of the Louvre picture nor can the Paris canvas be called a copy of ours; nor do I see any reason for the confident assertion that Leonardo never made a replica of one of his own pictures. Nothing is more common or natural for an artist than to abandon a picture when still incomplete to recast & improve the design & it seems to me specially characteristic of Leonardo's limitless care for his work.'

It is now universally accepted that Fairfax Murray and others were correct in attributing both works to Leonardo. His suggestion 'that the National Gallery picture was used by the painter as a draft of his subject & that he abandoned it' leads logically to the conclusion that in his view the London version was the earlier. At the time the inconclusive documentary evidence that forms the basis of later discussion of the two pictures had not then been discovered. Critics today are as far from unanimous as ever over this question of chronology, and the record is tantalisingly incomplete.

It is known that Leonardo and the two de Predis brothers (who were to paint the side panels) were commissioned to produce an altarpiece for the chapel of the Confraternity of the Immaculate Conception in San Francesco Grande, Milan in April 1483; and that their failure to complete the work by the date stipulated in 1485 resulted in a lengthy lawsuit in which they counter-claimed for payment. It is also known that a version of the panel was in its place in San Francesco Grande in August 1508; one school of thought holds that in settlement of the lawsuit, Leonardo and assistants painted a second version, now in the Louvre, and that only when this went to Louis XII was the, earlier, London version completed and set up in its place.

The London version was purchased by the English collector Gavin Hamilton in 1785, but the known events do not of themselves illuminate whether Hamilton bought the first version, later finished by the de Predis, or a second. If opinion is now broadly in favour of the London picture being the later it is on stylistic grounds and evidence of assistance from the de Predis. The de Predis were however party both to the original contract as well as the second, and Fairfax Murray's 'draft' Leonardo may yet prove to have been finished by them later. Unless further documentary evidence is found the question will not be settled conclusively.

Fairfax Murray's three draft articles are almost the only written evidence he left of his views on contemporary scholarship, his awareness of the limitations in knowledge of the day, and the only testimony to his own rigorous connoisseurship. They are a record also of his stimulating approach to works of art, and it is regrettable that he did not overcome his literary inhibitions and leave more witness to his authority in his time.

Endnotes

Chapter One: Early Days

1 A term first used by General William Booth, founder of the Salvation Army, in 1881

2 Fairfax Murray to William Silas Spanton, 14.6.1885, Dulwich Picture Gallery

3 William Silas Spanton, *An Art Student and his Teachers in the 60's*, p 69, Robert Scott, London 1927

4 Fairfax Murray to William Silas Spanton, 7.7.1886, Dulwich Picture Gallery

5 Fairfax Murray to William Silas Spanton, 13.1.1890, Dulwich Picture Gallery

6 A C Benson, *Memories and Friends,* John Murray 1924

7 William Silas Spanton, *An Art Student and his Teachers in the 60's*, p 63, Robert Scott, London 1927

8 Fairfax Murray, Diary 10.2.1888, Collection Frits Lugt, Institut Néerlandais, Paris

9 William Silas Spanton, *An Art Student and his Teachers in the 60's*, p 93, Robert Scott, London 1927

10 William Silas Spanton, *An Art Student and his Teachers in the 60's*, p 94, Robert Scott, London 1927; 'Murray often had difficulty in expressing himself…'

11 A C Benson, *Diaries*, ed Percy Lubbock, 11.12.1904, Hutchinson & Co, London 1926

12 Fairfax Murray to William Silas Spanton, February 1873, Dulwich Picture Gallery

13 William Silas Spanton, *An Art Student and his Teachers in the 60's*, pp 63–64, Robert Scott, London 1927

14 William Silas Spanton, *An Art Student and his Teachers in the 60's*, p 65, Robert Scott, London 1927

15 From the statement of aims of the Parliamentary Commission on the National Gallery, 1857

16 Georgiana Burne-Jones to Fairfax Murray, 16.11.1901, John Rylands Library, University of Manchester, Brit. Mss 1281

17 Fairfax Murray was of Scottish descent

18 Ruskin, *Works* XXXVI.503 n2, ed Cook & Wedderburn, G Allen 1903. Fairfax Murray trained at Thomas Heatherley's in the summer of 1866; Fairfax Murray to William Silas Spanton, November 1914, Dulwich Picture Gallery

19 Ruskin, *Works* XXXVII.669, ed Cook & Wedderburn, G Allen 1903

20 William Silas Spanton, *An Art Student and his Teachers in the 60's*, p 79, Robert Scott, London 1927

21 William Silas Spanton, *An Art Student and his Teachers in the 60's*, p 68, Robert Scott, London 1927; Spencer Stanhope also trained at Heatherley's

Chapter Two: 'On Becoming an Artist'

1 In a letter to Sir Ernest Chesnau written in 1882, Burne-Jones listed no major works between 1863 and 1867, partly the result of his practice of working on several canvasses concurrently over a period of years. He counted 60 unfinished paintings in the studio when he returned from Italy in 1870

2 Burne-Jones Papers, Fitzwilliam Museum, Cambridge

3 William Michael Rossetti, *Rossetti Papers 1862–70*, p 227. Howell bought in Burne-Jones's early work at the Anderson Rose sale on 23.3.1866. Rose was an early Pre-Raphaelite patron and Rossetti's solicitor

4 J W Mackail, *Notebooks*, London 1899

5 Dante Gabriel Rossetti to Charles Augustus Howell, 25.12.1866, Harry Ransom Humanities Research Center, Austin, Texas

6 Charles Fairfax Murray to Samuel Bancroft Jnr, 6.9.1893, Delaware Art Museum, Sloan Archive

7 Aymer Vallance, *Life of William Morris*, p 82, George Bell, 1897

8 Georgiana Burne-Jones, *Memorials of Edward Burne-Jones* i p 290, Macmillan 1904

9 Charles Harvey and Jon Press, *Art, Enterprise and Ethics; The Life and Works of William Morris*, Cass 1996

10 Penkill Papers, University of British Columbia

11 Author of *Les Affections Nerveuses Syphilitiques*, Prix Civrieux, Paris 1861

12 William Silas Spanton, *An Art Student and his Teachers in the 60's*, p 70, Robert Scott, London 1927

13 Edward Burne-Jones to Charles Fairfax Murray, July 1870; Harry Ransom Humanities Research Center; Burne-Jones had, however, written to George Howard, 26.8.1867, 'Little Murray is alternately insolent and abject, but a good boy: he has commenced a daring work for himself which if I praise he becomes intolerable and if I blame he becomes pitiable.' Castle Howard Archive J22/27/423

14 Edward Burne-Jones to Charles Fairfax Murray, 27.8.1867; Harry Ransom Humanities Research Center, Austin

15 Birmingham Museum and Art Gallery

16 Georgiana Lady Burne-Jones, *Memorials of Edward Burne-Jones* ii p 50, Macmillan 1904

17 Dante Gabriel Rossetti to Isa Craig, October 1866, Harry Ransom Humanities Research Center, Texas

18 Dante Gabriel Rossetti to Charles Fairfax Murray, March 1867, Harry Ransom Humanities Research Center, Texas. This was Charles Fairfax Murray's first commission for the Arundel Society

19 William Michael Rossetti, *Some Reminiscences*, Vol II, p 325, Brown, Langham & Co, London 1906

20 Joseph Knight, *Life of Dante Gabriel Rossetti*, W Scott, London 1887

21 Dante Gabriel Rossetti to Charles Fairfax Murray nd, Harry Ransom Humanities Research Center, Austin, Texas

22 It is unclear in the context of this entry for 3.6.1868 whether Ruskin was recording the emotional crisis in Burne-Jones's affair as has been assumed, or the continued bad weather

23 Edward Burne-Jones to Charles Fairfax Murray, 17.7.1868, Harry Ransom Humanities Research Center, Austin, Texas

24 Dante Gabriel Rossetti to Ford Madox Brown, 24.1.1869

25 Edward Burne-Jones to Dante Gabriel Rossetti, Fitzwilliam Museum

26 Dante Gabriel Rossetti to Jane Burden Morris, nd British Library

27 Edward Burne-Jones to Charles Fairfax Murray, nd 1869, Harry Ransom Humanities Research Center, Austin, Texas

28 Edward Burne-Jones to Charles Fairfax Murray, nd August ? 1870, Harry Ransom Humanities Research Center, Austin, Texas

29 Christina Rossetti to F S Ellis, 25.2.1870

30 Commissioned by William Morris as a gift to his mother, now in the William Morris Gallery, Walthamstow

31 Edward Burne-Jones to Charles Fairfax Murray, 24.12.1869, Harry Ransom Humanities Research Center, Austin, Texas

32 Edward Burne-Jones to Charles Fairfax Murray, 21.8.1871, Harry Ransom Humanities Research Center, Austin, Texas

33 Charles Fairfax Murray to Samuel Bancroft, 13.10.1895, Delaware Art Museum

34 Rowland Elzea, Occasional Paper Nr. 2, February 1980, Delaware Art Museum. Eileen Cassavetti, *Antique Collector*, March 1989 suggests without authority that the model concerned was Maria Zambaco, which would indeed have been *lèse majesté*. Nor was she a 'favourite model of Rossetti.'

35 There is a portrait of Clara Sentance in the Pierpont Morgan Library. A companion portrait of Emma is in a private collection

36 Charles Fairfax Murray to William Silas Spanton, 14.2.1876, Dulwich Picture Gallery

37 Charles Fairfax Murray to William Silas Spanton, March 1872, Dulwich Picture Gallery

38 John Rylands Library, University of Manchester

39 William Michael Rossetti 18.9.1869, *Rossetti Papers 1862–70*, p 407, Sands & Co, London 1903

40 *Lucretzia Borgia washing her hands*. Murray made two copies completed by Rossetti (Charles Fairfax Murray to Samuel Bancroft, 6.9.1893, Delaware Art Museum), one of which is in the Fogg Art Museum

41 Dante Gabriel Rossetti to Charles Fairfax Murray, ud ?April 1870, Harry Ransom Humanities Research Center; thought by Rowland Elzea to be the unfinished replica commissioned by William Graham, now in a private collection

42 Dante Gabriel Rossetti to Charles Fairfax Murray, ud c1870, Harry Ransom Humanities Research Center, Austin, Texas

43 William Silas Spanton, *An Art Student and his Teachers in the 60's*, Robert Scott, London 1927

44 Edward Burne-Jones to Charles Fairfax Murray, 10.11.1869, Harry Ransom Humanities Research Center, Austin, Texas

45 William Morris to Charles Fairfax Murray, 25.6.1870, Harry Ransom Humanities Research Center, Austin, Texas

46 J W Mackail, *Life of William Morris*, vol i p 208, Longmans, Green & Co, 1899

47 William Morris to Charles Fairfax Murray, 24.5.1869, Harry Ransom Humanities Research Center, Austin, Texas

48 J W Mackail, *Life of William Morris*, vol i p 299, Longmans, Green & Co, London 1899

49 Ruskin *Works* XXXVI p 339, Cook & Wedderburn, G Allen 1903

50 W Graham Robertson, *Time Was*, Hamish Hamilton 1931

51 Now in the Ashmolean Museum, Oxford
52 William Morris to Aglaia Coronio, 24.7.1874
53 Edward Burne-Jones to George Howard, 30.9.1870, Castle Howard Archive J22/27/224
54 Edward Burne-Jones to Charles Fairfax Murray, Nov 1870, Harry Ransom Humanities Research Center, Austin, Texas
55 William Morris to Charles Fairfax Murray, Sept. 1874, Harry Ransom Humanities Research Center, Austin, Texas
56 May Morris, Introduction to *Complete Works of William Morris,* Vol VI, Longmans, Green & Co, London 1903
57 Edward Burne-Jones to Charles Fairfax Murray, nd, Harry Ransom Humanities Research Center, Austin, Texas
58 Ionides Collection, now in the V&A Museum, London
59 Dante Gabriel Rossetti to Charles Fairfax Murray, nd ?August 1871, Harry Ransom Humanities Research Center, Austin, Texas
60 Dante Gabriel Rossetti to Charles Fairfax Murray, 22.8.1871, Harry Ransom Humanities Research Center, Austin, Texas
61 Edward Burne-Jones to Charles Fairfax Murray, Harry Ransom Humanities Research Center, Austin, Texas
62 Edward Burne-Jones to George Howard, nd July1871, Castle Howard Archive J22/27/241
63 Edward Burne-Jones to George Howard, nd Oct 1871, Castle Howard Archive J22/27/230

Chapter Three: A Visit to Italy

1 Charles Fairfax Murray to William Silas Spanton, ud March 1872, Dulwich Picture Gallery
2 Philip Webb to F S Ellis, nd 1872, Fitzwilliam Museum
3 Edward Burne-Jones to Charles Fairfax Murray, 26.12.1872, Harry Ransom Humanities Research Center, University of Texas, Austin
4 Charles Fairfax Murray to Dante Gabriel Rossetti, 8.1.1872, University of British Columbia
5 Charles Fairfax Murray to William Silas Spanton, nd January 1872, Dulwich Picture Gallery
6 Charles Fairfax Murray to William Silas Spanton, 21.2.1872, Dulwich Picture Gallery
7 Charles Fairfax Murray to William Silas Spanton, 21.2.1872, Dulwich Picture Gallery
8 Charles Fairfax Murray to William Silas Spanton, ud March 1872, Dulwich Picture Gallery
9 A C Benson, *Memories and Friends* p 212, John Murray, London 1924
10 Charles Fairfax Murray to William Silas Spanton, nd 1872, Dulwich Picture Gallery
11 Charles Fairfax Murray to William Silas Spanton, 1.3.1872, Dulwich Picture Gallery

12 There is a detailed account of the history of Bodley's work at Jesus College, and the part played by Morris, Marshall, Faulkner & Co, in *Morris & Co in Cambridge*, Duncan Robinson and Stephen Wildman, Cambridge University Press 1980

13 A C Sewter, *The Stained Glass of William Morris and his Circle,* vol i pp 47–48, Cambridge University Press 1980

14 Now in the Birmingham Museum and Art Gallery

15 A C Sewter, *The Stained Glass of William Morris and his Circle,* vol i pp 47–48, Cambridge University Press 1980

16 Charles Fairfax Murray to William Silas Spanton, 14.2.1876, Dulwich Picture Gallery

17 Richard and Hilary Myers, *William Morris Tiles,* Dennis 1996

18 Victoria & Albert Museum (E1293, 1297, 1298–1931), V&A (C104-1965), William Morris Gallery

19 Graily Hewitt, *The Illuminated Mss. of William Morris*

20 Diary of John Marshall, Professor of Anatomy at the RA Schools, 2.11.1888, '...went to her studio the other evening and found it all shut up, a man offered to ring the bell for us and while waiting supplied us with some information. There are only two studios, side by side, and one is "Mme Zambago's" like lumbago & the next Mr Burne-Jones's, "royal artist" our informant added with a flourish ... remembering the set out there was between them before it looks very odd. I feel quite disgusted that she is going on again in the old style ... if I were Mrs BJ I would have her wig off.'

21 William Michael Rossetti, *Diary,* November 1870

22 Edward Burne-Jones to Charles Fairfax Murray, 6.12.1872, Harry Ransom Humanities Research Center, University of Texas, Austin

23 John Ruskin, *Works* Vol XXX p1 ix, ed Cook & Wedderburn, G Allen 1903

24 John Ruskin, Oxford Lecture, *Ariadne Florentina*, 1874, *Works* XXII p 427, ed Cook & Wedderburn, G. Allen 1903

25 John Ruskin, 'The Shepherd's Tower' in *Mornings in Florence, being simple studies in Christian Art, for English travellers*, G Allen 1877

26 John Ruskin to Joan Severn, 3.1.1873, Ruskin Library, University of Lancaster

Chapter Four: Return to Italy

1 John Ruskin to Charles Fairfax Murray, nd 1873, Pierpont Morgan Library, New York

2 National Portrait Gallery, London

3 Philip Speakman Webb to Charles Fairfax Murray, 18.3.1873, Fitzwilliam Museum

4 Edward Burne-Jones to Charles Fairfax Murray, nd March 1873; Harry Ransom Humanities Research Center, Austin, Texas

5 George Price Boyce to Charles Fairfax Murray, John Rylands Library, University of Manchester

6 Charles Fairfax Murray to William Silas Spanton, nd March 1873, Dulwich Picture Gallery

7 Charles Fairfax Murray to William Silas Spanton, 25.5.1873, Dulwich Picture Gallery

8 Edward Burne-Jones to Charles Fairfax Murray, Good Friday 1873; Harry Ransom Humanities Research Center, Austin, Texas

9 Georgiana Burne-Jones, *Memorials of Edward Burne-Jones*, vol ii p 37, Macmillan 1904

10 John Ruskin to Charles Fairfax Murray, 3.5 and 23.5.1873, Pierpont Morgan Library

11 Charles Fairfax Murray to William Silas Spanton, 25.5.1873, Dulwich Picture Gallery

12 Now in the Ruskin Library, University of Lancaster

13 Edward Burne-Jones to Charles Fairfax Murray, 14.7.1873, Harry Ransom Humanities Research Center, Austin, Texas. Fairfax Murray was later at pains to defend Augustus Howell from claims that Rossetti forgeries had also emanated from him; Henry Treffry Dunn was more likely the culprit

14 There are for example some 215 sheets of Fairfax Murray's drawings in the Art Museum at Princeton University which were apparently purchased by their donor, Dan Fellows Platt, as by Burne-Jones. Many can be related directly to Fairfax Murray's identified paintings and few are copies from Burne-Jones

15 John Ruskin to Charles Fairfax Murray nd., Pierpont Morgan Library

16 Charles Fairfax Murray to William Silas Spanton, 22.8.1873, Dulwich Picture Gallery

17 Dante Gabriel Rossetti to Jane Morris, 17.11.1880, *Letters*, ed Bryson & Troxell, Clarendon 1971

18 Philip Webb to Charles Fairfax Murray, 13.11.1873, Fitzwilliam Museum, Cambridge

19 Philip Webb to Charles Fairfax Murray, nd January 1874, Fitzwilliam Museum, Cambridge

20 Luca Signorelli's *Last Acts and the Death of Moses*, Sistine Chapel, John Ruskin to Charles Fairfax Murray, 15.2.1874, Pierpont Morgan Library

21 John Ruskin to Charles Fairfax Murray, 12.2.1874, Pierpont Morgan Library

22 Philip Webb to Charles Fairfax Murray, 25.8.1874, Fitzwilliam Museum, Cambridge. Possibly a reference to George Basevi, the architect of the Fitzwilliam (1834) and a cousin of Benjamin Disraeli, who fell to his death from scaffolding on the west tower of Ely Cathedral in 1845

23 Edward Burne-Jones to Charles Fairfax Murray, 2.2.1874, Harry Ransom Humanities Research Center, University of Texas

24 Edward Burne-Jones to Charles Fairfax Murray, 2.2.1874, Harry Ransom Humanities Research Center, Austin, Texas.

25 Eileen Cassavetti suggests that the relationship continued in to the 1880s, citing Edward Burne-Jones's letter of introduction of Oscar Wilde to Maria Zambaco in 1883; *The Antique Collector*, Vol 60 No 3, March 1989

26 William Morris to Charles Fairfax Murray, 9.3.1874, Harry Ransom Humanities Research Center, Austin, Texas

27 Charles Fairfax Murray to William Silas Spanton, 23.3.1874, Dulwich Picture Gallery

28 Charles Fairfax Murray to William Silas Spanton, 27.3.1874 Dulwich Picture Gallery

29 R H Benson, letter to the *Times Literary Supplement*, 9.3.1919

30 John Ruskin to Charles Fairfax Murray, 29.4.1874, Pierpont Morgan Library

31 Charles Fairfax Murray to William Silas Spanton, 29.4.1874, Dulwich Picture Gallery

32 John Ruskin to Charles Fairfax Murray, 5.5.1874, Pierpont Morgan Library

33 Charles Fairfax Murray to William Silas Spanton, 7.5.1874, Dulwich Picture Gallery

34 Charles Fairfax Murray Diary, 19.5.1874, Collection Frits Lugt, Institut Néerlandais, Paris

35 John Ruskin to Charles Fairfax Murray, 2.6.1874, Pierpont Morgan Library

36 Charles Fairfax Murray to John Ruskin, 18.6.1874, Houghton Library, Harvard University, bms Am 1088 (6096)

37 John Ruskin to Charles Fairfax Murray, 3.7.1874, Pierpont Morgan Library

38 John Ruskin to Charles Eliot Norton, 20.7.1874, Houghton Library, Harvard University, bms Am 1088 (6096)

39 Charles Fairfax Murray, Diary 1874, 13.7.1874, Collection Frits Lugt, Institut Néerlandais, Paris

40 William Morris to Dante Gabriel Rossetti, 16.4.1874, *The Collected Letters of William Morris* ed. Kelvin, Princeton University Press 1984

41 Walter Theodore Watts added Dunton, to become Watts-Dunton, under the terms of a legacy

42 May Morris to Sydney Carlyle Cockerell, 11.5.1938, Hammersmith Local History Archive

43 Pass Book No. 1, Burne-Jones Papers, Fitzwilliam Museum

44 Edward Burne-Jones to Dante Gabriel Rossetti, nd 1874, Fitzwilliam Museum. This letter in typescript is among those available to Georgiana Burne-Jones when she was writing her *Memorials of Edward Burne-Jones* (and to J W Mackail in writing his *Life of William Morris*) copied from originals lent by friends, including Charles Fairfax Murray. Both chose to ignore this letter: May Morris said that she had always believed the myth of the perfect friendship between Morris and Burne-Jones, and that Fairfax Murray had shown her the correspondence in 1902, only when both were dead

45 Edward Burne-Jones to George Howard, 20.8.1874, Castle Howard Archive J22/27/276

46 Edward Burne-Jones to Charles Fairfax Murray, 5.9.1874, Harry Ransom Humanities Research Center, Austin, Texas

47 Edward Burne-Jones to George Howard, nd September 1874, Castle Howard Archive J22/27/162

48 Edward Burne-Jones to George Howard, nd late 1873, Castle Howard Archive J22/27/255

49 This letter from Edward Burne-Jones is dated in Fairfax Murray's hand, 6.10.1874

Chapter Five: Siena

1 Charles Fairfax Murray, Diary 1.6.1874, Collection Frits Lugt, Institut Néerlandais, Paris

2 Philip Webb to Charles Fairfax Murray, 25.11.1874, Fitzwilliam Museum

3 Charles Fairfax Murray, Diary, 24.1.1875, Collection Frits Lugt, Institut Néerlandais, Paris

4 William Morris to Charles Fairfax Murray, 11.3.1875, *The Collected Letters of William Morris* ed. Kelvin, Princeton University Press 1984

5 J W Mackail, *The Life of William Morris,* Longmans, Green & Co, 1899

6 John Ruskin to William Stillman, 3.5. 1874, John Rylands Library, University of Manchester

7 John Ruskin to William Stillman, 19.12.1874, John Rylands Library, University of Manchester

8 John Ruskin to Charles Fairfax Murray, 18.3.1875, Pierpont Morgan Library

9 Charles Fairfax Murray to William Silas Spanton, 25.3.1875, Dulwich Picture Gallery

10 Charles Fairfax Murray to William Silas Spanton,14.6.1875, Dulwich Picture Gallery

11 Charles Fairfax Murray, Diary, 4.5.1875, Collection Frits Lugt, Institut Néerlandais, Paris

12 Charles Fairfax Murray to William Silas Spanton, 14.6.1875, Dulwich Picture Gallery

13 William Morris to Charles Fairfax Murray, 27.5.1875, Harry Ransom Humanities Research Center, Austin, Texas; this was the year of Morris's *Acanthus Leaf* wallpaper design

14 J M Ludlow in *The Origins of the Working Men's College*, ed. Llewelyn Davies

15 John Ruskin to Charles Fairfax Murray, 21.11.1875, Pierpont Morgan Library

16 Philip Webb to Charles Fairfax Murray, 1.4.1876, Fitzwilliam Museum, Cambridge

17 The frescoes in the Choistro Verde, damaged by flood in 1966, are by Paolo Ucello

18 The frescoes in the Cappellone degli Spagnuoli, completed 1365, were attributed by della Valle in 1786 to 'Andrea da Firenze' on stylistic grounds related to frescoes in the Campo Santo in Pisa. Only in 1916 was documentary evidence discovered securely giving these frescoes to the same, Andrea Bonaiuti

19 Charles Fairfax Murray to William Silas Spanton, 10.8.1875, Dulwich Picture Gallery

20 Edward Burne-Jones to Charles Fairfax Murray, 14.8.1875, Harry Ransom Humanities Research Center, Austin, Texas

21 Walburga, Lady Paget; *Embassies of other days, and further recollections*, Vol 2 p 318, Hutchinson & Co, London 1923

22 A C Benson, *Memories and Friends*, p 210, John Murray 1924

23 Philip Webb to Charles Fairfax Murray, 23.3.1875, Fitzwilliam Museum, Cambridge

24 Walter Crane, *An Artist's Reminiscences,* Methuen 1907

25 David Sox, *Bachelors of Art*, Fourth Estate 1991

26 Edward Burne-Jones to George Howard, 2.2.1876, Castle Howard Archive, J22/27/50

27 Edward Burne-Jones to Charles Fairfax Murray, April 1871, Harry Ransom Humanities Research Center, Austin, Texas

28 Charles Fairfax Murray to William Silas Spanton, 1.2.1876, Dulwich Picture Gallery

29 Georgiana Burne-Jones to Charles Fairfax Murray, 9.1.1876, John Rylands Library, University of Manchester

30 Dr Gianni Mazzoni, *Siena between Purism and Liberty*, 1994

31 Charles Fairfax Murray to Frederick Burton, 6.12.1877, Harry Ransom Humanities Research Center, Austin, Texas

32 The volume of their correspondence alone is testimony; there are 107 letters 1873–84 from Burton to Charles Fairfax Murray in the Harry Ransom Humanities Research Center

33 NG 1147

34 Charles Fairfax Murray to Frederick Burton, 13.8.1877, National Gallery Archives

35 Charles Fairfax Murray to Frederick Burton, 25.12.1877, National Gallery Archives

36 Dante Gabriel Rossetti to Jane Burden Morris, 19.4.1878, *Letters*, ed Bryson & Troxell, Clarendon 1971

37 Dante Gabriel Rossetti to Jane Burden Morris, 27.11.1877, *Letters*, ed Bryson & Troxell, Clarendon 1971

38 A first edition of Ascanio Condivi's *Life of Michelangelo* published in 1553

39 Frederick Burton to Charles Eastlake, 26.9.1878, National Gallery Archive

40 John Ruskin to Charles Fairfax Murray, 30.7.1878 and 7.8.1878, Pierpont Morgan Library

41 Charles Fairfax Murray to Frederick Burton, 13.8.1877, National Gallery Archive

42 Frederick Burton to Charles Fairfax Murray, 15.12.1878, Harry Ransom Humanites Research Center, Austin, Texas

Chapter Six: Partings, Ruskin and Rossetti

1 Charles Herbert Moore spent winter 1876–77 in Venice with Ruskin, whom he had first met at Oxford, introduced by Charles Eliot Norton

2 John Ruskin to Charles Eliot Norton

3 John Ruskin to Charles Fairfax Murray, 28.2.1877, Pierpont Morgan Library

4 John Ruskin to Charles Fairfax Murray, 8.3.1877, Pierpont Morgan Library

5 John Ruskin to Charles Fairfax Murray, 4.4.1877, Pierpont Morgan Library

6 Charles Fairfax Murray, Diary, 24.4.1877, Collection Frits Lugt, Institut Néerlandais, Paris. This portrait has not been found

7 John Ruskin to Charles Fairfax Murray, 9.4.1877, Pierpont Morgan Library

8 John Ruskin to Charles Fairfax Murray, 2.6.1877, Pierpont Morgan Library

9 John Ruskin to Charles Fairfax Murray, 17.7.1877, Pierpont Morgan Library

10 Charles Fairfax Murray, Diary, 26.6.1877, Collection Frits Lugt, Institut Néerlandais, Paris

11 Charles Fairfax Murray, Diary, 7.7.1877, Collection Frits Lugt, Institut Néerlandais, Paris

12 The Ispettore of the Accademia, Venice and a noted conservator and restorer. In his official capacity Botti was also responsible for the issue of permits for the export of works of art

13 National Gallery of Scotland 2238, now attr. Workshop of Verrocchio, possibly by Domenico Ghirlandaio

14 John Ruskin *Fors* July 1877, *Works* XXI, ed Cook & Wedderburn, G. Allen 1903

15 Charles Fairfax Murray, Diary, 14.11.1877, Collection Frits Lugt, Institut Néerlandais, Paris

16 John Ruskin to Charles Fairfax Murray, 22.12.1877, Pierpont Morgan Library

17 Charles Fairfax Murray to Sir Frederick Burton, 4.1.1878, National Gallery Archive

18 Charles Fairfax Murray to William Silas Spanton, 17.3.1878, Dulwich Picture Gallery

19 John Ruskin to Charles Fairfax Murray, 20.3.1879, Pierpont Morgan Library

20 John Ruskin to Charles Fairfax Murray, 13.8.1879, Pierpont Morgan Library

21 John Ruskin to Charles Fairfax Murray, 15.8.1879, Pierpont Morgan Library

22 John Ruskin to Charles Fairfax Murray, 15.8.1879, Pierpont Morgan Library

23 John Ruskin to Charles Fairfax Murray, nd, Pierpont Morgan Library

24 Frederic Leighton to Charles Fairfax Murray, 12.11.1879, John Rylands Library, University of Manchester

25 Now in the National Gallery of Art, Washington, where it is attributed to Andrea della Robbia

26 John Ruskin to Charles Fairfax Murray, 25.12.1879, Pierpont Morgan Library

27 John Ruskin, Diary, 19.1.1880

28 John Ruskin to Charles Fairfax Murray, 17.5.1880, Pierpont Morgan Library

29 John Ruskin to Charles Fairfax Murray, 30.6.1880, Pierpont Morgan Library

30 John Ruskin to Charles Fairfax Murray, 1.8.1880, Pierpont Morgan Library

31 John Ruskin to Charles Fairfax Murray, 18 and 19.1.1881, Pierpont Morgan Library

32 John Ruskin to Charles Fairfax Murray, 3.9.1881, Pierpont Morgan Library

33 John Ruskin to Charles Fairfax Murray, 18.10.1881 and 20.10.1881, Pierpont Morgan Library

34 John Ruskin to Charles Fairfax Murray, 23.4.1882, Pierpont Morgan Library

35 John Ruskin to Charles Fairfax Murray, 25.4.1882, Pierpont Morgan Library

36 John Ruskin to Charles Fairfax Murray, 27.8.1882, Pierpont Morgan Library

37 John Ruskin to Charles Fairfax Murray, 28.10.1882, Pierpont Morgan Library

38 John Ruskin to Charles Fairfax Murray, 16.1.1883, Pierpont Morgan Library

39 John Ruskin to Charles Fairfax Murray, 16.1.1883, Pierpont Morgan Library

40 Charles Fairfax Murray to John Ruskin, 20.1.1883, Pierpont Morgan Library

41 John Ruskin to Charles Fairfax Murray, nd 1883, Pierpont Morgan Library

42 Charles Fairfax Murray to Thomas Wise, 23.10.1894, Harry Ransom Humanities Research Center, Austin, Texas

43 Charles Fairfax Murray to William Silas Spanton, Dulwich Picture Gallery

44 H C Marillier, *Dante Gabriel Rossetti, an illustrated memorial of his Art and Life,* p 183, Geo Bell 1890

45 Jane Burden Morris to Dante Gabriel Rossetti, nd, *Letters*, ed Bryson & Troxell, Clarendon 1971

46 Dante Gabriel Rossetti to Jane Burden Morris, nd, *Letters*, ed Bryson & Troxell, Clarendon 1971

47 Dante Gabriel Rossetti to Jane Burden Morris, 9.10.1879, *Letters*, ed Bryson & Troxell, Clarendon 1971

48 Dante Gabriel Rossetti to Jane Burden Morris 25.7.1879 *Letters*, ed Bryson & Troxell, Clarendon 1971

49 Dante Gabriel Rossetti to Jane Burden Morris, 25.7.1879, *Letters*, ed Bryson & Troxell, Clarendon 1971

50 Dante Gabriel Rossetti to Jane Burden Morris, August 1879, *Letters*, ed Bryson & Troxell, Clarendon 1971

51 Dante Gabriel Rossetti to Jane Burden Morris, 15.8.1879, *Letters*, ed Bryson & Troxell, Clarendon 1971

52 Dante Gabriel Rossetti to Charles Fairfax Murray, 2.5.1880, Harry Ransom Humanities Research Center

53 Dante Gabriel Rossetti to Charles Fairfax Murray, 2.5.1880, Harry Ransom Humanities Research Center

54 Dante Gabriel Rossetti to Charles Fairfax Murray 7.1.1880, Harry Ransom Humanities Research Center

55 Rossetti's 'big picture' was *Dante's Dream*, which previously had been sold first to Graham and then to Valpy, neither of whom had a wall large enough to hang it

Chapter Seven: Florence

1 Dante Gabriel Rossetti to Jane Burden Morris, 28.8.1879, *Letters*, ed Bryson & Troxell, Clarendon 1970

2 William Michael Rossetti, Diary, 7.1.1873, Hurst & Blackett, London 1900

3 Edward Burne-Jones to Charles Fairfax Murray, January nd 1879, Harry Ransom Humanities Research Center, Austin, Texas

4 Burne-Jones's Pass Book, 20.1.1879, Fitzwilliam Museum, Cambridge

5 Charles Fairfax Murray to William Silas Spanton, nd early 1881, Dulwich Picture Gallery

6 Charles Herbert Moore to Charles Fairfax Murray, 5.3.1878, John Rylands Library, University of Manchester

7 Royal W Leith, foreword to *A Quiet Devotion, the Life of Henry Roderick Newman*, the Jordan-Volpe Gallery, New York 1996. Henry Newman's books are now in the Houghton Library, Cambridge MA

8 Ruskin criticised Jarves in a letter to Charles Eliot Norton, omitting to mention his own criticisms of Newman to Joseph Lindon Smith

9 William Morris, letter to the *Daily News*, 21.10.1879

10 Charles Fairfax Murray to William Silas Spanton, 16.1.1880, Dulwich Picture Gallery

11 William Morris to Jane Burden Morris, 31.3 nd c1881, British Library mss.

12 Charles Fairfax Murray to William Silas Spanton, March 1872, Dulwich Picture Gallery

13 Henry Wallis (1830–1916), painter of *The Death of Chatterton* (1856) and *The Stonebreaker* (1857). Founder member of the Hogarth Club with George Price Boyce (1826–97); through Boyce, Wallis came in to Rossetti's orbit in the early days of the PRB. He was authoritative on majolica, about which he published several monographs

14 Charles Fairfax Murray to Newman Marks, Secretary to SPAB, 3.5.1881, ASPAB archive.

15 A. Tolomei in *La Capella degli Scrovegni e l'Arena di Padova*

16 Edward Burne-Jones to Charles Fairfax Murray, 12.5.1879, Harry Ransom Humanities Research Center, Austin, Texas

17 Edward Burne-Jones to George Howard, nd June 1879, Castle Howard Archive, J22/27/252

18 Dante Gabriel Rossetti to Jane Burden Morris, nd, *Letters*, ed Bryson & Troxell, Clarendon 1971

19 Edward Burne-Jones to Charles Fairfax Murray, 23.10.1880, Harry Ransom Humanities Research Center, Austin, Texas

20 Jane Burden Morris to Dante Gabriel Rossetti, 30.4.1881, *Letters*, ed Bryson & Troxell, Clarendon 1971

21 Presented to the Walker Art Gallery, Liverpool in 1926 by his son Arthur Rhodes Murray

22 Private collection, 1884

23 Frick Collection, New York

24 Frick Collection, New York

25 Charles Fairfax Murray to Wilhelm von Bode, 2.1.1885, Staatliche Museen Berlin, Zentral Archiv Nachlaß Bode Nr. 3832

26 Between 1882 and 1884, the National Gallery purchased six paintings from Fairfax Murray, *The Marriage of the Virgin* by Niccolo Buonaccorso de Siena (NG1109), *The Crucifixion* attr. Andrea del Castagno (NG1138), a *Virgin and Child with Saints Peter and Catherine of Siena and a Carthusian Donor* of Giovanni Bazzi – 'Il Sodoma' (NG1144), two Duccio's *The Annunciation* and *The Marriage of the Virgin* (NG1139 and 1140) and a Florentine School portrait of *A Bearded Man* attributed to Pontormo (NG1150)

27 Sir Frederick Burton to Charles Fairfax Murray, 29.1.1883 and 30.1.1883, National Gallery/Harry Ransom Humanities Research Center, Austin, Texas

28 Dr Wilhelm von Bode, the German expert on Italian art was first assistant and then (1883) Director of the Sculpture Department of the Berlin Museum. Appointed to Director of Paintings (the Gemäldegalerie) in 1903 and Director General in 1905 of the Prussian State Museums, and the Kaiser Friedrich Museum in Berlin

29 Sir Frederick Burton to Charles Fairfax Murray, 4.1.1884, Harry Ransom Humanities Research Center, Austin, Texas

30 Sir Frederick Burton to Charles Fairfax Murray, 29.1.1884, Harry Ransom Humanities Research Center, Austin, Texas

31 Sir Frederick Burton to Charles Fairfax Murray, 5.2.1884, Harry Ransom Humanities Research Center, Austin, Texas

32 Sir Frederick Burton to Charles Fairfax Murray, 14.3.1884, Harry Ransom Humanities Research Center, Austin, Texas

33 NG1143. Ridolfo Ghirlandaio (1483–1561), the son of Domenico Ghirlandaio, who numbered Michelangelo among his pupils

34 Sir Frederick Burton to Charles Fairfax Murray, 30.1.1883, Harry Ransom Humanities Research Center, Austin, Texas

35 Sir Frederick Burton to Charles Fairfax Murray, 8.3.1883, Harry Ransom Humanities Research Center, Austin, Texas

36 Sir Frederick Burton to Charles Fairfax Murray, 22.3.1883, Harry Ransom Humanities Research Center, Austin, Texas

37 Sir Frederick Burton to Charles Fairfax Murray, 3.4.1883, Harry Ransom Humanities Research Center, Austin, Texas

38 Sir Frederick Burton to Charles Fairfax Murray, 5.4.1883, Harry Ransom Humanities Research Center, Austin, Texas

39 Sir Frederick Burton to Charles Fairfax Murray, 11.5.1883, Harry Ransom Humanities Research Center, Austin, Texas

40 The Sodoma *Madonna and Child with Sts Peter and Catherine of Siena*, NG1144. Frederick Burton to Charles Fairfax Murray, 17.5.1883, Harry Ransom Humanities Research Center, Austin, Texas

41 NG 1139, *Annunciation*, and NG 1140, *Jesus Opens the Eyes of a Man Born Blind*

42 Charles Fairfax Murray to William Silas Spanton, 4.2.1884, Dulwich Picture Gallery

43 Charles Fairfax Murray to William Silas Spanton, 27.8.1885, Dulwich Picture Gallery

44 Philip Webb to Charles Fairfax Murray, 8.9.1885, Fitzwilliam Museum

Chapter Eight: Return to London

1 Charles Fairfax Murray, Diary, 30.1.1886, Collection Frits Lugt, Institut Néerlandais, Paris

2 Among Charles Fairfax Murray's papers at his death were 77 letters of Frederick Sandys to Charles Augustus Howell, almost without exception desperate pleas for money. Fairfax Murray bought them from Kitty Howell's estate to keep them out of the public domain, out of concern for the children's welfare. John Rylands Library, University of Manchester

3 see Simon Reynolds, *William Blake Richmond*, Norwich 1995

4 see Caroline Dakers, *The Little Holland Park Circle, Artists and Victorian Society*, Yale University Press 1999

5 Charles Fairfax Murray to William Silas Spanton, 10.8.1875, Dulwich Picture Gallery. The picture was exhibited at the Royal Academy, 1875

6 G C Williamson in *Murray Marks and his Friends*, John Lane, London & New York 1919, implies without supporting evidence that Marks introduced Charles Fairfax Murray to Dante Gabriel Rossetti. Charles Augustus Howell and Murray Marks were both prominent members of Rossetti's circle in the mid-1860s

7 Emily Eden. It was believed at time that the site was Nineveh, later discovered nearby

8 Charles Fairfax Murray to William Silas Spanton, 27.3.1878, Dulwich Picture Gallery

9 Charles Fairfax Murray to William Silas Spanton, 9.11.1885, Dulwich Picture Gallery

10 Charles Fairfax Murray to Samuel Bancroft Jnr, 9.10.1909, Delaware Art Museum, Sloan Archive

11 Charles Fairfax Murray, Notebook, private collection

12 Frits Lugt, recalling a conversation with Charles Fairfax Murray c1905 to Felice Stampfle of the Pierpont Morgan Library in 1965. Transcript of Ms Stampfle's notes, in the Collection Frits Lugt, Institut Néerlandais, Paris

13 Delaware Art Museum

14 Reproduced in *The English Pre-Raphaelite Painters,* Percy Bate, Bell 1901

15 Charles Fairfax Murray to Wilhelm von Bode, 3.3.1881, Staatliche Museen von Berlin, Zentralarchiv Nachlaß Bode Nr 3832

16 Marie Spartali Stillman to Charles Fairfax Murray, from 32 Terne, Rome 19.11.1889

17 In 1869 Giovanni Milanesi published contemporary documents in a paper *Documenti dei lavori fatti da Andrea Orcagna nel Duomo d'Orvieto,* casting doubt on Andrea Orcagna's involvement with these mosaics, signed JOANNES ET UGOLINUS DE URBEVETERI MCCCLXV (1365), citing the dates of di Cioni's residence in Orvieto as *capomaestro,* 1358–62. Joannes, Giovanni Leonardelli, a Francisan friar, was employed there as a mosaicist continuously from March 1360 to February 1370. Orcagna, employed to supervise the mosaic decoration of the west front, would have been deeply involved in the work, though it was probably incomplete when he left Orvieto. Luigi Fumi's original verdict in *Il Duomo d'Orvieto,* published in 1891 when the mosaic was still in Italy, was that 'it ... shows clearly the Giottoesque manner of Orcagna'. He made extensive use of Milanesi's article in his later rebuttal in *Rivista d'Arte* November 1905, but it has been generally accepted that the mosaic is at least in part Orcagna's work, commenced under his direction and probably to his designs.

18 On R H Benson's death in 1927, his collection passed in a single transaction to Joseph Duveen. Three of his Duccio predella panels are respectively in the Frick Collection in New York, in the Kimbell Art Museum, Fort Worth and in the National Gallery of Art, Washington DC (Samuel H Kress Collection). The fourth is in the Thyssen-Bornamisza Collection

19 Charles Fairfax Murray to Wilhelm von Bode, 21.1.1885, Staatliche Museen von Berlin, Zentralarchiv Nachlaß Bode Nr 3832

20 Charles Fairfax Murray to Wilhelm von Bode, 21.1.1885, Staatliche Museen von Berlin, Zentralarchiv Nachlaß Bode Nr 3832

21 Charles Fairfax Murray to Wilhelm von Bode, 17.7.1885, Staatliche Museen von Berlin, Zentralarchiv Nachlaß Bode Nr 3832

22 Charles Fairfax Murray to Wilhelm von Bode, 20.5.1893, Staatliche Museen von Berlin, Zentralarchiv Nachlaß Bode Nr 3832

23 Charles Fairfax Murray to Wilhelm von Bode, 11.4.1886, Staatliche Museen von Berlin, Zentralarchiv Nachlaß Bode Nr 3832

24 Charles Fairfax Murray to Wilhelm von Bode, 6.1.1896, Staatliche Museen von Berlin, Zentralarchiv Nachlaß Bode Nr 3832

25 Charles Fairfax Murray to Wilhelm von Bode, 8.2.1904, Staatliche Museen von Berlin, Zentralarchiv Nachlaß Bode Nr 3832

26 Richard Norton to Mrs Isabella Stewart Gardner, 16.9.1898, Isabella Stewart Gardner Museum Archives, Boston

27 Wilhelm von Bode to Charles Fairfax Murray, April 1914, John Rylands Library, University of Manchester

28 Edward Waldo Forbes, *Art Notes*, Ed IV Vol I p 38. (now Rondinelli, Fogg 1902.20)

29 Edward Waldo Forbes, *Art Notes*, Ed IV Vol I pp 41–44

30 More than one cabinet was made to this design; one shown at Vienna and purchased by Prince Lichtenstein, a client of Charles Fairfax Murray's, was later wrongly attributed to Edward Burne-Jones. There is no reason to doubt the contemporary attribution to Fairfax Murray (Walter Smith, *Examples of Household Taste*, R Worthington, New York 1877). Although living in Italy from 1873, Fairfax Murray painted at least 26 panels for George Lock in 1874–5 and many others earlier and later

31 Now in the Detroit Institute of Art

32 Fairfax Murray's diary for 1874 survives; neither he nor Ruskin mention Mackmurdo's presence in Rome. The possibility rests on Mackmurdo's own account

33 Anderson Rose, Rossetti's solicitor, had an extensive collection of Rossetti's drawings; Fairfax Murray was able to outbid Ricketts and Shannon in spite of surprisingly low prices at his sale

34 For a critical examination of British artists and schools, their aims and dissensions between the end of the nineteenth century and the First World War, see John Christian's Introduction to *The Last Romantics*, Barbican, London 1989

35 Charles Fairfax Murray to William Silas Spanton, 10.10.1913, Dulwich Picture Gallery

36 Fairfax Murray took Samuel Bancroft to meet her in 1892. Despite 15 years domicile in Italy, Fairfax Murray remained in contact with the survivors of his early days with Dante Gabriel Rossetti and William Morris. He was in touch with George Campfield, the first foreman of Morris, Marshall, Faulkner & Co, as late as 1903

37 William Silas Spanton, *An Art Student and his Teachers in the 60's*, Robert Scott, London 1927

38 William Silas Spanton, *An Art Student and his Teachers in the 60's*, Robert Scott, London 1927

Chapter Nine: 'How happy could I be with either...

1 Now in the Birmingham Museum and Art Gallery

2 Charles Fairfax Murray to William Silas Spanton, 17.4.1885, Dulwich Picture Gallery

3 Philip Speakman Webb to Charles Fairfax Murray, 30.4.1885, Fitzwilliam Museum

4 Philip Speakman Webb to Charles Fairfax Murray, 30.6.1885, Fitzwilliam Museum

5 Philip Speakman Webb to Charles Fairfax Murray, 23.10.1885, Fitzwilliam Museum
6 Charles Fairfax Murray to Dante Gabriel Rossetti, 28.1.1880, University of British Columbia. The dealer in question was Giuseppe Baslini, a favoured advisor to Layard and a friend of Giovanni Morelli
7 Charles Fairfax Murray to William Silas Spanton, 16.1.1887, Dulwich Picture Gallery
8 Charles Fairfax Murray to William Silas Spanton, 3.1.1887, Dulwich Picture Gallery
9 Charles Fairfax Murray, Diary 17.11.1886, Collection Frits Lugt, Institut Néerlandais,Paris
10 Charles Fairfax Murray to William Silas Spanton, nd April 1886, Dulwich Picture Gallery
11 Bombay Presidency Pension Records, Oriental & India Office papers, B. Library, where General Bates's career in India from his arrival in 1841 can be traced. He died at Shoeburyness in 1902
12 There are drawings of Blanche with a lute, sketches for a figure in *The Concert*, in the Ashmolean Museum, Oxford
13 Jean Strouse, *Morgan, American Financier*, Harvill Press, London, 1998
14 Marie Stillman to Sydney Carlyle Cockerell, 25.6.1919, British Library Add MS. 52754
15 Georgiana Burne-Jones to Charles Fairfax Murray, 13.11.1913, John Rylands Library, University of Manchester
16 Philip Webb to Ernest Gimson, 10.4.1899, Courtauld Institute, Webb papers
17 Sydney Carlyle Cockerell, Diary, 6.12.1913, British Library Add. MS. 52650
18 Sydney Carlyle Cockerell, Diary, 6.12.1913, British Library Add. MS. 52650

Chapter Ten: The Critics

1 Giorgio Vasari (1511–74), architect and painter, *Le Viti de più eccellenti architetti, pittori et scultori italiani*, first published in 1550. The *Lives of the Artists* was expanded and republished in 1568
2 Clarence Cooke writing in the *New York Tribune* in 1871
3 A C Benson, *Memories and Friends*, John Murray 1924
4 Charles Fairfax Murray to William Silas Spanton, 25.3.1875, Dulwich Picture Gallery
5 Harry Quilter, *What's What*, 1902
6 Charles Fairfax Murray to William Silas Spanton, 9.11.1885, Dulwich Picture Gallery
7 A C Benson, *Memories and Friends* John Murray, 1924
8 Lockett Agnew, 3.12.1912, giving evidence to the Curzon Committee appointed by the Trustees of the National Gallery to enquire in to the retention of important pictures in this country, Parliamentary Reports XXIX 1914–16
9 Jacob Burckhardt, *Die Kultur der Renaissance in Italien*, Schweighauser, Basel 1860
10 Als from Charles Fairfax Murray to Giovanni Battista Cavalcaselle are in the Biblioteca Marciana, Venice; those from Cavalcaselle to Murray are in the Huntington Library, San Marino, CA

11 NG1147

12 Edward Burne-Jones to Lord Rosebery, 8.4.1894; Rosebery Papers, National Library of Scotland Ms10150

13 For a full account of this correspondence, see Paul Tucker, '*Giovanni Battista Cavalcaselle, John Ruskin e Charles Fairfax Murray: interlocutori e antagonisti*' in: *Giovanni Battista Cavalcaselle, conoscitore e conservatore*, ed. A. C. Tommasi, Venezia: Marsilio, 1998

14 Marie Stillman to Charles Fairfax Murray, 19.11 nd, c 1885, from 32 Bocca Leone, Rome. John Rylands Library, University of Manchester

15 From one version of the discarded texts in the possession of Fairfax Murray's descendants in Italy; there is another in the Harry Ransom Humanities Research Center, Austin, Texas, c1894. None is dated

16 Giovanni Morelli, *Italian Painters; Critical Studies of their Works*, trans. Ffoulkes, with a foreword by Sir Austen Henry Layard, John Murray, 1892

17 Gustav Friedrich Waagen (1794–1868), Director of the Berlin Museum from 1832. Authoritative on works of art in private collections in Great Britain, he was consulted on the future direction of the National Gallery in 1853. Although many of his attributions failed to survive later critical scrutiny, he was nevertheless an important figure

18 Wilhelm von Bode, *Monthly Review*, November 1891

19 John Henry Middleton was an archaeologist, a friend of William Morris, who met him on his second visit to Iceland, and later married Bella Stillman. He was Slade Professor at Cambridge until 1888 when he was appointed Director of the Fitzwilliam, and he became Director of the South Kensington Museum in 1893

20 National Art Library Eng. Mss. 86.QQ Box I (b); Fairfax Murray here anticipates Berenson by 30 years

21 A C Benson, *Memories and Friends*, John Murray 1924

22 Charles Fairfax Murray to William Silas Spanton, 9.11.1885, Dulwich Picture Gallery

23 R H Benson to Charles Fairfax Murray, 29.8.1891, John Rylands Library, University of Manchester

24 Charles Fairfax Murray to Wilhelm von Bode, 20.5.1893, Staatliche Museen von Berlin, Zentralarchiv Nachlaß Bode Nr 3832

25 Charles Fairfax Murray, draft of an unpublished article c1902, Harry Ransom Humanities Research Center, University of Texas

26 Joseph Lindon Smith, known also as Zozo, was a landscape painter, a pupil of Charles Moore. He undertook a number of commissions in Europe for Mrs Gardner, acting as her scout for significant purchases of antiquities as well as pictures to add to her collection at Fenway Court. Small in stature, he also made copies and restored paintings for Mrs Gardner, who called him 'my gnome'

27 The Turenne version is catalogued among the replicas of the Chigi 'Madonna' but is not identified as a modern copy

28 Bernhard Berenson, unsigned article in the *Saturday Review*, 26.2.1898

29 Charles Fairfax Murray to Edward Waldo Forbes, 29.4.1916, Fogg Museum Archives

30 Charles Fairfax Murray to Robert Langton Douglas, 30.9.1904, John Rylands Library, University of Manchester

31 Charles Fairfax Murray to Robert Langton Douglas, 25.11.1904, John Rylands Library, University of Manchester

32 Robert Langton Douglas to Charles Fairfax Murray, 8.9.1906, John Rylands Library, University of Manchester

Chapter Eleven: High Water 1885–1900

1 John Henry Middleton to Charles Fairfax Murray, 28.12.1886, Fitzwilliam Museum, Cambridge

2 A G Dew-Smith to Charles Fairfax Murray from Trinity, 23.1.1887, John Rylands Library, University of Manchester

3 *Catologo dei libri poseduti da Charles Fairfax Murray provenienti dalla bibliotheca del Marchese Girolamo d'Adda*, 62 copies printed, of which 12 were on parchment, published London 1899 and 1902

4 Charles Fairfax Murray to William Silas Spanton, 26.7.1892, Dulwich Picture Gallery

5 *Catalogue of a collection of Early French books in the Library of Charles Fairfax Murray*, H W Davies, London 1910

6 *Catalogue of a Collection of Early German books in the Library of Charles Fairfax Murray*, H W Davies, London 1913

7 *Bernhard von Breydenbach and his journey to the Holy Land, 1483–4*, H. W. Davies, London 1911

8 Edward Burne-Jones to Charles Fairfax Murray, 11.5.1892, Harry Ransom Humanities Research Center, Austin, Texas

9 William Morris to Charles Fairfax Murray, 1.5.1891, Harry Ransom Humanities Research Center, Austin, Texas

10 William Silas Spanton, *An Art Student and his Teachers in the 60's*, p 63, Robert Scott, London 1927

11 Sir William Gregory to George Howard, 12.6.1889, Castle Howard Archive

12 The fourth was withdrawn from sale on William Agnew's advice, as being inferior in execution to the others. Fairfax Murray was acting in concert with Agnew's as early as June 1890; his prospective buyer was von Bode

13 Thomas Armstrong to George Howard, 14.6.1889, Castle Howard Archive

14 George Howard, 9th Earl of Carlisle, to Charles Fairfax Murray, 16.6.1889, John Rylands Library, University of Manchester

15 Lord Darnley to William Agnew, nd, National Gallery Archive

16 George Agnew to Charles Fairfax Murray, 14.3.1890, John Rylands Library, University of Manchester Eng Mss 1281

17 Duke of Portland to R H Benson, 9.2.1892, John Rylands Library, University of Manchester

18 Duke of Portland to R H Benson, 13.3.1892, John Rylands Library, University of Manchester

19 Duke of Portland to Charles Fairfax Murray, 31.1.1895, John Rylands Library, University of Manchester

20 Lord Beauchamp to Charles Fairfax Murray, 1.1.1902, John Rylands Library, University of Manchester

21 *St James's Gazette*, 19.1.1894
22 Charles Fairfax Murray to Wilhelm von Bode, 20.1.1894, Staatliche Museen Berlin, Zentral Archiv Nachlaß Bode Nr. 3832
23 Sir Edward Burne-Jones to Charles Fairfax Murray, 21.11.1893, Harry Ransom Humanities Research Center, Austin, Texas.
24 William Morris to the Trustees of the National Gallery, nd, National Gallery Archive
25 Edward Poynter became PRA during his term as Director of the National Gallery. Frederic Lord Leighton, PRA, who regarded Poynter's appointment to the Gallery as a disaster, died early in 1896 and was succeeded by Sir John Everett Millais, who died 13.8.1896 after less than six months in office. His successor was Sir Edward Poynter
26 Lord Rosebery's papers: National Library of Scotland; MS 10150
27 Edward Burne-Jones to Lord Rosebery, 8.4.1894; Rosebery Papers, National Library of Scotland MS 10150
28 W Lockett Agnew to Samuel Bancroft Jnr, 26.6.1894, Sloan Archive, Delaware Art Museum
29 Charles Fairfax Murray to Wilhelm von Bode, 27.5.1895, Staatliche Museen Berlin, Zentral Archiv Nachlaß Nr. 3832
30 Charles Fairfax Murray to Wilhelm von Bode, 11.12.1895, Staatliche Museen Berlin, Zentral Archiv Nachlaß Nr. 3832
31 Charles Fairfax Murray to Edward Poynter, 7.7.1902: NG 1699, now attributed to Michiel Nouts
32 Henry B Burton to Charles Fairfax Murray, 15.6.1900, John Rylands Library, University of Manchester
33 Edward Burne-Jones to Charles Fairfax Murray, 13.10.1891, Harry Ransom Humanities Research Center, Austin, Texas
34 Edward Burne-Jones to Charles Fairfax Murray, 25.1.1893, Harry Ransom Humanities Research Center, Austin, Texas
35 Edward Burne-Jones to Charles Fairfax Murray, 25.1.1893, Harry Ransom Humanities Research Center, Austin, Texas
36 Edward Burne-Jones to Charles Fairfax Murray, 12.8.1897, Harry Ransom Humanities Research Center, Austin, Texas
37 Edward Burne-Jones to Charles Fairfax Murray, 13.8.1897, Harry Ransom Humanities Research Center, Austin, Texas
38 Edward Burne-Jones to Charles Fairfax Murray, nd April 1898, Harry Ransom Humanities Research Center, Austin, Texas
39 Edward Burne-Jones to Charles Fairfax Murray, 6.5.1898, Harry Ransom Humanities Research Center, Austin, Texas
40 Edward Burne-Jones to Charles Fairfax Murray, 28.8.1893, Harry Ransom Humanities Research Center, Austin, Texas
41 Georgiana Burne-Jones, *Memorials of Edward Burne-Jones*, vol ii, p 341, Macmillan 1904
42 Philip Speakman Webb to Charles Fairfax Murray, 3.12.1894, Fitzwilliam Museum, Cambridge
43 Philip Speakman Webb to Charles Fairfax Murray, 3.1.1895, Fitzwilliam Museum, Cambridge

44 Philip Speakman Webb to Charles Fairfax Murray, 3.1.1895, Fitzwilliam Museum, Cambridge

45 Philip Speakman Webb to Charles Fairfax Murray, 8.2.1895, Fitzwilliam Museum, Cambridge

46 Now in the Delaware Art Museum, Wilmington

Chapter Twelve: Nunc Dimittis

1 Georgiana Burne-Jones to Charles Fairfax Murray, 7.1.1899, John Rylands Library, University of Manchester

2 The monetary equivalent of £7,500,000 in 1995, without allowing for inflation in the art market since 1905

3 A C Benson, *Memories and Friends*, John Murray 1924

4 Fairfax Murray selected the 50 *Old Italian Masters* engraved on woodblocks by Timothy Cole, published with accompanying essays by William Stillman in 1895 together with editorial footnotes, some clarifying and others contradicting Stillman's text, by Fairfax Murray

5 Samuel Bancroft to Charles Fairfax Murray, 20.8.1893, Delaware Art Museum, Sloan Archive

6 see Julie Codell, *Charles Fairfax Murray and the Pre-Raphaelite 'Academy': writing and forging the artistic field*, Ashgate 1998

7 William Silas Spanton, *An Art Student and his Teachers in the 60's*, p 73, Robert Scott, London 1927

8 A C Benson, *Memories and Friends*, John Murray 1924

9 H C Marillier to Charles Fairfax Murray, 8.9.1899, John Rylands Library, University of Manchester

10 Georgiana Burne-Jones to Charles Fairfax Murray, 7.10.1899, John Rylands Library, University of Manchester

11 Charles Fairfax Murray to Sydney Carlyle Cockerell, 16.4.1915, in *Friends of a Lifetime,* ed. Viola Meynell, Jonathan Cape, 1940

12 M R James to his father, December 1904, from Richard W. Pfaff, *M. R. James*, in which Fairfax Murray is described as 'an unpublicised and less high-powered Berenson'

13 A C Benson, 11.12.1904, *Diaries*, ed Percy Lubbock, Hutchinson & Co, London 1926

14 A C Benson to Montague Rhodes James, 12.9.1907, *Diaries* ed Percy Lubbock, Hutchinson & Co, London 1926

15 William Agnew was created Knight Baronet by Lord Rosebery in 1895 for political and public services

16 Geoffrey Agnew, *Agnew's 1817–1967*, the history of the firm written to celebrate 150 years in business, pp 41–43

17 Lockett Agnew was godfather to Elizabeth, Blanche's and Fairfax Murray's daughter, b 1901

18 Geoffrey Agnew, *Agnew's 1817–1967*, p 42, generous recognition from a later generation

19 Frits Lugt, in conversation with Felice Stampfle of the Pierpont Morgan

Library, transcript of her notes in the Collection Frits Lugt, Institut Néerlandais, Paris

20 Colin Agnew to Sir Martin Davies, February 1948, National Gallery Archive; there is a similar letter from him in the Fogg Archive

21 Frank Herrmann, *Sotheby's, Portrait of an Auction House*, Chatto & Windus 1980. The sale netted Sotheby's a huge profit at Fairfax Murray's expense; later sales in his lifetime went to Christie's, although Sotheby's was much the stronger house in books and manuscripts

22 This collection, the nucleus of the Morgan Library collection, was catalogued in 1905. Fairfax Murray wished them to remain together and waited for a suitable buyer

23 Sydney Carlyle Cockerell to Charles Fairfax Murray, 17.10.1911, Fitzwilliam Museum, Cambridge

24 Charles Fairfax Murray to Sydney Carlyle Cockerell, 29.10.1911, Fitzwilliam Museum, Cambridge

25 Charles Fairfax Murray to May Morris, 1.4.1914, Hammersmith & Fulham Records Office

26 Charles Fairfax Murray to William Davies at J & J Leighton, 11.6.1914, Pierpont Morgan Library

27 William Silas Spanton, *An Art Student and his Teachers in the 60's*, Robert Scott, London 1927

28 Charles Fairfax Murray to William Silas Spanton, 26.10.1914, Dulwich Picture Gallery

29 John Edward Murray to Edward Waldo Forbes, 10.8.1916, Fogg Art Museum, Harvard

30 Sydney Carlyle Cockerell to J R Holliday, 27.11.1916, Fitzwilliam Museum, Cambridge

31 Charles Ricketts to Sydney Carlyle Cockerell, 6.1.1917 quoted in *Friends of a Lifetime* ed. Viola Meynell, Jonathan Cape, 1940

32 Marie Spartali Stillman to Sydney Carlyle Cockerell, 9.1.1917, B. Library Add. MS.52754

33 Sydney Carlyle Cockerell, Diary, 2.3.1917, B. Library Add. MS.52654

34 Sydney Carlyle Cockerell, Diary, 7.8.1917, B. Library Add. MS.52654

35 Sydney Carlyle Cockerell, Diary, 1.2.1918, B. Library Add. MS.52655

36 Sydney Carlyle Cockerell, Diary, 8.2.1918, B. Library Add. MS.52655

37 Sydney Carlyle Cockerell to J R Holliday, 2.3.1918 and 8.3.1918, Fitzwilliam Museum, Cambridge

38 Charles Fairfax Murray to Samuel Bancroft Jnr, 27.12.1897, Delaware Art Museum, Sloan Archive

39 Charles Fairfax Murray to Henry Yates Thompson, 8.5.1918, Alleyn's School, Dulwich Archives

40 Sydney Carlyle Cockerell, Diary, 27.6.1918, 1918, B. Library Add. MS.52655

41 Sydney Carlyle Cockerell, Diaries, 23.1, 25.1 and 26.1.1919, B. Library Add. MS.52656

42 Arthur Richmond Murray, b 1888, Elizabeth Mary Murray, b 1901, and Edmund Rhodes Murray, b 1905

43 Sydney Carlisle Cockerell, Diary, 30.1.1919, British Library Add. MS.52656

44 Georgiana Burne-Jones to Sydney Carlyle Cockerell, 31.1.1919, National Art Library Eng. Mss. 86.SS.44-5
45 May Morris to an unknown correspondent, 1935, Hammersmith & Fulham Local History Archive
46 William Silas Spanton, *An Art Student and his Teachers in the 60's*, p 73, Robert Scott, London 1927

Appendix

1 *Quarterly Review*, July 1891
2 29.8.1891, John Rylands University of Manchester Library
3 Charles Fairfax Murray to Wilhelm von Bode 12.4.1893, Staatliche Museen von Berlin, Zentralarchiv Nachlaß Bode Nr 3832
4 Paul Bourget's *The Lady Who Has Lost her Painter*, 1906, was followed in 1907 by Frank Jewett Mather's short story *The Collectors*. Paul Bourget was a former friend of both Berenson and Mary Costelloe. They appear to have fallen out in the early 1890's; see Meryle Secrest *Being Bernard Berenson*. p. 121, Weidenfeld & Nicholson 1980
5 NG1126: originally the altarpiece of a funerary chapel in the Benedictine nunnery of San Piero Maggiore, purchased at the Hamilton sale of 26.6.1882. 'The *Assumption* has the distinction of being the only picture from the *quattrocento* known to have been painted to illustrate a heresy. The donor, Matteo Palmieri, believed that human souls are the angels who stayed neutral when Satan rebelled against God.' *Oxford Dictionary of Art*
6 The National Gallery version of the 'Virgin of the Rocks', NG 1093, acquired 1880 under the Directorship of Sir Frederick Burton
7 Charles Fairfax Murray to John Henry Middleton, 2.11.1885; NAL MS86 QQ Box 1 xxii
8 *Italian Painters I*, p. 284 describes the London version as a copy of the Louvre picture by a 'distinguished anonymous imitator' of Leonardo.

Chronology

Charles Fairfax Murray	Contemporary Events
1808 James Dalton Murray, father, born 9.7	Napoleon invades Spain Ludwig van Beethoven, Symphony No 5
1812	Napoleon's retreat from Moscow J M W Turner; *Snowstorm, Hannibal Crossing the Alps*
1816 Elizabeth Murray née Scott, mother, born	Jane Austen; *Emma*
1819	John Ruskin born, 8.2
1828	Dante Gabriel Rossetti born, 12.5 Francisco de Goya dies, 82 John Wharlton Bunney born, 20.6
1833	Edward Burne-Jones born, 28.3
1834	William Morris born, 24.3 Palace of Westminster destroyed by fire
1837	Accession of Queen Victoria Thomas Carlyle; *The French Revolution* Charles Dickens; *Pickwick Papers*
1842 Lucy Maria Murray, sister, born 25.2	Alfred Tennyson; *The Lady of Shallot* China cedes Hong Kong to Britain
1843	Marie Spartali born, 29.4 John Ruskin; *Modern Painters Vol 1*
1844 Arthur Murray, brother, born 14.3	J M W Turner; *Rain, Steam and Speed* Alexandre Dumas; *Les Trois Mousquetaires*
1845	John Henry Newman converts to the Church of Rome
1846 John Dalton Murray, brother, born 25.4	Famine in Ireland 1846–7 Millais discovers Lasinio's engravings of the Campo Santo, Pisa
1848	Ruskin marries Euphemia Gray, 10.4 Pre-Raphaelite Brotherhood formed Arundel Society formed

	Charles Fairfax Murray	Contemporary Events
1849	Charles Fairfax Murray born, 30.9	
1850		Joseph Paxton; Crystal Palace, Hyde Park
		Catholic hierarchy restored in Britain
1851		Ruskin defends the PRB
		John Ruskin; *The Stones of Venice Vol 1*
1852		William Morris enters Exeter College, Oxford, 2.6
1853	Elizabeth Murray, mother, dies 2.11	Last meeting of the PRB
		Burne-Jones meets Morris at Oxford
		Guiseppe Verdi; *Il Trovatore*
1856		Henry Wallis; *The Death of Chatterton*
		William Morris articled to George Street
		Burne-Jones becomes Rossetti's pupil
1857		Oxford Union murals, Morris meets Jane Burden, Swinburne joins Rossetti's circle
		Indian Mutiny breaks out at Meerut
1858	Angelica Albina Isolina Colivicchi born, Volterra 4.1	Ruskin meets Rose La Touche, 10
		William Frith; *Derby Day*
1859		William Morris marries Jane Burden, 26.4
1860		Burne-Jones marries Georgiana Macdonald
		William Dyce; *Pegwell Bay*
1861		Morris, Marshall, Faulkner & Co founded
		American Civil War begins
1862	Fairfax Murray attends his brother Arthur's wedding in Manchester	Elizabeth Siddal dies 11.2
		Christina Rossetti; *Goblin Market*
1863	Fairfax Murray (13) employed as 'shopboy' in the drawing office of Peto & Betts	Edouard Manet; *Le Déjeuner sur l'Herbe*

	Charles Fairfax Murray	**Contemporary Events**
1865	He is commissioned by Sir Samuel Morton Peto to draw portraits of his family Blanche Waddams Richmond born, Dec.	Ford Madox Brown; *Work* Abraham Lincoln assassinated
1866	Feb, Fairfax Murray sends his drawings to Ruskin who instructs Howell to give him lodgings and further training. Sept, he becomes Burne-Jones's first studio assistant	Algernon Swinburne; *Poems and Ballads* Burne-Jones/Maria Zambaco affair begins
1867	Fairfax Murray exhibits *Children in the Wood* at the Royal Academy. He re-paints 12 Zodiac panels for Philip Webb's Green Dining Room at the South Kensington Museum (V&A)	Walter Bagehot; *The British Constitution*
1869	He leaves Burne-Jones's studio but continues to assist him, now works also for Morris and Rossetti	Maria Zambaco attempts suicide, 23.1 Girton College founded Suez Canal opened
1870	He paints illustrations for William Morris's *Book of Verse*, copies for Rossetti, paints glass for MMF&Co. Morris takes him to Bruges for his 21st birthday	Burne-Jones, *Phyllis & Demophöon*, he resigns from the OWS Ruskin breaks with Ch. Augustus Howell Franco-Prussian War, Siege of Paris
1871	Morris and Fairfax Murray find Kelmscott Manor; he exhibits *Head of a Young Man* at Royal Academy. In Dec., he goes to Italy to study	James Abbott McNeill Whistler; *Arrangement in Grey and Black*
1872	He returns Apr., becomes MMF&Co's principal stained glass painter; the Vyner Memorial window in Christ Church, Oxford. Nov., Burne-Jones recommends him to Ruskin to copy in the Sistine Chapel for the Arundel Society	Rossetti attempts suicide 7.7 *Marie Celeste* found abandoned Christina Rossetti; *Sing Song: A Nursery Rhyme Book*
1873	Rome, Pisa, Florence and Siena for Ruskin; Easter, Burne-Jones and Morris visit Spencer Stanhope in	Walter Pater; *Studies in the History of the Renaissance*

Charles Fairfax Murray	Contemporary Events
Florence; he accompanies Burne-Jones to Siena; summer in London assisting Morris. Now resident in Italy	Jules Verne; *Round the World in 80 Days*
1874 Paints secret commission for Burne-Jones for Maria Zambaco; starts work on Sistine Chapel copies, joined by Ruskin, Apr.–May; London, Aug.–Oct. working with William Morris on his ms. *Horace*	Frederick Burton appointed Director of the National Gallery Edward Burne-Jones; *The Beguiling of Merlin* Benjamin Disraeli becomes Prime Minister James Abbott McNeill Whistler; *Nocturne in Black and Gold*
1875 He meets Giovanni Cavalcaselle in Rome; marries Angelica Colivicchi in Pisa 18.4, moves to Siena; George Howard visits Siena; Fairfax Murray travels to London 11.12, Christmas with the Burne-Joneses, Poynters, Cranes, Kiplings, Howards etc	Gilbert & Sullivan; *Trial by Jury* Rose La Touche dies, 25.5 MMF&Co wound up, Morris & Co founded
1876 Jan; Angelica's first daughter born, baby dies; Apr., they spend 3 months in Stanhope's studio in Florence and travel to London in Aug. His painted furniture panels for Collinson & Lock praised at Philadelphia Centennial Exhibition; his father dies in Sept. Dec., Ruskin calls him to Venice	Queen Victoria proclaimed Empress of India Auguste Renoir; *Au Moulin de la Galette*
1877 Venice, Feb.–May, he copies scenes from Carpaccio *St Ursula* series and in San Marco, working with Ruskin; June–July in London assisting Morris; Aug., second daughter born. Fairfax Murray appointed Italian Correspondent of Anti-Scrape. He buys a Botticelli for Ruskin which he dislikes	Grosvenor Gallery opens Morris initiates Society for Protection of Ancient Buildings (Anti-Scrape)
1878 London in April, returns with William Morris to meet Janey, the children and Rosalind Howard. Aug., third daughter born; Beatrice (second) dies in Nov. National	Ruskin's first mental collapse Ruskin v Whistler libel case re *Nocturne in Black and Gold* William and Marie Stillman move to Florence

Charles Fairfax Murray	Contemporary Events
Gallery acquire A Lorenzetti *Poor Clares* through Fairfax Murray	
1879 In debt, borrows £10 from the Firm. May, he exhibits two works at Grosvenor Gallery, remains in London until Aug.; Sept., he moves to Florence; Cavalcaselle and Fairfax Murray travel to Orvieto, Siena to study pictures; he meets Henry Roderick Newman	James Renwick; St Patrick's Cathedral, New York Henrik Ibsen; *A Doll's House* Johannes Brahms; Violin Concerto
1880 He buys Andrea della Robbia relief for delighted Ruskin; but increasing problems over payment for copies. John, eldest son, born 24.6. He negotiates purchase of Shelley-Clairmont papers	Camille Pissarro; *The Outer Suburbs* Edward Burne-Jones; *The Golden Stairs*
1881 Fairfax Murray exhibits at the Grosvenor Gallery, visits Vienna and Bucharest. Opposed to Anti-Scrape's public demonstrations against San Marco restorations which only anger the Italians, he embarks on a quiet crusade to mitigate excesses, mediates on restorations to Giotto's Arena Chapel	Ruskin seriously ill Gilbert & Sullivan; *Patience* Pablo Picasso born
1882 Fairfax Murray gifts P Lorenzetti *St Sabinus before the Governor of Tuscany* to the National Gallery	Mackmurdo founds the Century Guild Edouard Manet; *Bar at the Folies Bergère* Dante Gabriel Rossetti dies, 9.4.
1883 He breaks with Ruskin over long overdue payments; resumes negotiations in Siena for Matteo di Giovanni *Assumption* for NG, bidding simultaneously for a Ghirlandaio *Procession to Calvary* in Florence; both succeed against Wilhelm von Bode for Berlin who recognises a worthy rival, leading to a close relationship. Eduardo, second son, born 18.10	Ruskin, third madness Krakatoa erupts, 36,000 die Mark Twain; *Life on the Mississippi* Inaugural run of the Orient Express, Paris–Istanbul

Charles Fairfax Murray	Contemporary Events
1884	Fernand Khnopff; *The Sphinx* Georges Seurat; *Bathers at Asnières*
1885 Mar.–May, Philip Webb and John Henry Middleton tour Italy with Fairfax Murray, visit Brescia, Bergamo, Venice, Ravenna, Forli, Vicenza, Mantua and Milan; he makes a copy of Carpaccio's *St George* for Webb; Aug.–Sept., and again in November in London, he resolves to move back	William Morris; *Woodpecker Tapestry* 'China' Gordon dies at Khartoum Burne-Jones elected ARA, assumes hyphen
1886 Apart from 3 weeks in Florence in March, Fairfax Murray remains in London for a year, painting, acting for his private clients and giving expert opinions; returns to Italy for a short holiday before setting out for Venice, Siena and Rome. In Oct., he comes back to London to find a permanent studio, accompanied by Angelica	Henry James; *The Bostonians* Frederic Auguste Bartholdi; *The Statue of Liberty*
1887 Angelica returns to Florence in March. Fairfax Murray spends time in Cambridge with Middleton and the Darwins, painting portraits. He is in Italy between July and early Oct.; he returns via Paris. The year is spent in a daily round of contacts with such as Mackmurdo, Crane, De Morgan, Horne, Image, Ricketts and Shannon; and Watts, Leighton, Prinsep, Sandys, the Ionides, the Coronios; and acting for his clients Ch. Butler, R H Benson and Bode. He exhibits *The Last Parting of Helga and Gunnlaug*	Ruskin, fifth mental collapse Henry James; *The Aspern Papers* Vincent van Gogh; *Moulin de la Galette*
1888 Feb., Blanche Richmond sits for him; they become lovers. Fairfax Murray exhibits two portraits at the New Gallery. Angelica's third son born	New Gallery opens Arts & Crafts Exhibition Society's first show C R Ashbee founds Guild of Handicraft

Charles Fairfax Murray	Contemporary Events
1890	He negotiates purchase of Orcagna mosaics from Duomo in Orvieto for South Kensington Museum; he shows *The Music Party* at the New Gallery, bought by Rupert D'Oyly Carte for the Palace Theatre. He expands his collection of early books and manuscripts	Vincent van Gogh; *Portrait of Dr Gachet* Edward Burne-Jones; *The Briar Rose* series
1891	He buys the imposing Villa Murray near Florence for the family, retains his city studio for his own use; he catalogues the Duke of Portland's collection leading to opinions for Lords Balcarres, Beauchamp and the Duke of Bedford	William Morris; *News from Nowhere*
1892	Meets Samuel Bancroft who forms an important Pre-Raphaelite collection in Wilmington, Delaware; prepares the Kelmscott *Epistola* of Savonarola	Aubrey Beardsley; *Salome*
1893	Put forward by George Howard and Burne-Jones as their alternative candidate to Edward Poynter to succeed Sir Frederick Burton as Director of the National Gallery; he catalogues the Roscoe collection for Liverpool; expert advisor to BFAC Signorelli Exhibition	Edvard Munch; *The Scream* Antonin Dvorak; Symphony No 9 (From the New World)
1895	Fairfax Murray catalogues the collection of his friend George Price Boyce; copying for Agnew's; he completes the Portland catalogue	August Rodin; *The Burghers of Calais* Oscar Wilde; *The Importance of Being Earnest* Bernhard Berenson investigated by J Pierpont Morgan
1896	He draws William Morris in death, Kelmscott House 3.10	Kelmscott *Chaucer*
1898	May, he helps Burne-Jones repair the damaged *Love Among the Ruins*; June, Burne-Jones dies; Oct., Fairfax Murray takes over The Grange; he buys much of Morris's library; Cavalieri catalogue of his early Italian books describes 2,276 volumes	Emile Zola; *J'Accuse* John Philip Souza; *The Stars and Stripes Forever* Kelmscott Press closes

Charles Fairfax Murray	**Contemporary Events**
1899 He buys the Marchese Girolamo d'Adda's library of early books	
1900 Partnership with Agnew's and Haskard's Bank formalised	Boer War, relief of Mafeking Ruskin dies, 7.1 Paul Cezanne; *Mt Ste Victoire*
1903 Fairfax Murray sells 260 Rossetti and 226 Burne-Jones drawings to Birmingham below market value	Arnold Schoenberg; *Verklarte Nacht* Antoni Gaudi; *Sagrada Familia Church*
1904 He gives 35 Burne-Jones stained glass cartoons to Birmingham	Japan invades Manchuria Frederick Sandys dies
1905 He helps assure the Velasquez *Venus at her Toilet* for the nation, the future King lends him his help	Mutiny on the *Potemkin*, Lenin returns to Russia from exile
1906 He buys William Morris manuscripts at Hodson sale	San Francisco earthquake
1907 He sells 300 Millais, Madox Brown and Sandys drawings to Birmingham below market value; his picture sales give rise to rumours that he needs money; his ancient books now number 4,144	Henry Hardenburgh; Plaza Hotel, New York Claude Monet; *Water Lilies, Giverny*
1909 He sells 1450 Old Master Drawings collection to J Pierpont Morgan for the equivalent of £3,000,000	Algernon Swinburne dies Robert Delaunay; *The Eiffel Tower*
1910 The catalogue of Fairfax Murray's German books is published, dedicated to William Morris; Oct., he gives up The Grange to Richard Norton, moves to Agnew's Albemarle St apartment	Igor Stravinsky; *The Firebird* Henri Matisse; *Blue Nude*
1911 He gives 46 portraits painted in England to Dulwich Picture Gallery	*Mona Lisa* stolen from the Louvre
1913 He resolves to live in Italy, moves his books to his library in Florence; he offers to assist the NG to get the Layard Bequest out of Italy	Suffragettes slash pictures in the National Gallery Mar., J Pierpont Morgan dies in Rome
1914 May., he travels to New York to advise Jack Pierpont Morgan on his father's collections, returning in June for the Paris sale of many of	War with Germany, 4.8 Ghandi returns to India

	Charles Fairfax Murray	**Contemporary Events**
	his Old Masters. Sept., he returns to New York, and to London in Nov.	
1915	Ill in London, travels to Florence in July, suffers first stroke in Aug.	*Lusitania* torpedoed with loss of 1198 lives
1916	He recovers but suffers more severe stroke in June; by Oct., he is barely able to drag himself to Paris and on to London where he arrives unexpectedly at Blanche's family home in Chiswick	Richard Strauss; Ariadne auf Naxos
1917	He divides his time between London and Cambridge, makes further gifts to the Fitzwilliam including Titian's *Tarquin and Lucretia*	Amadeo Modigliani; *Crouching Female Nude*
1918	Feb., Eduardo, his second son, visits him in Albemarle Street. When health permits he visits Cambridge. Oct., he goes to Blanche in Chiswick	Feb., Lockett Agnew dies Lytton Strachey; *Eminent Victorians* Nov., Armistice
1919	24.1 he suffers third stroke and dies at noon	

Select Bibliography

Charles Fairfax Murray

CFM papers, John Rylands Library, University of Manchester, 1560 als
CFM papers, Harry Ransom Humanities Research Center, University of Texas, 1240 als
CFM papers, Dulwich Picture Gallery, 107 als
CFM papers, Fitzwilliam, 66 als
CFM papers, Huntington Library, 127 als uncatalogued
CFM to Middleton NAL MS86 QQ Box 1 xxii
CFM to Cavalcaselle, Biblioteca Marciana
Bancroft papers, Delaware Art Museum, Sloan Archive,192 als
Sydney Cockerell Papers, B Library
Seymour de Ricci, *English Collectors of Books and Manuscripts 1530–1930*, Burt, Franklin New York 1960
Jackson, *Book Collector*, Summer 1960, CFM's French Books
CFM Catalogue of Early French Books
CFM Catalogue of Early German Books
CFM Catalogue of Bernhardt von Breydenbach's Journey to the Holy Land
W S Spanton, *An Art Student and his Teachers in the 60's*, Robert Scott, London 1927
A C Benson, *Memories and Friends*, John Murray, London 1924
Sandra Beresford: *Preraffaelismo ed Estetismo a Firenze negli ultimi del XIX*, in *L'Idea di Firenze; Temi e interpretazione nell'arte straniera dell'Ottocento, secolo*, Florence, 1986
Pierpont Morgan Old Master drawings, catalogue
Burlington Magazine, March 1919 p 122
Seymour de Ricci, *Census of Mediaeval and Renaissance Mss. in the USA*, H W Wilson & Co, New York & Paris 1935
Times, 29.1.1919
May Morris, *Times Literary Supplement* 29.6.1934
Paul Tucker, *Giovanni Battista Cavalcaselle, John Ruskin e Charles Fairfax Murray: interlocutori e antagonisti* in *Giovanni Battista Cavalcaselle, conoscitore e conservatore*, ed. A C Tommasi, Venezia: Marsilio, 1998

Pre-Raphaelitism & the History of Victorian Art

Percy H Bate, *The English Pre-Raphaelite Painters*, Bell, London 1901
Pre-Raphaelite Papers, ed Parris 1984
Ford Madox Brown, *Diaries* ed Surtees, Yale University Press
William Michael Rossetti, *Pre-Raphaelite Diaries and Letters*, Hurst & Blackett, London 1900
William Holman Hunt, *Pre-Raphaelitism and the PRB*, Chapman & Hall, London 1913
William Bell Scott, *Autobiographical Notes* ed Minto, Osgood, McIlvaine, London 1892
K K Andrews, *The Nazarenes*, Clarendon, Oxford 1964
J Maas, *Victorian Painters*, Barrie & Rockcliff 1969
Julian Treuherz, *Victorian Painting*, Thames & Hudson, London 1993
W E Fredeman, *Pre-Raphaelitism; A Bibliocritical Study*, Harvard University Press 1965

John Ruskin

William Michael Rossetti, *Ruskin, Rossetti and PRism*, G Allen 1899
Morley, *John Ruskin; Late Work, St George Educational Experiment*, Sheffield 1984
Diaries of John Ruskin, ed Evans & Whitehouse, 1956
The Brantwood Diaries of John Ruskin
Selected writings, *Ruskin Today*, K Clark, Penguin 1981
Praeterita, intr. K Clark, Penguin 1983
Ruskin, *Works*, ed Cook & Wedderburn, G Allen 1903
Ruskin *Letters on Art & Literature* ed Wise 1894

Dante Gabriel Rossetti

Selected Letters ed R. W. Peattie, Penn State University Press 1990
William Michael Rossetti, *Diaries 1870–1873*, ed O Bornand, Clarendon, Oxford
Treffry Dunn, *Recollections of DGR and his Circle*, Elkin Matthews 1904
Rossetti and His Circle, Max Beerbohm, 1922
H Rossetti Angeli, *Pre-Raphaelite Twilight, Story of Ch. Augustus Howell*, Richards Press 1954
William Michael Rossetti, *Rossetti Papers 1862–1870*, Sands 1903
William Michael Rossetti, *Some Reminiscences*, Brown, Langham & Co 1906
V Surtees, *Paintings and Drawings of DGR*, Clarendon, Oxford 1971
Helen Rossetti Angeli, *DGR Enemies and Friends*, Hamish Hamilton 1949
Letters of Dante Gabriel Rossetti, Doughty & Wahl, Clarendon, Oxford 1965–67
William Michael Rossetti, *Rossetti Papers 1854–1862*, Geo Allen 1899
J C Troxell, *Three Rossettis*, Harvard University Press 1937
Dante Gabriel Rossetti and Janey Morris, *Correspondence* ed Bryson & Troxell, Clarendon 1971
H C Marillier, *Dante Gabriel Rossetti, an illustrated memorial*, Geo Bell 1899
C L Cline, *The Owl and the Rossettis*, Penn State Univ Press

William Morris

William Morris, *Collected Letters* ed Kelvin, Princeton University Press 1984
William Morris to Sydney Cockerell, Letters
Wilfred Scawen Blunt, *Diaries*, Fitzwilliam Museum
Jane Morris to Wilfred Scawen Blunt ed Faulkner, Exeter 1991
May Morris, *Introductions to William Morris Complete Works*, Oriole, NY 1973
Fiona McCarthy, *William Morris*, Faber & Faber 1994
MMF&Co Minutes, Hammersmith Public Library
J W Mackail, *The Life of William Morris*, Longmans & Green 1908
William Morris; *Letters to his family and friends*, P Henderson 1950
Robinson & Wildman, *Morris & Co in Cambridge*, Cambridge University Press 1980
Charles Harvey and Jon Press, *Art, Enterprise and Ethics; The Life and Works of William Morris*, Cass 1996

Edward Coley Burne-Jones

Edward Burne-Jones Papers, Fitzwilliam
Georgiana Burne-Jones Letters, NAL

Edward Burne-Jones Papers, to Gladstone 1894, Layard, British Library
Georgiana Burne-Jones, *Memorials of Edward Burne-Jones*, Macmillan 1904
Penelope Fitzgerald, *Edward Burne-Jones*, Michael Joseph 1975
John Christian, *The Last Romantics*, London 1975
T M Rooke, *Burne-Jones Talking*, ed. Lago 1977

Arts & Crafts Movement

W Crane, *Morris to Whistler*, 1911
W Crane, *An Artist's Reminiscences*, Methuen 1907
W Crane, The Arts & Crafts (2nd Exh;) Catalogue 1889
A M W Stirling, *William De Morgan and his Wife*, 1922
In Pursuit of Beauty; America and the Aesthetic Movement, Metropolitan NY 1987
Victorian & Edwardian Decorative Art; the Handley-Read Collection, RA 1972
Collinson & Lock, *Sketches of Artistic Furniture*, Catalogue 1871
The Arts & Crafts Movement in America 1876–1916, ed R J Clarke
Isobel Spencer, *Walter Crane*, Studio Vista, London 1975
Walter Smith, *Examples of Household Taste*, NY 1877

Figures and Issues of the period

The Nineteenth Century, ed Huish 1884
George Price Boyce, *Diaries* ed Surtees, Norwich 1980
Frank Herrmann, *Portrait of an Auction House*, Chatto & Windus 1990
Christopher Newall, *Grosvenor Gallery Exhibitions*, Cambridge University Press 1995
Ian Fletcher, *Rediscovering Herbert Horne*, ELT Press, 1990
Henry Yates Thompson Papers, British Library
J G P Delaney, *Charles Ricketts, A Biography*, OUP 1989
J Darracott, *All for Art, The World of Charles Ricketts*, 1979
Arthur Jacobs, *Gilbert & Sullivan*, Max Parrish, London 1951
Joseph Archer Crowe, *Reminiscences of 35 Years of my Life*, John Murray 1895
S Reynolds, *W B Richmond, An Artist's Life*, Norwich 1995
A M W Stirling, *The Richmond Papers*, 1927
William Blunt, *Cockerell*, 1962
G C Williamson, *Murray Marks and His Friends*. John Lane, London 1919
James Jackson Jarves, *The Art Idea*, ed Rowland, Harvard University Press 1960
Edmund Gosse, *Life of A C Swinburne*, Macmillan & Co, London 1917
P Henderson, *Swinburne, Portrait of a Poet*, Routledge & Kegan Paul 1974
W Graham Robertson, *Time Was*, Hamish Hamilton 1931
John Collins, *Two Forgers, Biography of Harry Buxton Forman and Thomas J Wise*,
    Ashgate 1992
V Meynell, *Friends of a Lifetime*, Jonathan Cape, London 1940
Harry Quilter, *What's What, a Guide to Life Today*, 1902
E C Brook, *Sir Samuel Morton Peto, Bt.*, 1997
H Crackanthorpe, *Vignettes*,
J Comyns Carr, *Some Eminent Victorians*, Duckworth & Co 1908
A M W Stirling, *The Richmond Papers*, 1927
Gordon Waterfield, *Layard of Nineveh*, John Murray, London 1963
John Christian, *Marie Spartali*, Apollo 1984

Times 8.3.1927 Marie Stillman, obituary
W J Stillman, *Autobiography of a Journalist*, 1901
Mark Hamilton, *Rare Spirit, A Life of William De Morgan*, Constable 1997
Papers of George Howard, 9th Earl of Carlisle, Castle Howard
Papers of the 5th Earl of Rosebery, MS 10150, National Library of Scotland
A C Benson, *On the Edge of Paradise*, ed David Newsome
A C Benson, *Diaries*, ed Percy Lubbock, Hutchinson & Co, London 1926
J Llewellyn Davis , *The Working Men's College*, 1904
Working Men's College; Correspondence Boxes I–III
Emilia Barrington, *Life, Letters and Works of Frederic Lord Leighton*, Geo Allen 1902
Leonée & Richard Ormond, *Lord Leighton*, Yale University Press, 1975
W Gaunt, *Victorian Olympus*, Jonathan Cape 1952
Burton, *History of the Hyderabad Contingent*
Millicent Rose, *The East End of London*, Cresset Press, London 1951
Luke Ionides, *Memories*, Herbert Clark, Paris 1925
Alecco Ionides, *A Grandfather's Tale*
Frank Davis, *Victorian Patrons of the Arts*, 1963
Ernest Samuels, *Bernhard Berenson*, Belknap Press, 1979
Meryle Secrest, *Being Bernhard Berenson*, Weidenfeld & Nicholson 1980
Mary Berenson, Letters
S Behrman, *Duveen*, Andre Deutch, London 1986
S Sprigge, *Berenson*, Allan & Unwin, London 1960
Colin Simpson, *The Partnership*, Bodley Head, 1987
G F Ioni, *Affairs of a Painter*, London 1936
Letters, Berenson/Isabella Gardner, N E University
D Levi, *Cavalcaselle*, 1988
Donata Levi, *Cognoscitori, mercanti e amateurs a Firenze nell' Ottocento, La Cultura artistica a Siena nell'Ottocento, Carlo Sisi, Ettore Spaletti*, Pizzi, Milano, 1994
John Fleming, *Art Dealing and the Risorgimento*, Burlington Magazine 115
Federico Zeri and Burton B Fredericksen, *Census of pre-19th Century Italian Paintings in N. American Public Collections*, Harvard 1976
F Steegmuller, *The Two Lives of James Jackson Jarves*
Le Farge and A Jaccaci, *Noteworthy Paintings in American Collections*, 1907
Gazette des Beaux Arts 1892–3
Jane Abdy and Charlotte Gere, *The Souls*, Sidgwick & Jackson, London 1984
Lady Gregory, *Hugh Lane, Life and Legacy*
Collecting the Pre-Raphaelites, ed M F Watson, Ashgate 1997
Re-framing the Pre-Raphaelites, ed E Harding, Ashgate 1996
David Sox, *Batchelors of Art*, Fourth Estate 1991
Royal W Leith, *A Quiet Devotion, The Life & Work of Henry Roderick Newman*, NY 1996
Carol Gibson-Wood, *Studies in the Theory of Connoisseurship from Vasari to Morelli*, 1988
B Waters, *George Howard and his Circle*, catalogue, Carlisle
Calvin Tombs, *Merchants and Masterpieces*, 1970
J Pope-Hennesey, *Italian Sculptures in the V&A*
Lili Helbig Morani, *Jugend im Abendrot, Romische Erinnungen*, Stuttgart 1953
Phillipa Bernard, *Antiquarian Books, a Companion*
Lady Eastlake, *The Patriot & the Critic, Quarterly Review* July 1891
John Christian, *The Oxford Union Murals*, University of Chicago 1974
Arthur Chamberlain, *Hours in the Birmingham Art Gallery*, 1928
Saturday Review of Politics, Literature, Science and the Arts, Spring issues, 1898

Sydney Cockerell; Kelmscott papers, Walthamstow
James Cuno, *Harvard's Art Museums, 100 Years of Collecting*, catalogue
R R Rooksby, *A C Swinburne, A Poet's Life*. Scolar Press 1997
M J C Cattermole & A F Wolfe, *Horace Darwin's Shop*, Bristol 1987
Edna Lindeman, *The Art Triangle*, Rockwell Hall State, 1989
P Bourdieu, *The Field of Cultural Production*, Cambridge Polity Press 1993

Index